ESSENTIALS of
Appreciative Inquiry

For Leaders of Change

ESSENTIALS of
Appreciative Inquiry

David L. Cooperrider, Ph.D.
Case Western Reserve University
Weatherhead School of Management

Diana Whitney, Ph.D.
Corporation for Positive Change
and Saybrook Graduate School and Research Center

Jacqueline M. Stavros, EDM
Lawrence Technological University
College of Management

Foreword by Ronald Fry

Crown Custom Publishing, Inc.
Brunswick, OH

Crown Custom Publishing, Inc.
1656 Pearl Road
Brunswick, Ohio 44212
(330) 273-4900
(877) 225-8820
www.crowncustompublishing.com

Ordering Information

Individual sales: This book can be ordered direct from Crown Custom Publishing, Inc. at the address above.

Quantity sales: Special discounts are available on quantity purchases by corporations, associations, and others. For details, contact Crown Custom Publishing, Inc. at the address above.

Orders for college textbook/course adoption use: Please contact Crown Custom Publishing, Inc. at (877) 225-8820.

Orders by U.S. wholesalers: Please contact Crown Custom Publishing:
    Tel: (800) 509-4887; Fax (800) 838-1149;
    E-mail: carl@crowncustompublishing.com or visit
      www.crowncustompublishing.com

    ISBN 978-1-933403-205
    Printed in the United States of America

Library of Congress Cataloging-in-Publication Data
First Edition   10 9 8 7 6 5 4 3 2 1

Publisher: Carl Wirick
Production Editor: Roger Williams
Copyediting: Marianne Miller
Design: Tia Andrako

Contents

Detailed Contents

PART 2   Application of the 4-D Cycle of Appreciative Inquiry

Chapter 4: Discovery: *What Gives Life?*

Chapter 5: Dream: *What Might Be?*

Chapter 6: Design: *How Can It Be?*

List of Tables, Figures, and Exhibits

Foreword

"Be the change you want to see in the world."
—Gandhi

This essential edition of the *Appreciative Inquiry Handbook* signals a period of tremendous growth in the application and dissemination of AI throughout the world. No fewer than 20 new books on AI have appeared during the four short years since the Handbook first appeared—books ranging in focus from organizational capacity building to building of dynamic relationships, from peace making to knowledge management, from leadership to coaching and program evaluation, and from socially responsible enterprises to multistakeholder strategy creation. A steadily growing number of workshops, certificate programs, and master's degree programs emphasizing AI and related strength-based change methods are being conducted in most continents and in multiple languages. There is no doubt that AI has established itself as a maturing community of practice that carries on the legacy of Kurt Lewin's memorable notion that nothing is so good as a practical theory.

As the praxis of AI matures, so does our understanding of the theoretical underpinnings that remain valid and that provide confidence for the practitioner, as well as our recognition of new frontiers for thought and action. This *ESSENTIALS* version of the handbook instructs and guides us in both areas. I would like to offer a few observations on the healthy "state of the discipline" as we receive this new edition:

- **The fundamentals are sound.** I believe the core principles (Chapter 1) and their theoretical roots (mini-lectures) remain the bedrock of this practice. Fundamentally, AI is still about changing attitudes, behaviors, and practices through appreciative conversations and relationships—interactions designed to bring out the best in people so that they can imagine a preferred future together that is more hopeful, boundless, and inherently good. It is still about socially constructing a shared future and enacting human systems through the questions asked. And it is still about anticipatory learning—finding those positive, anticipatory images of the future that compel action toward them. Even the academic critics (another sign of a maturing science!) of AI avoid any serious debate of the basic principles; these basic assumptions still signal a verifiable way (not *the* way) to understand and activate positive change in human systems.

- **The scale is limitless.** From pairs to populations, from a team to a global network of thousands of stakeholders, the scope of AI in practice is ever-expanding. The advent of the AI Summit methodology and other adaptations of large-group interventions using AI combined with today's information technology enable global systems to connect in ways never imagined. World Vision can engage nearly 5,000 of its members and stakeholders to create strategic goals in four days, working 24 hours a day in three languages. The BBC can engage all 22,000 employees worldwide in the design and creation of a culture for innovation. In ten summits, the U.S. Navy can engage thousands across seven different commands to foster a culture of engaged and empowered leaders at every level. A cadre of more than 1,000 appreciative leaders throughout Nepal can mobilize to shape a peaceful and prosperous future for their country (including the voices of more than 150,000 village women!). Those are just a few examples. Every day AI practitioners are discovering more effective way to engage all stakeholders—the whole system at once—in the center of strategy formation, planning, and implementation.

- **A greater scope is calling.** One of the great scholars of leadership and management over the past century, Peter Drucker, has said that all of the world's greatest challenges are business opportunities. Since AI has become an established means for designing, transforming, and growing effective organizations, it is well suited to help address the more difficult issues and/or questions of our time. This is an important frontier for AI—to increasingly tackle the difficult questions that will require engaging stakeholders and parties with wildly opposing world views, mental models, learned values, and the like. The methods, tools, and insights in this Handbook enable the reader/learner to find the strengths (positive core) of organizations (particularly businesses) and to apply those strengths toward shaping business to be an agent for world benefit, toward eco-innovations, toward business as an agent of peace, toward business models to eradicate poverty, and so on. They have helped the United Nations Global Compact and the Academy of Management create a new, enduring partnership to merge research of consequence to assist the aims of businesses in fulfilling the Millennium Development Goals. For Green Mountain Coffee Roasters, AI has been instrumental in its record setting economic growth and its continuing recognition as one of the world's most socially responsible organizations.

- **The focus is on generativity.** As with any maturing phenomena, there is a danger of superficial understanding or application that manipulates for an outcome rather than that opens for inquiry and searches for new understanding. I believe the field of AI is at that stage, particularly with respect to the tendency for many to be drawn to the "positive-ness" of AI as an end or outcome. There is little doubt that one of the attractions to AI is that it honors or privileges the experience of positive effect—and that our need for this, or attraction to it, is a commentary on the state of today's social systems that tend to provoke the opposite (vicious) effect much of the time. However, the place of positive effect in AI is more a means than an end. The burgeoning fields of Positive Psychology and Positive Organization Scholarship are revealing that human systems are not entropic; rather, they are capable of virtuous acts resulting from members finding more energy to cooperate with each other—that the desire to put more effort, more time, and more attention toward an activity of mutual benefit is the consequence of certain kinds of inquiry and conversation. Negative, critical, radical, or fringe voices are not excluded from this formula. AI choreographs dialogic inquiry to increase the likelihood of generating new cooperative acts. This is the meaning of the use of positive in labeling a type of scholarship, a field of psychology, or a type of change.

- **The inquiry is what really counts.** Similar to the "trap" of seeking just to be positive is the tendency for those using AI to seek only to be acting or engaging in appreciative ways. So often I hear of AI "exercises" being used to begin key meetings, strategic planning workshops, and so on, as warm-ups to get all of the voices in the room to reconnect with some highpoints and to begin on an "appreciative note." It would be a tragedy for this Handbook to serve merely for that purpose. Rather, let it be your guide to *inquiry*, to a particular type of search and exploration for shared meaning that can lead to powerful images of the future that then call for action to realize that preferred future. In other words, AI is more about learning and understanding something (the affirmative topic, Chapter 2)—and thereby *valuing* it—than it is about expressions of appreciation.

This Handbook remains the best and most complete and practical set of materials for anyone wanting to read about AI and to begin to practice the AI 4-D methodology. It remains the basic primer for "what to do," "how to do it," and "why to do it" and for using AI theory and methods. This second edition contains more examples of applications and measured impacts, more evidence of positive change from longitudinal interventions, and more tools and new insights about the *Design* phase of the AI process (4 Ds) in Chapter 6. The resources brought forth are a rich companion to anyone engaged or wanting to engage in AI. I expect no matter your prior experience with AI ideas and processes, you will want to reference this book again and again. Once again the authors have amassed in one place all of the foundation concepts and latest concepts, cases, and resources necessary to learn and apply AI at any level.

However, there is one shortcoming of this great foundation book about AI in that it cannot really convey what the authors model in their practice: the "be-ing" of AI. David, Diana, and Jackie are great practitioners and teachers, not just because of what they know, but because of how they "be AI" in their everyday lives. When, in their company, you experience the gift of their ability to be what they write about, as I have, you suddenly realize the essence of this wonderful idea of appreciative inquiry—that we can actually be in the moment we are in, working toward the change we want to realize, and that this be-ing with each other is the change happening, as we engage. We do not have to plan for it, measure it, wait for a date to have it, or announce that it is here; positive change is what life—living—can be all about. It is not a Cartesian concept to be objectified or even measured as much as it is a quality of experience—of being connected to others in shared hopes, activities, and exchanges that help each of us to flourish in the moment.

Ronald Fry
Weatherhead School of Management
Case Western Reserve University
Cleveland, Ohio
Fall 2007

Preface

> *"The ageless essence of leadership is to create an alignment of strengths in ways that make a system's weaknesses irrelevant."*
> —Peter Drucker

Better ways of leading change are spreading throughout the world. Could it be, as Drucker's provocative manifesto so clearly implies, that the leadership of change is *entirely* about the discovery and elevation of strengths? Certainly we know that *strengths perform*. But what about the idea that strengths do far more than perform—*that strengths transform*? As many are now experiencing, an exciting nondeficit model of positive change is rapidly spreading that puts something powerful and full of life deep inside the heart of every type of business and organizational change.

Some call it the "strengths revolution"—a movement that has profound implications for everyone interested in leading with hope and optimism and winning the future through the highest engagement of human strengths. Fascinating questions on this topic are many. Why, for example, would discovering and moving from strength to strength in human systems activate, energize, and elevate change? What would it mean to ignite an entire change paradigm around new combinations, configurations, and chemistries of strengths? What good are positive emotions, words, images, inquiries, and constructions as we seek to understand the positive psychology and expansive economy of human strengths—especially in turbulent, difficult, and complex times? And what if we took the strengths logic to the hilt: where are all of the new tools, and where would we—as managers, change leaders, parents, and friends—start? Equally important, what becomes of all of the "deficiencies," "threats," "breakdowns," "gaps," and "problems" if we truly explore what's involved in Drucker's ever-curious phrase in *ways that make a system's weaknesses irrelevant*?

This book is that invitation to an imaginative and fresh perception of organizations and the process through which they change. Its "metacognitive" stance is choicefully affirmative. Its central thesis—as an extension of the Lewinian premise that human action depends on the world as constructed rather than the world as it is—is pragmatic and hopeful. This book teaches how to build and sustain an organization from its strengths—positive core. This book offers a fresh approach to using the contributions of any and all stakeholders to design and redesign the systems within organizations for a more effective and sustainable future.

In its most practical construction, Appreciative Inquiry (also referred to as AI) is a form of transformational inquiry that selectively seeks to locate, highlight, and illuminate the life-giving forces of an organization's existence. It is based on the belief that human systems are made and imagined by those who live and work within them. AI leads these systems to move toward the creative images that reside in the positive core of an organization. This approach is based on solid, proven principles for enabling creativity, knowledge, and spirit in the workplace. These principles call people to work toward a common vision and a higher purpose.

AI seeks out the best of "what is" to help ignite the collective imagination of "what might be." The aim is to generate new knowledge that expands the "realm of the possible" and helps members of an organization envision a collectively desired future. Furthermore, it helps to implement vision in ways that successfully translate images of possibilities into reality and belief into practice. The methodology results in a win-win situation.

This book provides a comprehensive presentation, the theory and the practical application of AI methods. Theories and activities in this book have been developed from the work of small and large corporations, government organizations, and international organizations working on issues of sustainability. Research on AI has been conducted in organizations in more than 100 countries around the world.

Material in this book is designed to facilitate theoretical understanding and the effective use of AI by organization leaders, managers, members, and consultants. This book is the essentials edition that provides new developments of AI, updated case information and additional resources. It contains everything needed to plan, design, and lead an AI initiative. We invite readers to adapt it to their needs, in accordance with the copyright guidelines.

For the reader interested in *applications* of AI, we offer the accompanying compact disk, which contains case clippings, extensive worksheets, over 100 Powerpoint slides and assorted other tools to aid the change leader in the facilitative role. The CD also contains the Classic Articles [including, "Positive Image... Positive Action"] which are reprinted in the longer *Handbook*. The CD-ROM can be obtained from Crown Custom Publishing at www.crowncustompublishing.com.

As Goethe reminds us, "Whatever you can do or dream you can, begin it. Boldness has genius, power and magic in it." When you are prepared to believe in people, trust them, and acknowledge that they know best about what needs to be done—at work and in their lives—Appreciative Inquiry is for you.

David L. Cooperrider, Diana Whitney and Jacqueline M. Stavros

Acknowledgments

Creating a second edition for a book takes a great deal of time, effort, and depth of conversations with and contributions from many people. We wish to acknowledge these efforts that took place over the past year.

We would like to thank the following people who contributed to the creation and content of the first *Appreciative Inquiry Handbook*: Frank Barrett, Steve Cato, David Chandler, Joep de Jong, Marsha George, Mette Jacobsgaard, Ralph Kelly, Jackie Kelm, Jim Lord, Jim Ludema, Ada Jo Mann, Adrian McLean, Bernard Mohr, Ravi Pradhan, Anne Radford, Diane Robbins, Judy Rodgers, Marge Schiller, Barbara Sloan, and Jane Watkins.

Other colleagues and friends who contributed resources to this Handbook include Stan Baran, Gervase Bush, Diane Ruiz Cairns, John Carter, Dawn Cooperrider Dole, Ronald Fry, Pamela Johnson, Ed and Martha Kimball, Jason Kirk, Claudia Leibler, Anne Kohnke Meda, Mary Grace Neville, Karla Phlypo, Charleysee Pratt, Thomas Price, Maryanne Rainey, Leslie Sekerka, Tony Silbert, Suresh Srivastva, Paul Stavros, Amanda Trosten-Bloom, Rita Williams, and Susan Wood.

We also would like to thank Michael Feinson, Jen Hetzel-Silbert, Sally Lee, Bernard Mohr, Ada Jo Mann, and Heidi Ramsbottom for helping to update the AI Initiative Table with the great work they are doing across the world.

Our clients and first edition readers have contributed to this book in ways both visible and subtle. Our readers shared with us what they liked about the first edition and what content to keep and what to add more of. At each of these organizations, hundreds, if not thousands, of people deserve credit.

We want to once again thank Ron Fry, our dear colleague and friend, who made many contributions to the field of AI since it emerged. He took the time to write the foreword for this second edition, capturing the growth and impact of AI across the globe in a variety of ways and industries.

We thankfully acknowledge the direction, commitment, and support of the editorial, design, and production team from Crown Custom Publishing and Berrett-Koehler for taking this book to its second edition. These behind-the-scenes people are the ones who bring the book to you!

And once again, we thank our families and friends for their support and patience during this adventurous journey.

With loving appreciation,
David, Diana, and Jackie

Introduction

Welcome to the Essentials edition of *Appreciative Inquiry Handbook*, the brief, cogent resource for learning and creating an Appreciative Inquiry (AI) initiative. This material is usable as is or may be customized to meet specific needs. This section of the book will:

- Provide background information about AI.
- List what is new in this Essentials edition.
- Describe the contents of this book.
- Set the stage for launching an AI initiative.

The Focus of Appreciative Inquiry

AI is a philosophy that incorporates an approach, a process (4-D Cycle of *Discovery, Dream, Design, and Destiny*) for engaging people at any or all levels to produce effective, positive change. Currently, AI is used throughout the world in both small- and large-scale change initiatives. It has been used as an adaptable change method in combination with other organizational processes such as strategic planning, coaching, leadership and management development, redesign of structures and systems, mergers and acquisitions, cultural transformation, team building, valuing diversity, and social and sustainable development issues.

AI is an exciting way to embrace organizational change. Its assumption is simple:

Every organization has something that works right—things that give it life when it is most alive, effective, successful, and connected in healthy ways to its stakeholders and communities. AI begins by identifying what is positive and connecting to it in ways that heighten energy, vision, and action for change.

AI begins an adventure. Its call to adventure has been experienced by many people and organizations, and it will take many more to fully explore this emergent paradigm. Current practitioners and organizations sense an exciting direction in AI's language and theories of change; they sense an invitation to "a positive revolution."

The words *positive revolution* were first used by GTE (now Verizon) to describe the impact of years of work to create an organization in full voice, a center stage for a positive revolution. Based on significant and measurable changes in stock prices, morale survey measures, quality/customer relations, union-management relations, and so on, GTE's whole system change initiative was given professional recognition by the American Society for Training & Development (ASTD). GTE won the National ASTD award for best organization change program in the country. AI was cited as the backbone of that change.

AI has exhibited staying power and longevity within organizations such as Hunter Douglas, Tendercare, British Airways, and Roadway/Yellow Trucking—all of which are highlighted in this section and discussed in more detail in other chapters. Long-term applications of AI are iterated in Table I.1. Recently, the AI process has undergone change, particularly in the *Design* phase, where the concept of altering an organization's "social architecture" has been somewhat refined and broadened, consistent with the broader notions of design as a discipline.

Approach of the Essentials Edition

This book provides an approach to launching an AI initiative. It is written to help people and their organizations take a long-term view of current activities and to achieve positive results by involving stakeholders. AI has proven to be a positive experience of a new way of living and organizing at work. Through the 4-D Cycle, people can transform the present state of their organization into a future state by building on a "positive core" of strengths to create its destiny. AI is an engaging participative process that, once begun, moves quickly to remarkable results.

Audience

This book is for trainers, executives, consultants, and students who want to be catalysts for organizational and social change. AI has been used by senior executives, line and staff managers, specialists in human resources and organizational development, leaders of nongovernmental organizations, and union management teams. The book is designed for those familiar with AI and its potential, as well as for those just beginning to explore the possibilities of AI.

The first edition of this book has been a valuable resource in many MBA and doctorate programs in business, organizational development, organizational behavior, and human resource development. This essentials edition also serves the needs of students who will be leading strategic change efforts, as well as practitioners. It is a positive response to those who have urged upon us a "core book" consisting of theoretical background and the four components of the process.

Because the AI focus is innovation and creativity, its effectiveness is not limited to organizations of a particular type, size, demographic, or industry. Both for-profit and nonprofit organizations have found AI to be effective, and it works equally well at all levels of an organization. AI is ideal for anyone who wants to be part of a positive revolution in change.

What's in This Book?

This book contains the following:
- Seven chapters of text material and resources
- Exciting examples of AI topic choices, interview guides and reports
- An AI reference and bibliography list
- "Appreciative Insights" by AI users
- Contact information
- Course outlines and agendas
- Detailed description of the 4-D Cycle: Discovery, Dream, Design, and Destiny
- A glossary of terms
- An invitation to be a member of Appreciative Inquiry Consulting, LLC

This book contains everything needed to understand the principles of AI and the way they apply. It includes a complete set of tools to design and deliver AI initiatives as well as detailed instructions and agendas for setting up multiple types of AI sessions:
- One-Hour AI Introduction
- Two-Hour Executive Overview
- Four-Hour Introductory Meeting
- Two-Day AI Program and Detailed Project Plan
- Detailed Project Plan

Each session can be used by itself or in combination with a planned initiative. Although this book covers a great deal of material, it is not exhaustive. The reader is encouraged to develop an appreciative learning library (refer to the bibliography).

What's New in the Second Edition

- Table updates are provided on new and existing uses by organizations, demonstrating the sustainability of AI.
- Chapter 1 includes the mini-lecture "Why AI Works."
- To exemplify sustainability in the AI process (in the sense of longevity of the initiative), all Case Clippings in Chapters 4–7 have been updated.
- Throughout this book, the larger meaning of sustainable enterprise has been referred to in terms of the "triple bottom line," rephrased in AI

terms as "people, prosperity, and planet."
- Chapter 3 provides a detailed employee development and healthcare project plan, an agenda, and an interview guide.
- Chapter 3 offers an expanded list of questions (up to 71) to consider when getting started.
- Chapter 6 provides two new powerful ways in which the Design phase can unfold to allow for creativity and innovation.

How to Use This Book

Used in combination with the CD-ROM (www.crowncustompublishing.com), this book contains everything needed to launch an AI initiative—background information on the topic, sample project plans, designs, agendas and interview guides, overheads, participant worksheets, and resources.

Before starting an AI initiative, the reader should review the structure and content of the entire book in order to understand the complete process. Chapter 3, Introducing, Defining, and Planning an Appreciative Inquiry Initiative, provides several illustrations and agendas that can help in designing a project plan. Part 2: Application of the 4-D Cycle of Appreciative Inquiry, evolves chapter by chapter to fully explain each phase: Discovery, Dream, Design, and Destiny. The bibliography presents new and updated information that has appeared in books, newsletters, and articles and on Web sites—an ongoing process.

AI is a robust intervention that can be molded to fit any organization's situation. However, the examples in the book are just that—examples. Creativity and innovation in developing or modifying the existing materials are encouraged and are a natural offshoot of an evolving process.

This book is designed for the novice as well as the experienced AI practitioner. For those just starting out, developing the first AI intervention will likely prove to be a time-consuming task. Sufficient time must be allowed to prepare and modify the plan. New practitioners should be patient and flexible and experience fun in embracing change. Experienced users will find this book a useful reference for further developing their AI initiatives.

This book details the transformational process needed to design, lead, and implement an AI initiative anywhere in an organization. The process starts with four simple, powerful questions being asked in an appreciative interview:

The Appreciative Interview
1. What would you describe as being a high-point experience in your organization, a time when you were most alive and engaged?
2. Without being modest, what is it that you most value about yourself, your work, and your organization?

3. What are the core factors that give life to your organization, without which the organization would cease to exist?
4. Assume you go into a deep sleep tonight, one that lasts ten years. But while you are asleep, powerful and positive changes take place, real miracles happen, and your organization becomes what you want it to be. Now you awaken and go into the organization. It is 2018, and you are very proud of what you see. As you take in this vision and look at the whole, what do you see happening that is new, changed, better, or effective and successful?

Those questions start a dialogue to discover and dream a new, more compelling image of the organization and its future. From anecdotal images, the future of the human systems within the organization is designed and the organization begins to move toward its destiny.

An AI initiative is more than just a training program. It is an opportunity to create an exciting and *dynamic* organization. To explain, the following definition is offered:

Dynamic: characterized by continuous change, activity, or progress; characterized by vigor and energy.[1]

AI recognizes that every organization is an open system that depends on its human capital to bring its vision and purpose to life. AI focuses on what gives life to an organization's system when it is operating at its best. An organization will cease to exist without a human system to lead and support it. AI identifies and leverages the positive core of an organization to ensure its ongoing success.

The outcome of an AI initiative is a long-term positive change in the organization. AI has helped many organizations increase employee satisfaction; enhance productivity; increase levels of communications among stakeholders; decrease turnover; stimulate creativity; and align the whole organization around its vision, mission, objectives, and strategies. AI is applicable to any profit, nonprofit, or governmental organization.

To be effective, business leaders need to move away from the traditional problem-solving approach to organizational change and move toward viewing organizations as a mystery to be embraced. AI provides a fresh approach to organizational change that motivates all stakeholders to contribute to the organization. When an organization uses AI to solve problems, embrace challenges, create opportunities, make decisions, and initiate action, the whole sys-

---

1 Stavros, J., & Torres, C. (2005). *Dynamic relationships: Unleashing the power of appreciative inquiry in daily living.* Chagrin Falls, OH: Taos Institute Publishing.

tem works toward a shared vision.

AI is a powerful approach to positive change. The process is simple, and it can engage everyone in the organization. Through collaborative inquiry and a connection to their positive core, many organizations have cocreated **whole systems processes** to:

- Create a common-ground vision and strategy for the future.
- Accelerate organizational learning—speeding the spread of innovation and amplifying the power of even the smallest victories.
- Unite labor and management in new, jointly envisioned partnerships.
- Create dialogue to foster shared meanings.
- Improve communications.
- Strengthen implementations of major information technology changes.
- Work toward sustainability.
- Demonstrate positive intent and trust with stakeholders.
- Build dynamic relationships and high-performance teams to facilitate change.

AI can revitalize virtually every process or program that may have been deficit-based, such as quality programs, focus groups, surveys, and reengineering efforts. AI is important because it works to bring the whole organization together to build on its positive core, one that allows for engagement in both transactional (action planning) and/or transformational change (values-vision-mission identification and alignment). AI encourages people to work together to promote a more complete understanding of the human system, the heartbeat of the organization.

AI Insight

Appreciative Inquiry can get you much better results than seeking out and solving problems. That's an interesting concept for me—and I imagine for most of you—because telephone companies are among the best problem solvers in the world. We troubleshoot everything. We concentrate enormous resources on correcting problems that have relatively minor impact on our overall service performance . . . . When used continually and over a long period of time, this approach can lead to a negative culture. If you combine a negative culture with all the challenges we face today, it could be easy to convince ourselves that we have too many problems to overcome—to slip into a paralyzing sense of hopelessness.

And yet if we flip the coin, we have so much to be excited about. We are in the most dynamic and most influential business of our times. We ought to be excited, motivated, and energized. We can be if we just turn ourselves around and start looking at our jobs (and ourselves) differently—if we kill negative self-talk and celebrate our successes. If we dissect what we do right and apply the lessons to what we do wrong, we can solve our problems and re-energize the organization at the same time . . . . In the long run, what is likely to be more useful: Demoralizing a successful workforce by concentrating on their failures or helping them over their last few hurdles by building a bridge with their successes?

Don't get me wrong. I'm not advocating mindless happy talk. Appreciative Inquiry is a complex science designed to make things better. We can't ignore problems. We just need to approach them from the other side.

Thomas H. White
President, GTE Telephone Operations
Vital Speeches of the Day, 1996

Hundreds of organizations are embracing this positive revolution through AI. Table A.1 highlights some of these organizations and their initiatives.

Table A.1 Appreciative Inquiry Initiatives

Organization	AI Initiative/Award

Academy for Educational Development, Addis Ababa, Ethiopia
More than 100 educators, government ministers, donors, and NGOs reflected on their many accomplishments and envisioned the future of education in Ethiopia for the next ten years.

ANZ Bank, Melbourne, Australia
ANZ Bank launched an inquiry into its purpose, involving more than 1,000 people—the largest engagement activity ever at the bank. Within a month, the bank crafted its purpose and had it adopted by the board of directors.

Avon Mexico
Avon Mexico addressed the issue of gender equity and a pilot project for Avon globally. It won the 1997 Catalyst Award as the best place in the country for women to work.

BAE Systems
BAE Systems created a five-year strategic plan for its Armament Systems Division with internal stakeholders and customers using the SOAR framework.

Boulder County Aging Services Division
This organization was awarded the 2007 Local Government Award "Planning with Vision" by the Denver Regional Council of Governments.

British Airways North America
British Airways created and sustained delivery of "Excellence in Customer Service."

City of Longmont, Colorado
Longmont completed the AI Core Project of the Year by the International Association for Public Participation and was awarded "All America City" by the National Civic League (2006).

Cleveland Clinic
The Cleveland Clinic discovered what made the clinic function successfully (first AI initiative).

DTE Energy Services
Its employees created a culture of choice.

EcoLogic Development Fund
This firm guided a participative strategic planning process that made it a world leader in collaborative, community-led conservation of biological and cultural diversity.

Fairmont Minerals
This firm launched a Sustainable Development Summit that created a vision and plan for 3 Ps: people, profits, and planet. It included a sustainable development design of the organization's purpose and principles in day-to-day operations, products, and services in addition to employees' personal lives.

FCI Automotive
It improved supply chain management and inventory quality.

Green Mountain Coffee Roasters
The firm increased its *Positive World Benefit through Phenomenal Sustainable Growth* while making a profit. AI is being used at all levels by providing employees with a process that fits with the strategy and culture.

Group Health Cooperative
This healthcare organization improved performance of its healthcare delivery system in the areas of cost, quality, and service.

GTE Telecommunications
GTE received the Best Organization Change Project Award from the American Society of Training & Development, 1997.

Guyana Democratic Consolidation and Conflict Resolution (GDCCR) Project—Guyana, South America
This agency inspired peace building and community development initiatives through increased citizen participation in policy reform and decision making, specifically targeting youth education, inter-religious collaboration, and participative governance.

Hunter Douglas Window Fashions Division
The company created shared vision and reinstilled the "positive core" factors (creativity, flexibility, intimacy, and sense of community) that had contributed to the division's original success, while building a sustainable leadership within the organization. It was ranked in the "Top Ten Places to Work" in Denver, Colorado (2004) and in Colorado (2006).

Imagine Chicago
This organization was the first to use AI intergenerational interviews, where young people interviewed elders to discover civic engagement and to nurture hope. Imagine Chicago has received many awards and today is helping to spawn "Imagine" projects on six continents focused on long-term sustainable development in large cities.

Imagine Nagaland (India)

This organization brought various ministries together with young people to discover the future they wanted to create. UNICEF helped guide the project, and a major film producer created a movie documentary showing the movement from hopelessness and conflict to new vision and collaboration.

Jefferson Wells

Jefferson Wells created a strategic operational plan that resulted in accelerated growth and performance, moving the selected office from rankings of sixth in the firm in revenues and eighth in profits to first in both revenues and profits with a turnover rate of 30% moving to under 10%. The office won the 2006 Global Office of the Year Award given by Manpower.

John Deere Harvester

To break through years' worth of apathy and distrust, John Deere initiated a five-day summit, the last two days focused exclusively on "tactical implementation." Participants selected ten projects they believed were most critical to organizational effectiveness and long-term performance.

Lancaster County, Pennsylvania Historical Society

The Society created a strategic plan to guide the institution for the next five years. The initiatives focused on twentieth-century history, affirmed Lancaster County's diversity, and championed the growth of technological capabilities to increase presence in the community.

Lawrence Technological University

The school completed an environmental scan and identified the core values of the university in support of the strategic plan.

Lovelace Health Systems

It improved nursing quality and retention.

Managua, Nicaragua

Nicaraguan citizens from a variety of political persuasions sponsored a two-day, 500-person AI event on civil society to create a society around shared interests, purposes, values, and vision. One of the projects resulted in a 100,000-person peaceful march (with all political parties represented) through the streets of Managua to draw attention to citizen responsibility in the electoral process.

McDonald's

McDonald's applied the Appreciative Inquiry approach in the Human Resources area and became among the best employers in each community around the world by putting "People First."

Milton Hershey School

This school designed a pioneer program that enables seniors nearing graduation to experience an advanced level of independence in life outside the residential school setting. AI is also used in the evaluation of this program.

Myrada

This organization built capacity within a network of Southern India NGOs.

NASA

NASA created a strategic plan for its OHR division to align with the larger NASA vision. This resulted in a more inclusive, participative culture.

Newark Beth Israel Medical Center

The hospital increased patient safety by redesigning the process of handing off patients from one nurse to another in a 670+ bed hospital. The staff built on their most effective handoff experiences, resulting in a 23.3% increase in patient satisfaction.

North American Steel, Inc.

This company celebrated its 40th year and tapped into the positive core of its history. The information was used for strategic planning, as 250 factory workers and managers were interviewed relative to positive experiences.

Nutrimental

The company created an innovative whole-system approach to strategic planning and decision making to achieve qualitative and quantitative outcomes; for example, a 600% increase in profits as well as a 75% reduction in absenteeism rates. The company has used the AI Summit method to do strategic planning for the past six years.

PA Community Hospitals

This group enhanced patient care delivery by improving the retention of nurses—Program: Building Capacity for Better Work and Better Care.

Princeton Group Health

Five hundred medical people—doctors, nurses, administrators, union leaders, patients, and many others—participated in whole-system planning by using AI and Future Search.

Roadway Express

This company engaged its unionized workforce to strategize about its future and increased throughput and productivity to move it from being a good organization to a great organization. The initial initiative was to reduce costs and rapidly increase business. Unionized workers, management, and staff worked together on this plan.

Save the Children

The organization changed how it could be re-created and achieved and sustained its mission.

Scandinavian School System
It received the Award for Educational Achievement, 1998.

Star Island Corporation
This firm obtained widespread, substantial involvement in the strategic planning system by including the Star Community in the process.

Syntegra – 109
The firm built a new leadership team and strategy to better approach and service its market.

Tendercare, Inc.
The company identified the positive care core needed to increase census while placing the residents in the center of the circle of quality care.

United Nations
The UN supported the Global Compact through a Leaders Summit that included more than 1,400 organizational members from business, civil society, and government to constructively engage in cocreating action plans in support of its principles.

United Religions Initiative
This group created a global interfaith organization dedicated to peace and cooperation among people of different religions, faiths, and spiritual traditions.

United States Agency for International Development (USAID)
This organization offered innovative management and leadership training to Private Voluntary Organizations (PVOs) to understand how NGOs built their capacities.

United States Navy
The focus of the initiative was to create enlightened leadership at every level of the Navy. The Navy brought together admirals and sailors at all levels for an AI Summit that included more than 250 people, and 30 projects were created to support the vision. A film was created of the event. Currently, AI Summits have occurred throughout the Navy, including the entire Pacific Fleet, to build leadership at every level.

Unity
Unity created a high-performance organizational culture congruent with its spiritual "new thought" philosophy.

Utah Education System
The teacher's union (UEA) has been using AI for more than three years. A statewide summit with legislators, media, people from the community, the board of education, teachers, administrators, university faculty, parents, and students joined together for a "Leap of Learning" facilitated by members of the Positive Change Core. In 2007, the school district committed to infusing the AI philosophy in classrooms.

World Vision Relief and Development
The organization built collaborative alliances to bring help and developmental assistance to thousands of children in hundreds of orphanages across Romania. More than 300 organizations were connected in a partnership, building on a strength- based analysis of each. Many papers were written about the effort, making possible the new "knowledge alliance" and resulting in millions of dollars in medical support.

Structure of the Book

AI Insight

AI was first used in 1980, when David Cooperrider, a doctoral student at Case Western Reserve University, was helping Al Jensen undertake his dissertation on physician leadership at one of the top tertiary care medical centers in the world, the Cleveland Clinic. They asked physician leaders to tell stories of their biggest successes as well as their biggest failures. But when Cooperrider looked at the data, he was drawn only to the success stories. Listening to their narratives of strength and strong leadership, he was amazed by the level of positive cooperation, innovation, and egalitarian governance at the clinic—by consensus, this was when organizational members were most effective. With the intellectual collaboration and prodding of his adviser, Suresh Srivastva, and the permission of the clinic's chair, David decided to look at the data exclusively in search of the positives—everything that served to give life to the system and to people when they were most alive, effective, committed, and empowered. Everything else was considered irrelevant.

The method of analysis was to systematically and deliberately "appreciate" everything of value, then use the positive analysis to speculate on the potentials and possibilities for the future. A theory of future possibility was created, and momentous stories were used to vivify the potentials. History was used as a source of positive possibility. In a report to the board of governors, Cooperrider and Srivastva called their method Appreciative Inquiry (AI). Thus, this was the first organizational analysis using AI. The results of the study created such a powerful positive stir that the board requested that this AI method be used at all levels of the 8,000-person organization to facilitate change. Cooperrider wrote his dissertation on the holistic process and created a scholarly logic for this, a new form of action research. This experience set the stage for the AI learning community!

To facilitate conceptual understanding and effective practical use of AI, the material in the book is presented in two parts. *Part 1: Essential Elements of Appreciative Inquiry* provides a powerful learning approach to (1) gaining an understanding of basic AI principles, (2) selecting an affirmative topic on which to build from the positive core, and (3) starting an AI initiative. The material presented in this section is a call to working with people, groups, and organizations in a more positive, collaborative, and constructive approach than perhaps they have utilized in the past. It provides all of the essential ingredients to design and lead strengths-based positive change in one's organization or community.

The 4-D appreciative learning model is the focus of *Part 2: Application of the 4-D Cycle of Appreciative Inquiry.* The process is dynamic and interactive. It builds on imagination and flexibility for its success. It starts with Discovery. At this stage, the "best of what is" in a system is identified as the positive core. The second stage is Dream. This stage teaches a visioning process to suggest "what might be." The third stage is Design. The Design chapter outlines the steps to create the ideal system for an organization. It builds on the positive core and the envisioned results of the first two stages. It allows for coconstructing the ideal design, "how it can be." The final stage is termed Destiny. The Destiny chapter covers the implementation and model for sustaining an appreciative learning environment, "what will be." Thus, Part 2 moves through the phases of discovery, dream, design, and destiny—the "4 Ds."

A glossary, index, and a list of additional resources are also included. Today more than 500 scholarly papers pertaining to AI have been published worldwide; in addition, a dozen books and many Web sites are devoted to the practice of AI.

How Can AI Make a Difference?

This book is not a recipe; it is an adventure. AI is an effective way to get members of an organization involved in unleashing a positive revolution in today's dynamic global environment. The objectives of the book are to teach the founding principles and theories of AI, present a wide range of applications of the theory and the AI 4-D Cycle, and facilitate the training of trainers who will introduce and use AI. Therefore, the final section of this book includes resources to facilitate group teaching, learning, and application.

An organization's guiding force is its people. This book offers those people a framework for an appreciative learning journey that has proven to be successful in cocreating organizational systems that feature each organization operating at its best.

Where Can AI Make a Difference?

AI can make a difference with a single person or with any collective human system. To illustrate, AI has been successfully used in the following ways:

- Innovations leading toward the ideal organization
- Strategic planning
- Leadership and management development
- Work process redesign
- Team development
- Organizational culture change
- Employee development
- HR practices: staffing, orientation, and performance management
- Coaching
- Communications
- Collaborative alliances and joint ventures
- Community relations and customer relations
- Diversity initiatives
- Focus groups
- Generative benchmarking
- Surveys
- Meetings
- Global change initiatives
- Evaluation to valuation of performance systems
- New product development

AI is a proven paradigm for accelerating organizational learning and transformation. It can be used in any situation where the leaders and organizational members are committed to building positive, life-centered organizations.

You are ready to begin the journey.

PART 1
Essential Elements of Appreciative Inquiry

Part I: Essential Elements of Appreciative Inquiry (AI)

Since the publication of the first edition in 2003, much has happened in the practice of Appreciative Inquiry (AI) and in the creation of new and connecting theories, as is apparent from the additional 125 resources and 40 studies/dissertations that were completed. (You can find these in the updated Bibliography.) The field of AI has "come of age" and has taken its place as a prominent change process within the field and textbooks of organizational development, behavior, and change.

Part 1 seeks to impart a powerful learning approach to gaining a better understanding of basic AI principles, theories, and applications. Chapter 1 touches briefly on the evolutionary changes in AI over the past several years. In addition, as in the first edition, this book gives a brief but *precise* review of the theory of AI with nine mini-lectures that includes one new piece on why AI works and sustains itself. These mini-lectures have been found to be useful in introducing AI to an organization.

AI as a strength-based approach and a process (4-D Cycle) has recently exhibited resonance with broader definitions of *sustainable development* and *sustainable enterprise*. Sustainable development is defined by the World Business Council for Sustainable Development (WBCSD) as "forms of progress that meet the needs of the present without compromising the ability of future generations to meet their needs" (http://www.wbcsd.org). The sustainable enterprise is a firm or an organization that maintains and re-creates itself over time while simultaneously attending to the triple bottom line of social, environmental, and economic benefits being distributed to the entire world. These concepts are connected to AI in Chapter 2.

Chapter 3 presents the basics of starting an AI initiative that includes 60 new questions to consider in the planning phases, together with sample agendas ranging from a one-hour brief introduction to a two-day AI workshop. A new case application in healthcare, The University of Kentucky Hospital/UK Children's Hospital, is included with a project overview, agendas, the interview guide, and summit materials.

1

The Theoretical Basis of Appreciative Inquiry

Ap-pre'ci-ate, *v.*, 1. *to value; recognize the best in people or the world around us; affirm past and present strengths, successes, and potentials; to perceive those things that give life (health, vitality, excellence) to living systems. 2. to increase in value, e.g., the economy has appreciated in value. Synonyms: value, prize, esteem, and honor.*

In-quire', *v.*, 1. *to explore and discover. 2. to ask questions; to be open to seeing new potentials and possibilities. Synonyms: discover, search, systematically explore, and study.*

This chapter begins by introducing the theory and creation of AI. **Appreciative Inquiry** is an organization development (OD) process and approach to change management that grows out of social constructionist thought and its applications to management and organizational transformation. Through its deliberately positive assumptions about people, organizations, and relationships, AI leaves behind deficit-oriented approaches to management and vitally transforms the ways to approach questions of organizational improvement and effectiveness. Such questions include culture change, survey analysis, strategic planning, organizational learning, customer focus groups, leadership development, team building, quality management, measurement systems, joint ventures and alliances, diversity training, performance appraisal, communications programs, internal online networks, corporate history writing and others.

Presented here is a thesis, a proposition regarding the future of OD and change management. The thesis is a significant shift from "traditional" problem-solving methodologies. AI exhibits embedded wisdom that is reminiscent of early pioneers such as Kurt Lewin, Mary Parker Follett, Herb Shepard, and others. The thesis might be summarized this way:

> We may have reached the end of traditional problem solving. AI is a powerful approach to transformation as a mode of inquiry capable of inspiring, mobilizing, and sustaining human system change. The future of OD belongs, instead, to methods that affirm, compel, and accelerate anticipatory learning involving larger and larger levels of collectivity.

The new methods are distinguished by the art and science of asking powerful and unconditional positive questions. (Someday there will be an "encyclopedia of questions" that brings together classic formulations such as Maslow's interview protocols on peak human experience and Peters and Waterman's studies of organizational excellence or Vereena Kast's exceptional studies of joy, inspiration, and hope.) The new methods view realities as socially constructed. Therefore, they will become more radically relational, widening the circles of dialogue to groups of hundreds, thousands, and perhaps (due to cyberspace) millions. The arduous task of intervention will give way to the speed of imagination and innovation. Instead of negation, criticism, and spiraling diagnoses, there will be discovery, dream, design, and destiny.

AI: A Brief Introduction

AI has been described in many ways. Here is a practitioner-oriented definition:

> *Appreciative Inquiry is the cooperative co-evolutionary search for the best in people, their organizations, and the world around them. It involves the discovery of what gives "life" to a living system when it is most effective, alive, and constructively capable in economic, ecological, and human terms. AI involves the art and practice of asking questions that strengthen a system's capacity to apprehend, anticipate, and heighten positive potential. The inquiry is mobilized through the crafting of the "unconditional positive question," often involving hundreds or thousands of people. AI interventions focus on the speed of imagination and innovation instead of the negative, critical, and spiraling diagnoses commonly used in organizations. The discovery, dream, design, and destiny model links the energy of the positive core to changes never thought possible.*

AI is based on the simple assumption that every organization has something that works well, and those strengths can be the starting point for creating positive change. Inviting people to participate in dialogues and share stories about their past and present achievements, assets, unexplored potentials, innovations, strengths, elevated thoughts, opportunities, benchmarks, high-point moments, lived values, traditions, core and **distinctive competencies**, expressions of wisdom, insights into the deeper corporate spirit and soul, and visions of valued and possible futures can identify a "positive core." From this, AI links the energy of the positive core directly to any change agenda. This link creates energy and excitement and a desire to move toward a shared dream.

AI, an approach to organizational analysis and learning, is also intended for discovering, understanding, and fostering innovations in social organizational arrangements and processes. In this context, AI refers to:

- A search for knowledge.
- A theory of collective action designed to evolve the vision and will of a group, an organization, or a society as a whole.

AI is deliberate in its life-centric search. Carefully constructed inquiries allow the practitioner to affirm the symbolic capacities of imagination and mind as well as the social capacity for conscious choice and cultural evolution. The art of "appreciation" is the art of discovering and valuing those factors that give life to a group or an organization. The process involves interviewing and storytelling to draw out the best of the past, to understand what one wants more of, and to set the stage for effective visualization of the future.

The following propositions underlie the practice of AI:

1. **Inquiry into "the art of the possible" in organizational life should begin with appreciation.** Every system works to some degree. Therefore, a primary task of management and organizational analysis is to discover, describe, and explain those "exceptional moments" that give life to the system and activate members' competencies and energies. The appreciative approach takes its inspiration from "what is." This is the first step of the process in the 4-D Cycle: *Discovery*. Valuing, learning, and inspired understanding are the aims of the appreciative spirit.

2. **Inquiry into what is possible should yield information that is applicable.** Organizational study should lead to the generation of knowledge that can be used, applied, and validated in action.

3. **Inquiry into what is possible should be provocative.** An organization is an open-ended, indeterminate system capable of becoming more than it is at any given moment and learning how to actively take part in guiding its own evolution. Appreciative knowledge of "what is" becomes provocative to the extent that the learning stirs members to action. In this way, AI allows use of **systematic management** analysis to help an organization's members shape an effective future according to their imaginative and moral purposes.

4. **Inquiry into the human potential of organizational life should be collaborative.** This principle assumes an immutable relationship between the process of inquiry and its content. A unilateral approach to the study of social innovation is a direct negation of the phenomenon itself.

In its most practical construction, AI is a form of organizational study that selectively seeks to locate, highlight, and illuminate what are referred to as the life-giving forces of the organization's existence, its positive core.

In this sense, two basic questions are behind any AI initiative:

1. What, in this particular setting and context, gives life to this system—when it is most alive, healthy, and symbiotically related to its various communities?

2. What are the possibilities—expressed and latent—to provide opportunities for more effective (value-congruent) forms of organizing?

AI seeks out the exceptional best of "what is" (*Discovery*) to help ignite the collective imagination of "what might be" (*Dream*). The aim is to generate new knowledge of a collectively desired future. It carries forth the vision in ways that successfully translate images into possibilities, intentions into reality, and beliefs into practice.

As a method of organizational analysis, AI differs from conventional managerial problem solving. The basic assumption of problem solving is that "organizing is a problem to be solved." The task of improvement traditionally involves removing deficits by (1) identifying the key problems or deficiencies, (2) analyzing the causes, (3) analyzing solutions, and (4) developing an action plan.

In contrast, the underlying assumption of AI is that an organization is a "solution to be embraced" rather than a "problem to be solved." The phases are shown in Figure 1.1, Appreciative Inquiry 4-D Cycle. It starts with selecting a topic: affirmative topic choice. What follows are *Discovery* (appreciating and valuing), *Dream* (envisioning), *Design* (coconstructing the future), and *Destiny* (learning, empowering, and improvising to sustain the future). These are the essence of dialogue woven through each step of the process.

Figure 1.1: Appreciative Inquiry "4-D" Cycle

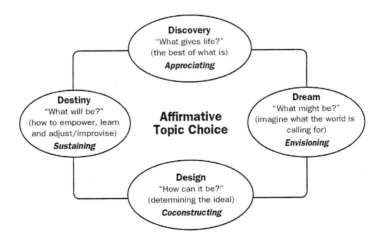

The first step in this process is to discover and value those factors that give life to the organization. For example, the organization might discover and value its commitment and identify when that commitment was at its highest (affirmative topic choice: highest commitment). Regardless of how few or infrequent the moments of highest commitment were, the organization's task is to focus on them and discuss the factors and forces that served as fertile ground for that exceptional level of commitment.

The First D is *Discovery*

The list of positive or affirmative topics for *Discovery* is endless: high quality, integrity, empowerment, innovation, customer responsiveness, technological innovation, team spirit, best in class, and so on. In each case, the task is to discover the positive exceptions, successes, and most vital or alive moments. Discovery involves valuing those things that are worth valuing. It can be done within and across organizations (in a benchmarking sense) and across time (organizational history as positive possibility).

As part of the *Discovery* process, individuals engage in **dialogue** and meaning-making. This is simply the open sharing of discoveries and possibilities. Through dialogue, a consensus begins to emerge whereby individuals in the organization say, "Yes, this is an ideal or a vision that we value and should aspire to." Through conversation and dialogue, individual appreciation becomes collective appreciation, individual will evolves into group will, and individual vision becomes a cooperative or shared vision for the organization.

AI helps create a deliberately supportive context for dialogue. It is through the sharing of ideals that social bonding occurs. What makes AI different from other OD methodologies at this phase is that every question is positive.

From *Discovery* to *Dream*

Second, participants *Dream,* or envision what might be. It occurs when the best of "what is" has been identified; the mind naturally begins to search further and to envision new possibilities. Valuing the best of "what is" leads to envisioning what might be. Envisioning involves passionate thinking, creating a positive image of a desired and preferred future. The *Dream* step uses the interview stories from the *Discovery* step to elicit the key themes that underlie the times when the organization was most alive and at its best.

Articulated *Dream(s)* to *Design*

Third, participants **coconstruct** the future by the *Design* of an **organizational architecture** in which the exceptional becomes everyday and ordinary. This design is more than a vision. It is a provocative and inspiring statement of intention that is grounded in the realities of what has worked in the past combined with what new ideas are envisioned for the future. It enhances the organization by leveraging its own past successes and successes that have been experienced elsewhere with a "strategic intent." Strategic intent signals what the organizations wants more of and recognizes that the future is built around what can be and what is.[1]

Design to *Destiny*

Fourth, the *Design* delivers the organization to its *Destiny* through innovation and action. AI establishes a momentum of its own. Once guided by a shared image of what might be, members of the organization find innovative ways to help move the organization closer to the ideal. Again, because the ideals are grounded in realities, the organization is empowered to make things happen. This is important because it is precisely through the juxtaposition of visionary content with grounded examples of the extraordinary that AI opens the status quo to transformations via collective action. By seeking an imaginative and fresh perception of organizations (as if seen for the very first time), the appreciative eye takes nothing for granted, seeking to apprehend the basis of organizational life and working to articulate the possibilities for a better existence.

Part 2 of the book covers the 4-D Cycle of AI in detail.

The principles that underlie AI are deeply grounded in scientific research and are highlighted in the remainder of this section in Mini-lectures I–IX. While the practitioner need not have a thorough understanding of these principles, it is often helpful when introducing AI to an organization to provide some of the supporting theory and research. The following presentation ideas are organized into nine brief mini-lectures. Each one refers to the theoretical constructs on which AI is based. Practitioners can successfully introduce AI by introducing and adapting these key concepts to the language and culture of the organization.

---

1 deKluyver, C., & Pearce, J. A. (2006). *Strategy: A view from the top.* Upper Saddle River, NJ: Prentice Hall.

Mini-lecture I: Five Principles of AI

The following five principles inspired and moved the foundation of AI from theory to practice:

1. The Constructionist Principle
2. The Principle of Simultaneity
3. The Poetic Principle
4. The Anticipatory Principle
5. The Positive Principle

Launching an AI initiative requires an understanding of these principles to fully grasp AI theory and to internalize the basis of the 4-D Cycle.

The full conceptual article on these principles, "Appreciative Inquiry into Organizational Life," is located in Chapter 11.

1. **Constructionist Principle:** Social knowledge and organizational destiny are interwoven. A constructionist would argue that the seeds of organizational change are implicit in the first questions asked. The questions asked become the material out of which the future is conceived and constructed. Thus, the way of knowing is fateful.[2] To be effective as executives, leaders, **change agents**, and so on, one must be adept in the art of reading, understanding, and analyzing organizations as living, human constructions. Knowing organizations is at the core of virtually every OD task. Because styles of thinking rarely match the increasingly complex world, there must be a commitment to the ongoing pursuit of multiple and more fruitful ways of knowing.

    The most important resource for generating constructive organizational change is cooperation between the imagination and the reasoning function of the mind (the capacity to unleash the imagination and mind of groups). AI is a way of reclaiming imaginative competence. Unfortunately, people's habitual styles of thought include preconscious background assumptions, root metaphors, and rules of analysis that come to define organizations in a particular way. These styles have often constrained the managerial imagination and mind.

---

2 For more information, refer to Gergen, K. *Realities and relationships.* (1994). Cambridge, MA: Harvard University Press and *Social construction: Entering the dialogue.* (2004). Chagrin Falls, OH: Taos Institute Publishing.

2. **Principle of Simultaneity:** This principle recognizes that inquiry and change are not truly separate moments; they can and should be simultaneous. Inquiry is intervention. The seeds of change are the things people think and talk about, the things people discover and learn, and the things that inform dialogue and inspire images of the future. They are implicit in the very first questions asked. One of the most impactful things a change agent or OD practitioner does is to articulate questions. The questions set the stage for what is "found" and what is "discovered" (the data). These data become the stories out of which the future is conceived, discussed, and constructed.

3. **Poetic Principle:** A useful **metaphor** in understanding this principle is that human organizations are an "open book." An organization's story is constantly being coauthored. Moreover, pasts, presents, and futures are endless sources of learning, inspiration, or interpretation (as in the endless interpretive possibilities in a good work of poetry or a biblical text). The important implication is that one can study virtually any topic related to human experience in any human system or organization. The choice of inquiry can focus on the nature of alienation or joy in any human organization or community. One can study moments of creativity and innovation or moments of debilitating bureaucratic stress. One has a choice.

4. **Anticipatory Principle:** The most important resource for generating constructive organizational change or improvement is collective imagination and discourse about the future. One of the basic theorems of the anticipatory view of organizational life is that the image of the future guides what might be called the current behavior of any organism or organization. Much like a movie projected on a screen, human systems are forever projecting ahead of themselves a horizon of expectation that brings the future powerfully into the present as a mobilizing agent. In the final analysis, organizations exist because people who govern and maintain them share some sort of discourse or projection about what the organization is, how it will function, what it will achieve, and what it will likely become.

5. **Positive Principle:** This last principle is more concrete. It grows out of years of experience with AI. Put most simply, momentum for change requires large amounts of positive affect and social

bonding, attitudes such as hope, inspiration, and the sheer joy of creating with one another. Organizations, as human constructions, are largely affirmative systems and thus are responsive to positive thought and positive knowledge. The more positive the questions used to guide a group building an OD initiative, the more long-lasting and effective is the change.[3] In important respects, people and organizations move in the direction of their inquiries. Thousands of interviews into "empowerment" or "being the easiest business in the industry to work with" will have a completely different long-term impact in terms of sustaining positive action than a study of "low morale" or "process breakdowns."

These five principles are central to AI's theoretical basis for organizing for a positive revolution in change. These principles clarify that it is the positive image that results in the positive action. The organization must make the affirmative decision to focus on the positive to lead the inquiry.

For more detailed information and application of the AI principles, refer to *Dynamic Relationships: Unleashing the Power of Appreciative Inquiry in Daily Living* by Jackie Stavros and Cheri Torres (Chagrin Falls, OH: Taos Institute Publishing, 2005).

Mini-lecture II:
Positive Image — Positive Action

The power of positive imagery, as illustrated in the fifth principle, is a key factor in the AI dialogue. There are six main areas of research to support this premise: research into the placebo effect, Pygmalion effect, positive effect, internal dialogue, positive imagery, and metacognitive competence. This section briefly elaborates on each area. The original article "Positive Image, Positive Action: The Affirmative Basis of Organizing" appears in the accompanying CD-ROM (www.crowncustompublishing.com).

1. **Powerful Placebo:** The **placebo effect** is a fascinating process in which projected images, as reflected in positive belief, ignite a healing response that can be as powerful as conventional therapy or any

---

3 See Bushe, G., & Coetzer, G. (March 1994). Appreciative inquiry as a team-development intervention: A controlled experiment. *Journal of Applied Behavioral Science*, 31, 13.

other intervention. In the twentieth century, the placebo effect is accepted by most medical professions as genuine. Between one-third and two-thirds of all patients show marked physiological and emotional improvement in symptoms simply by believing they were given an effective treatment, even when that treatment was a sugar pill or some other inert substance. While the complex mind-body pathways are far from being completely understood, there is one area of clear agreement: positive changes in anticipatory reality through suggestion and belief play a central role in all placebo responses.

2. **Pygmalion Effect:** In the classic Pygmalion study,[4] on the basis of "credible" information, teachers are led to believe that some of their students possess exceptionally high potential while others do not. Thus, the teachers are led, on the basis of some expert opinion, to hold a positive image (PI) or expectancy of some students, and a negative image (NI) or expectancy of others. Unknown to the teachers, however, is the fact that the so-called high-potential students were selected at random. In objective terms, all student groups were equivalent in potential and were merely dubbed as high, regular, or low in learning potential. As the experiment unfolds, differences quickly emerge— not on the basis of any innate intelligence factor or some other predisposition, but solely on the basis of the manipulated expectancy of the teacher. Over time, subtle changes among students evolve into clear differences, as the high-PI students began to significantly overshadow all others in actual achievement.

    The key lesson is that cognitive capacities are cued and shaped by the images projected through another's expectations. For example, what is seen is believed. As a result, actions and behaviors take on a whole new tone based on the perceived image. In turn, the resulting differential behavioral treatment makes the people receiving this treatment begin to respond to the positive images that others have of them. The greatest value of the Pygmalion research is that it provides empirical understanding of the relational pathways of the positive image—positive action dynamic.

3. **Positive Effect and Learned Helpfulness:** While still in the formative stages, early results on this issue suggest that positive imagery evokes positive emotions and positive emotions move people

---

4 Rosenthal, R. (1969). *Pygmalion in the classroom.* New York: Holt, Rinehart and Winston.

toward a choice for positive actions. Positive emotions are inti-
mately connected with social helpfulness. This line of research is
an expansion on an earlier, empirically validated theory of learned
helplessness articulated by Martin Seligman and others in the
growing field of positive psychology. Somehow, positive emotions
draw people out of themselves, pull them away from self-orient-
ed preoccupations, enlarge their focus on the potential good in the
world, increase feelings of solidarity with others, and propel people to act in more altruistic and positive ways.[5] For more than a
dozen years, Dr. Barbara Fredrickson has been studying the effect
of positive emotions in the workplace. Her work has demonstrated the improvement in individual and collective functioning, psychological well-being, and physical health due to positive imagery.[6]

4. **Inner Dialogue (2:1):** It is argued that all human systems exhibit
a continuing "cinematographic show of visual imagery" or ongoing "inner newsreel" that is best understood through the notion
of inner dialogue. For example, a study of a stressful medical procedure indicated that people may have thoughts that impede the
aim of the clinical intervention (this procedure may kill me, a negative image) or that facilitate the goals of the care (this will save
my life, a positive image). Hence, the inner dialogue functions as
an inner dialectic between positive and negative adaptive statements. One's guiding imagery is presumably an outcome of such
an inner dialectic. In addition, studies show that there is a definite
imbalance in the internal dialogue in the direction of positive
imagery for those groups of individuals identified as more psy-
chologically or socially functional. Functional groups are characterized by a 2:1 ratio of positive images to negative images,
whereas mildly dysfunctional groups demonstrate equal fre-
quencies—a balanced 1:1 internal dialogue.

   The AI dialogue creates guiding images of the future from the
collective whole of the group. It exists in an observable, energizing, and tangible way in the living dialogue that flows through
every living system, expressing itself anew at every moment,
thereby enhancing the chances of the 2:1 imagery to prevail in a
group setting.

---

5 Seligman, M. (1992). *Helplessness: On development, depression, and death.* New York: W. H. Freeman.

6 For more information on the broaden-and-build theory, refer to Fredrickson, B. (2003). The value of positive emotions. *American Scientist*, 91, 330–335.

5. **Positive Imagery as a Dynamic Force:** Various scholars have noted that the underlying images that a civilization or a culture holds have an enormous influence on its fate. In his study of Western civilization, the Dutch sociologist Fred Polak argued this point concerning the tendency of the positive image. For him, the positive image of the future is the single most important dynamic and explanatory variable for understanding cultural evolution. Therefore, as long as an organization's or society's image is positive and flourishing, the dynamic culture is growing toward the positive images of the future. When there is a vision or a bright image of the future, the people flourish.

6. **Metacognition and Conscious Evolution of Positive Images:** Metacognition is awareness of one's own cognitive systems and knowledge and insight into its workings. It is the awareness that prompts a person to write reminders to himself or herself to avoid forgetting something.[7] The **heliotropic** hypothesis states that human systems have an observable tendency to evolve and move in the direction of those positive images that are the brightest and boldest, most illuminating, and promising. To the extent that the heliotropic hypothesis has some validity, questions of volition and free agency come to the fore.

   - Is it possible to develop metacognitive capacity and thereby choose positive ways of construing the world? If so, with what result?
   - Is the quest for affirmative competence, the capacity to project and affirm an ideal image as if it is already so, a realistic aim or merely a romantic distraction?
   - Is it possible to develop the affirmative competence of large collectives, that is, of groups, organizations, or whole societies affirming a positive future together?[8]

With the exception of the last question (where not enough research has been completed), most of the available evidence suggests quite clearly that affirmative competence can be learned, developed, and honed through experience and disciplined, formal training. One example is that imagery techniques are becoming important to the successful training of athletes. Experimental evidence indicates that the best athletes may be successful because of a high-

---

7 Ashcraft, M. (1997). *Fundamentals of cognition.* Englewood Cliffs, NJ: Prentice Hall.
8 Ibid.

ly developed **metacognitive** capacity of differential self-monitoring. In brief, this capacity involves being able to systematically observe and analyze successful performances (positive self-monitoring) or unsuccessful performances (negative self-monitoring) and to be able to choose between the two cognitive processes when desired. The professional athlete wills himself or herself to succeed by envisioning (imagining) a positive outcome to his or her next action or series of actions.

These examples demonstrate the power of positive imagery leading to positive actions and demonstrate that such imagery on a collective basis may be the strongest approach to cocreating a positive future. It is time to concentrate as never before on the power of positive images in leading to positive actions. Through such studies, new knowledge and images of possibility have been created.

Mini-lecture III:
Social Constructionism

A central premise of AI is that the appreciative process of knowing is socially constructed. In other words, knowing takes place through interaction with and within a social system. That is why AI views organizations as centers of human relatedness. Thus, by getting people to unite on a central theme or idea, AI allows people who share a related objective to project or construct their future—in this case, the future of an organization.

The idea that a social system creates or determines its own reality is known as **social constructionism**. AI takes this theoretical framework and places it in a positive context. This positive spin on social constructionism is central to AI. Many of its principles flow from the idea that people control their destiny by envisioning what they want to occur and developing actions to move toward this end result. There is considerable overlap between the AI model and social constructionism theory. Some areas of overlap include the following:

1. The social order at any given point is viewed as the product of broad social agreement.

2. Patterns of social/organizational action are not fixed by nature in any direct biological or physical way; the vast share of social conduct is virtually stimulus-free, capable of infinite conceptual variation.

3. From an observational point of view, all social action is open to multiple interpretations, not one of which is superior in any objective

sense. The interpretations favored in one historical setting may be replaced in the next.

4. Historical narratives and theories govern what is taken to be true or valid. To a large extent, such narratives determine what scientists and laypersons are able to see. An observation, therefore, is filtered through conventional stories, belief systems, and theoretical lenses.

5. To the extent that action is predicated on the stories, ideas, beliefs, meanings, and theories embedded in language, people are free to seek transformations in conventional conduct by changing patterns of narration.

6. The most powerful vehicle communities have for changing the social order is through the act of dialogue made possible by language. Therefore, alterations in linguistic practices hold profound implications for changes in social practice.

7. Social theory can be viewed as a highly refined narrative account with a specialized grammar all its own. As a powerful linguistic tool (created by trained linguistic experts), theory may enter the conceptual meaning system of a culture and, in this way, alter patterns of social action.

8. Whether intended or not, all theoretical accounts are normative and have the potential to influence the social order. Therefore, all narrative accounts (including social theory) are morally relevant. They have the potential to affect the way people interact with one another. This point is a critical one because it implies that there is no such thing as a detached, technical, scientific mode for judging the ultimate worth of value claims.

9. Value knowledge or social theory is, therefore, a narrative creation, not an aspect of the physical world. Social knowledge is not "out there" in nature to be discovered through detached, value-free, observational methods (**logical empiricism**); nor can it be relegated to the subjective minds of isolated individuals (**cognitivism**). Viewed from this perspective, social knowledge resides in the stories of the collectivity; it is created, maintained, and put to use by the human group. Dialogue, free from constraint of distortion, is necessary to determine the "nature of things" (social constructionism).

More information on the social constructionist viewpoint can be found in Kenneth and Mary Gergen's work listed in the References and Bibliography at the end of the book. Visit http://www.taosinstitute.net for a detailed listing of their publications.

Mini-lecture IV:
Beyond Problem Solving to AI

Since the 1930s, organizations have used a **deficit-based approach to problem solving**. It begins with seeking out the problem, the weak link in the system. Typically, there is a diagnosis; then alternative solutions are recommended. AI challenges this traditional paradigm with an "affirmative" approach, embracing an organization's challenges in a positive light. AI offers an alternative—to look for what is good in the organization, its success stories.

In Figure 1.2, Paradigm 1's basic assumption is that an organization is a problem that needs to be solved. Paradigm 2's basic assumption is that an organization is a mystery that should be embraced as a human center of infinite imagination, infinite capacity, and potential. The word mystery signifies, literally, a future that is unknowable and cannot be predicted. And this is true of organizations because nobody knows when or where the next creative insight will emerge that can shift everything or how a fresh combination of strengths will open to horizons never seen before. Paradigm 1 depicts organizations as broken-down machines in need of fixing; they are problems to be solved. Therefore, every analysis begins with some variation of the same question: What is wrong? What are the problems? What are the causes?

Figure 1.2 Two Paradigms for Organizational Change

Paradigm 1: Problem Solving	Paradigm 2: Appreciative Inquiry
"Felt Need" Identification of Problem	Appreciating "Valuing the Best of What Is"
⇓	⇓
Analysis of Causes	Envisioning "What Might Be"
⇓	⇓
Analysis of Possible Solutions	Dialoguing "What Should Be"
⇓	⇓
Action Planning (Treatment)	Innovating "What Will Be"
Organizing is a problem to be solved.	*Organizing is a mystery (infinite capacity) to be embraced.*

Paradigm 2 says something quite different. Organizations are not problematic. Indeed, no organization was created as a "problem." Organizations, if anything, are meant as solutions. But even more than that, organizations are not even singular solutions. They are creative centers of human relatedness, alive with emergent and unlimited capacity. Paradigm 2 is "life-centric." It searches for everything that gives life to a human system when it is most alive. It is creative and in a healthy relationship with its extended communities. AI is an approach to organizational change that is unique and refreshing. Detached observers of AI say that it is one of the most powerful, yet largely unrecognized models available to the OD and change management fields.

Mini-lecture V: Vocabularies of Human Deficit

AI Insight

While AI was still evolving, Frank Barrett and David Cooperrider teamed up to work with a hotel that was experiencing low occupancy, with the staff and management locked in a setting of distrust and backbiting. Both sides were extremely negative toward each other, and neither was able to move past this to see a more positive option. In order to turn this hotel around, the AI team knew the first step was to shift the focus from a negative mind-set to one of openness. The AI team took the group to experience a four-star hotel. The staff and management did an inquiry to focus on what made this property an award-winning hotel. They focused on what worked well. From this inquiry, they learned they could work in similar ways to transform their hotel to a four-star hotel. Negative conversations turned into discussions of how they could be more than what they were. The transformation began, and the hotel became a top-rated four-star hotel. Frank Barrett and David Cooperrider coauthored a major paper on the breakthrough called "Generative Metaphor Intervention," and it received Best Paper of the Year Award at the Academy of Management's OD Division in 1988.[9]

---

9 See Barrett, F., & Cooperrider, D. (1991). Generative metaphor intervention: A new approach to intergroup conflict. *Journal of Applied Behavioral Science*, 26.

A fundamental assumption underlying AI is that the language one uses creates one's reality. Therefore, the emotional meaning of words such as dysfunctional, codependent, and stressed out affect one's thinking and acting, as illustrated earlier in the Pygmalion effect. This deficit-based vocabulary can inhibit the vision for a better and brighter future and limit growth.

Examples of deficit-based vocabularies are prolific in everyday conversation. Organizations, too, have adopted this mentality and spend considerable resources to train managers to remain vigilant at uncovering problems and identifying issues. As a result, many believe that a manager's job is to solve problems. This mentality constantly seeks to reinforce the idea that only by focusing on the problems can a better organization be created.

These tremendous expansions in vocabularies of human and organizational deficit can best be illustrated in Table 1.1, Vocabularies of Human Deficit,[10] and Table 1.2, Vocabularies of Organizational Deficit.

Table 1.1: Vocabularies of Human Deficit

Depressed	Midlife Crisis	Extremely Controlled
Bulimic	Kleptomaniac	Obsessive-Compulsive
Antisocial Personality	Neurotic	Low Self-Esteem
Paranoid	Anorexic	Identity Crisis
Posttraumatic Stress	Psychopathic Co-dependent	
Sadomasochistic	Dysfunctional Family	
Brief Psychotherapy		

Table 1.2 Vocabularies of Organizational Deficit

Organizational Stress	Theory X	Job Dissatisfaction
Work Alienation	Turfism	Neurotic Organization
Authoritarian Management	Low Morale	Executive Burnout
Role Conflict	Groupthink	Intergroup Conflict
Defensive Routines	Peter Principle Inflexibility	Structural
Bureaucratic Red Tape	Labor-Management Mistrust	Dilbert Bureaucracy
Interpersonal Incompetence	Organizational Diagnosis	Organization Learning Disabilities

10 All of these terms have come into common usage only within the past century (several only in the last two decades). See Gergen, K. (1991). *The saturated self.* New York: Basic Books.

To break through this negative vocabulary framework, AI proposes an affirmative vocabulary of organizing for the future. Why? As noted earlier, human systems and organizations move in the direction of what they study. The sooner the unconditional positive question is asked, the sooner the right answers can be obtained. This principle leads to the affirmative theory of organizing.

Mini-lecture VI: Toward a Theory of Affirmative Organization

The AI adventure truly begins with the appreciative mind-set, eye, thoughts, and vocabulary based upon the following concepts:

1. Organizations are made and imagined.

2. No matter what the durability to date, virtually any pattern of action is open to alteration and reconfiguration.

3. Organizations are "heliotropic" in character in the sense that organizational actions have an observable and largely "automatic" tendency to move in the direction of images of the future.

4. The more an organization experiments with the conscious evolution of positive imagery, the better it will become. There is an observable self-reinforcing, educating effect of affirmation. Affirmative competence is the key to the self-organizing system.

5. Paradoxically, the following is also true: the greatest obstacle in the way of group and organizational well-being is also the positive image, the affirmative projection that guides the group or organization.

6. Organizations do not need to be fixed. They need constant reaffirmation.

7. Leadership = Affirmation.

8. The challenge for organizational learning and development is creating the condition for organization-wide appreciation. This is the single most important act that can be taken to ensure the conscious evolution of a valued and positive future.

Once these simple, yet powerful concepts are internalized, the conditions that are essential to becoming an affirmative organization of change fall into place.

Mini-lecture VII: Assessing Organizational Inner Dialogue

Too often there is a tendency for OD interventions and even business meetings and organizational task forces to become gripe sessions or exercises in problem solving. Transforming the human system and its organization toward an affirmative learning and working environment requires a conscious effort to maintain a positive focus on the dialogue. In so doing, positive affirmations or comments should be encouraged, while negative dialogues should be minimized or avoided altogether. Listening for key phrases and/or activities can facilitate this process.

By way of example, the following positive discourse categories are offered:[11]

I.   Positive Categories

1.   Positive Valuing: Any mention of positive values, past or present.

2.   Hope toward future: Any mention of hope, optimism, or positive anticipation toward the future.

3.   Skill or Competency: Any mention of skill, competency, action, or positive quality about self or others.

4.   Openness, Receptivity, Learning: Any mention of receptivity in self or others accompanied by a positive outcome; also, any noticing of one's or others' learning or interests.

5.   Active Connection, Effort to Include, Cooperation, or Combination: Any noticing of efforts to include, cooperate, connect, and relate that may be accompanied by at least an inferred positive outcome.

6.   Mention of Surprise, Curiosity, or Excitement: Any mention of curiosity, surprise, openness to fresh insights, or excitement in self or others.

7.   Notice of Facilitating Action or Movement toward a Positive Outcome: Any mention of a facilitating action or movement toward a real or imagined positive outcome or any mention of a facilitating object or circumstance. Also, noticing of any event that enhances another event, an effective state, or a person; noticing facilitative or positive cause and effect.

---

11 From Barrett, F., Cooperrider, D., Tenkasi, R., & Joseph, T. Unpublished manuscript, Case Western Reserve University, Cleveland, OH.

8. Effort to Reframe in Positive Terms: Any mention of a negative emotion or action accompanied by the possibility of a positive desired outcome; also, any mention of a change in mood from negative to positive, including any mention of an obstacle that is temporary or getting over a negative static state, or reframing a negative situation into more positive terms.

9. Envisioned Ideal: Any mention of a vision/value end-state articulation of a positive outcome envisioned for a future that is **utopian** or **pragmatic**.

Then for the organization to process, there must be a commitment to let go of the negative discourse categories that drain the organization's resources. These include the following:

II. Negative Discourse Categories

1. Negative Valuing: Any mention of negative valuing; for example, fatalism, apathy, or dislike. Any description of person, a group, a circumstance, or an event as a problem or an obstacle.

2. Concern, Worry, Preoccupation, Doubt: Any mention of concern, worry, or preoccupation without mention of a possible model to alleviate concern or to enhance understanding; any mention of doubt, suspicion, or lack of confidence in future outcomes.

3. Unfulfilled Expectation: Any mention of any event, action, state, or person that does not match intention, wish, desire, goal, or other unfulfilled expectation.

4. Lack of Receptivity, Absence of Connection: Any mention of a lack of receptivity in self or others, including a lack of collaboration, a lack of understanding, a failure to listen or failure to agree, or any explicit mention of an absence of connection.

5. Deficiency in Self or Others: Any mention of a sense that something is missing; for example, a deficiency in self or others or a lack of motivation, appropriate effort, skill, or competence or an absence of resources (such as time or money).

6. Negative Effect: Any mention of feelings of dissatisfaction, selfishness, sadness, defensiveness, irritation, or anger without mentioning a possible antidote or relief or effort to understand.

7. Withdrawal or Suppression: Any mention of avoidance, ignoring, withdrawal of energy or surrender, or suppressing of self or others.

8. Control or Domination: Any notice of effort or action to disrupt, dominate, wield control, or halt a mood or an action in self or other.

9. Wasted Effort: Any mention of excessive investment of time, resources, or energy without mention of reward or positive outcome.

10. Prediction, Image of a Negative Future: Any mention of prediction, vision, image, or expectation of a negative future.

11. Attribution of Control by Others in Combination with Self-Deprecation: Any notice of effort or action in others to disrupt, dominate, or wield control in combination with attribution of helplessness to self or self-pity.

12. Negative Cause-and-Effect Relation: Any explicit notice of a cause-and-effect relationship leading to a negative outcome.

13. Reframing a Situation in Negative Terms: Any mention of a positive emotion with the possibility of a negative outcome; mention of experiencing a change in mood from positive to negative or getting into a negative state, focusing on possible obstacles, or reframing a positive situation into more negative terms.

The responsibility of the AI moderator—whether a consultant, a manager, or an appointed team leader—is to facilitate positive discourse and minimize negative discourse to foster constructive change dialogue.

Mini-lecture VIII:
History as Positive Possibility

Three factors that give life to healthy organizations are continuity, novelty, and transition. Research[12] has established that visionary organizations and their leadership have the capacity to learn and apply lessons from the best of the past (**continuity**), to surface and develop ideas for creative acts (**novelty**), and to enact actual changes in systems and behaviors to progress toward a desired state (**transition**). The importance and effectiveness of AI stems in part from its natural focus on all three of these generative factors.

---

12 See Collins, J., & Porras, J. (1994). *Built to last: Successful habits of visionary companies.* New York: Harper Business and Jonas, H., Fry, R., & Srivastva, S. (1989). The office of the CEO: Understanding the executive experience. *Academy of Management Executive,* 3(4).

Continuity

AI begins with a focus on organizational continuity, the understanding and appreciation of the system's connective threads of identity, purpose, pride, wisdom, and tradition that perpetuate and connect day-to-day life in the organization. It is paramount to recognize that continuity is a necessary part of change or transformation. As Jim Collins, coauthor of Built to Last: Successful Habits of Visionary Companies, puts it, ". . . change is good, but first know what should never change."[13]

Steven Covey also emphasizes the importance of valuing continuity in human development:[14]

> *People cannot live with change if there's not a changeless core inside them. The key to the ability to change is a changeless sense of who you are, what you are about, and what you value.*

In attending to continuity, the dialogue is built around the system's founding stories, turning points, proudest achievements, best practices, empowering traditions, intergenerational wisdom, legacies, and amazing moments. It is a discovery of the organization's history-as-positive-possibility. This inquiry reveals the bases on which healthy management of continuity can be sustained by:

- Knowing what people do best.
- Ensuring human and technical resources to support basic core tasks.
- Orienting to maintain the most valued aspects of the culture.

The function of continuity is between the individual and the organization.

Table 1.3 Functions of Continuity

For the Individual	For the Organization
Social Connectedness	Strengthened Commitment
Moral Guidance	Better Sense-Making and Decision Making
Confidence to Act	Consistent Values and Mission
Personal Welfare	Decentralized Control
Pride, Hope, and Joy	Basis for Organizational Learning
Freedom	Long-Term Thinking
	Customized Change

13 Ibid.
14 See Covey, S. (1990). *The 7 habits of highly effective people.* New York: Simon & Schuster.

Novelty

In attending to novelty, the AI dialogue and process provides the opportunity for unexpected newness to be offered up. A space for true valuing of novel thinking and acting is created. Hierarchy is suspended; harmony is postponed in favor of curious questioning. Symphonies of logical rationales are replaced with cacophonies of wild, half-baked notions; and typical incentives to conform are supplanted with celebration of those who constructively challenge the status quo. Such flowerings in an organization—what Dee Hock terms "creative chaos"[15] — enable the healthy management of novelty through:

- Intentional processes for learning from collective experience.
- Practices that actively search for new ideas: internally and externally.
- Investments in individual growth and development as a stimulus for new paradigm thinking.

This is where the affirmative topic choices come into the AI process.

Transition

In attending to transition, the dialogue uncovers ways in which new ideals (novelty) are transformed into visible changes that are experienced by everyone as positive movement toward a change target with minimal disruption (threat to continuity). The system is enlivened through a shared sense of enacting a "common script," whereby everyone recognizes the positive reason to change, the desired state to be achieved, and the next few steps to be taken. This allows for healthy management of transition through:

- A common vision, from which priorities are determined.
- Helpful feedback/measurement mechanisms on key success factors.
- Support for purposeful experimentation.
- Involvement strategies to promote a common script.

AI: The Foundational Questions

For visionary organizations, continuity, novelty, and transition are necessary capacities that exist in healthy tension. Too much attention on continuity may create myopic, rule- bound systems that constrain. Too much attention to nov-

---

15 Hock, D. *Birth of the chaordic age* (1999). San Francisco: Berrett-Koehler.

elty can result in ivory-tower leadership that loses credibility with those do the core work. Too much emphasis on transition can create a sense of directionless change-for-the-sake-of-change. As a process, AI is instrumental in finding and sustaining a healthy balance among these life-giving capacities. The following foundational questions provide an opportunity to address the three necessary elements of continuity, novelty, and transition. The first three AI generic questions focus on continuity:

- What would you describe as being a high-point experience in your organization, a time when you were most alive and engaged?
- Without being modest, what do you value most about yourself, your work, and your organization?
- What are the core factors that give life to your organization, without which the organization would cease to exist?

continuity questions

The next step for the organization is to open itself to novelty, the unexpected newness or the new possibilities in its human systems. It is a time to dream. What is it that the organization can become?

- Imagine you have awakened from a long, deep sleep. You get up to realize that everything is as you always dreamed it would be. Your ideal state has become the reality. What do you see? What is going on? How have things changed?

Finally, there is the transition, the intentional change of the human systems in the organization. How will the organization achieve the dream that was discovered? It is in the Design phase that transition begins, continuing through the Destiny phase. The final AI foundational question addresses the future:

- What three wishes do you have to enhance the health and vitality of your organization?

All organizations have something to value about their past. This element must be appreciated so that change becomes a positive experience without unnecessary resistance from a sense of disruption. The AI process helps in honoring the past (continuity) and searching for newness (novelty) in order to embrace movement toward the new future (transition), as illustrated in Figure 1.3. Simultaneously, AI brings all three areas into balance and harmony.

Figure 1.3 Managing Change: Continuity, Novelty, and Transition[16]

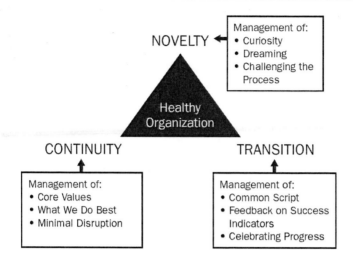

Mini-lecture IX: Why AI Works: The Liberation of Power

Adapted with permission from Whitney, D., & Trosten-Bloom, A. (2003). The power of appreciative inquiry. San Francisco: Berrett-Koehler.

For over two decades, organizations and communities around the globe have experienced extraordinary transformations through the use AI for organizational and social change. Those working with AI began asking the following questions:

- Why do people get so excited and want to participate in AI efforts?
- Why does participation so readily lead to positive results such as innovation, productivity, employee satisfaction, and profitability?
- What creates the space for people to be their best at work and for personal transformation?
- What are the conditions that foster cooperation throughout a whole system of highly diverse groups of people?

16 From Srivastva, S., & Fry, R. (1992). *Executive continuity.* San Francisco: Jossey-Bass.

In keeping with the spirit of AI, an inquiry into *why Appreciative Inquiry works* was conducted by Diana Whitney and Amanda Trosten-Bloom. They created a set of questions, held focus groups, and conducted formal and informal interviews in several organizations—most notably Hunter Douglas Window Fashions Division. (The Hunter Douglas Case Clipping is at the end of Chapter 7.) Their key finding is that AI works by generating six essential conditions within an organization. These conditions through which AI liberates power and unleashes human potential are called the Six Freedoms. Following is a brief description of each "freedom," along with quotes from stakeholders involved in the process.

1. **AI creates a context in which people are "Free to Be Known in Relationship."** Human identity forms and evolves within relationships; yet all too often in work settings, people are related in their roles rather than as unique individuals. AI interrupts the cycle of depersonalization that masks people's sense of being and belonging. It offers people the chance to truly know one another—both as unique individuals and as a part of the web of relationships. AI doesn't just build relationships. It also levels the playing field and builds bridges across boundaries of power and authority.

    > *For instance, at Hunter-Douglas, a machinist exclaimed, "Appreciative Inquiry blew the communication gap wide open." Similarly, a printer commented on the ways in which AI in general—and the interviews in particular—helped to make other people and their ideas more accessible: "Appreciative Inquiry gave us opportunities to be known across the boundaries. As our inquiry got fully under way, other people became excited, just like me. I didn't feel alone. For the first time, it was 'me with the world.'"*

2. **AI makes a space in which people are "Free to Be Heard."** Someone can listen without truly hearing or getting to know the other person. On the other hand, "being heard" is relational. To be heard requires that someone listen actively with sincere curiosity, empathy, and compassion. It requires an openness to know and to understand another person's story.

    Through one-on-one **appreciative interviews**, people who might otherwise feel as though they are ignored and do not have a voice are invited to come forward with information, ideas, and innovations that are subsequently put into action throughout the organization.

    To illustrate, a supervisor of a technical maintenance group initiated an inquiry among his team's internal customers: engineers, technical support staff, etc. He and his staff conducted interviews and collected stories of exceptional service. They invited people to dream about the service they had always wanted and to describe it in detail. In the process, the group built relationships across functions—in particular, between engineering and technical support.

3. **AI opens the opportunity for people to be "Free to Dream in Community."** In today's complex world, visionary leadership means unleashing the dreams of people at all levels of organizations. It means creating organizations as safe places where large, diverse groups of people dream and share their dreams in dialogue with one another.

    For example, in a nonprofit organization, interviews with more than 1,200 stakeholders worldwide yielded a vision of an entirely new model of service: from sending people out to do good to linking people and organizations of similar intent around the globe. This vision was so compelling—and its momentum so great—that by the first anniversary of the summit, close to 30 new initiatives were launched using this "sister organization" model as a template. Then in the two years that followed, close to 200 new initiatives—dreams—unfolded.

4. **AI establishes an environment where people are "Free to Choose to Contribute."** Work can separate people from what matters most to them, or it can provide a forum for enacting and realizing their deepest calling. Freedom of choice liberates power, but it also leads to commitment and a hunger for learning. When people choose to do a project and commit to others to do it, they become very creative and determined. They do whatever is necessary and learn whatever is needed to get the job done.

    For example, a frontline employee who had volunteered to lead an innovation team went to her personnel department to ask for coaching. She stated that for her team to succeed, she needed to learn how to facilitate meetings and how to help her team make decisions. Her determination paid off for the team, the organization, and herself. The team's project was finished in record time and led to significant process improvements in the company. She was promoted to a supervisory position, and her new team is thriving with her leadership.

5. **AI provides the context for people to be "Free to Act with Support."** To act with support is the quintessential act of positive interdependence. When people know that large numbers of people recognize and care about their work and are anxious to cooperate, they feel safe to

experiment, innovate, and learn. In other words, whole-system support stimulates people to take on challenges and draws people into acts of cooperation that bring forth their best self and work.

To break through several years' worth of apathy and distrust, John Deere Harvester Works initiated a five-day summit—the last two days focusing exclusively on what it called "tactical implementation." Participants selected ten projects they believed were most critically important. Then to their surprise, they began working with one another there in the summit to plan, line up resources, and initiate the projects.

When people are truly free to act with support, their contributions are profound and their lessons sometimes surprising. Another employee at Hunter Douglas shows that this freedom liberates individual and organizational power—even when the intended actions fail to reach fruition:

> *My coworkers and I worked hard to make the case for and create a cross-training program. It was ready for implementation, and then . . . nobody signed up!!! I was deeply disappointed—but ultimately OK. In the end, the only thing I really accomplished was getting an answer: people simply weren't that interested. But an answer was a big thing. It meant that I had the power to get an answer.*

6. **AI opens the way for people to be "Free to Be Positive."** In organizations today, it is not the norm to have fun, to be happy, or to be positive. Time and again people allow themselves to be swept away in collective currents of negativity, despite the pain it causes. A long-term employee of an organization mired in deficit discourse shared the following with dismay:

> *"I have ulcers because of this negative thinking and talking. Every day I come to work and hear nothing but complaints and criticism and blaming. I hate coming to work."*

Over and over again, people say that AI works, in part because it gives people permission to feel positive and to be proud of their working experiences.

The effect of AI is so strong and powerful that it can even transform deficit discourse and negative thinking. In the words of one employee,

> *"I am a very positive thinker, so this suits me very well. But I believe*

this process is powerful enough to influence all of the staff—not just those of us who are already this way."

AI works because it unleashes all of the Six Freedoms over the course of a 4-D Cycle. It creates a surge of power and energy that, once liberated, won't be recontained. A supervisor at Hunter Douglas said, "As people tried and got results, they gained confidence. That led to five times as much input and the desire to get more involved." In short, through the liberation of power, AI creates a self-perpetuating momentum for positive change.

Summary

The nine mini-lectures provide the theoretical foundations and research citations that move human and organizational systems toward a positive, generative future. In addition, it is manifest that human systems within organizations move in the direction of what they study and that the study begins with an inquiry. The best way to understand AI is to discover how it works. That will be the focus of the next chapter: to show how these theoretical foundations move people into action—a way forward.

2

The Appreciative Inquiry Process: How It Works

Overview

AI is premised on the idea that organizations move toward what they study. For example, when groups study human problems and conflicts, they often find that the number and severity of complex and problematic issues grow. In the same manner, when groups study lofty human ideals and achievements (such as teamwork, quality, or peak experiences), these phenomena tend to flourish. People in organizations construct and enact worlds that, in turn, affect their behavior. What they study is what they become knowledgeable about and skilled in carrying out. Problem-focused study builds organizational knowledge, wisdom, and capacity about those problems. On the other hand, the study of organizations operating at their best builds knowledge, wisdom, and replicable capacity about how to bring out the best in the organizations. In this sense, the AI approach accepts the notion that knowledge and organizational destiny are interwoven: *the way we seek to know people, groups, and organizations is fateful*. To understand AI at a fundamental level, one simply must understand these two points. First, organizations move in the direction of what they study. Second, AI makes a conscious choice to study the best of an organization, its **positive core**.

Chapter 1 laid out the theoretical foundation for AI: the principles upon which it is founded, *what* AI is and *why* it works. From this point forward, the focus will be on *how* AI works. This chapter begins with an overview of the positive core. The central theme of the positive core is fundamental to AI. It is the dominant principle and established basis for the 4-D Cycle and how it facilitates the AI intervention. The chapter concludes with an overview of the 4-D process.

The **4-D Cycle** is a method that allows the user to follow a well-coordinated series of steps (or phases) to help an organization identify its positive core and initiate the concrete operational steps needed to achieve its vision and desired goals. *Discovery, Dream, Design*, and *Destiny* were discussed briefly in the previous chapter. The concept of the affirmative topic choice, however, is new to this discussion. Yet that is where the AI process begins.

The first step in the AI process involves choosing the life-affirming factors as the focus of inquiry. What is it that you want more of? This step is important because what is studied becomes reality. Therefore, the right topics need to be created or chosen. These topics ultimately guide the formulation of questions and, through inquiry, create the learning agenda for an organization. This approach, known as the affirmative topic choice, lies at the center of the 4-D Cycle, illustrated in **Figure 2.1**.

Figure 2.1 Appreciative Inquiry 4-D Cycle

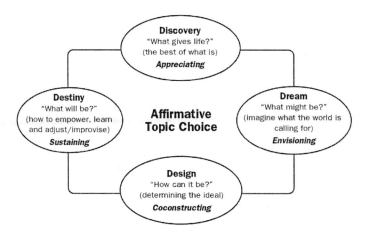

The Positive Core

The *positive core* of organizational life is one of the greatest, yet least recognized resources in the change management field today. AI has demonstrated that human systems grow in the direction of their persistent inquiries, and this propensity is strongest and most sustainable when the means and ends of inquiry are positively correlated. In the AI process, the future is consciously constructed on the positive core strengths of the organization. Linking the energy of this core directly to any change agenda suddenly and democratically creates and mobilizes topics never before thought possible.

The concept of the positive core is separate from yet central to the 4-D Cycle. As has been stated several times, AI is more than the 4-D Cycle. It is a strength-based philosophy (based on its core principles in Mini-lecture I: Five Principles of AI) created as "a way of being" in organizational life. The 4-D Cycle is the approach or process that allows the practitioner to access and mobilize the positive core. The positive core lies at the heart of the AI process. In this respect, the organization's positive core is the beginning and the end of the inquiry. This is where the whole organization has an opportunity to value its history and embrace novelty in transitioning into positive possibilities.

This positive core is woven throughout the 4-D Cycle. It is identified in the *Discovery* phase, mobilizing a whole-system inquiry into the positive core—*that which gives meaning to the organization*. It is amplified throughout the *Dream* phase, creating a clear results-oriented vision in relation to the discovered potential and in relation to questions of higher purpose. It is woven into the organizational architecture through the *Design* phase, creating provocative propositions of the ideal organization—an organizational design that people believe is capable of magnifying the positive core. Finally, it is implemented throughout the *Destiny* phase, strengthening the affirmative capability of the whole system. Thus, AI begins and ends with valuing that which gives life to an organization. In this sense, the organization's positive core can be expressed in any one of a number of ways, all of which can be identified through the inquiry. Following are some of the ways in which the positive core is expressed:

- Achievements and awards
- Best business practices
- Core and distinctive competencies
- Elevated thoughts
- Embedded knowledge
- Financial assets
- Innovations
- Leadership and management capabilities
- Market and/or strategic opportunities
- Organizational achievements
- Organizational wisdom
- Positive emotions
- Positive macro trends
- Product, service, and/or operational strengths
- Relational resources
- Social capital
- Technical assets
- Values and value chain
- Visions of possibility
- Vital traditions
- Strengths of partners and organizational stakeholders
- Capacities worldwide

Affirmative Topic Choice: A Fateful Act

Once the basic concept of the positive core is understood, the 4-D Cycle can be better explained. The first step in an AI application is selecting the **affirmative topic choice**.

This is, in short, the selection of topic(s) that will become the focus of the intervention.

Selecting the affirmative topic choice begins with the constructive discovery and narration of the organization's "life-giving" story. The topics, in the initial stages, are bold hunches about what gives life to the organization. Most importantly, the topics (usually three to five for an inquiry) represent what people really want to discover or learn more about. The topics will likely evoke conversations about the desired future.

The seeds of change are implicit in the first questions asked. The following two broad questions form a basis by which groups and organizations can create their own customized topics.

- *What factors give life to this organization when it is and has been most alive, successful, and effective?* This question seeks to discover what the organization has done well in the past and is doing well in the present.

- *What possibilities, expressed and latent, provide opportunities for more vital, successful, and effective (vision-and-values congruent) forms of organization?* This question asks the participants to dream about and design their most preferred future.

Since human systems typically grow in the directions about which people inquire, affirmative topic choices encourage people to select topics they want to see grow and flourish in their organizations. The choice sets the stage for AI through the application of the 4-D Cycle.

Careful, thoughtful, and informed choice of topics defines the scope of the inquiry, providing the framework for subsequent interviews and data collection. When AI was first being used, the design was an open topic choice, the "homegrown topic." The power of this type of discovery and dream led to the affirmative topic(s) that the organization would study, beginning with the AI foundational questions, as follows:

- What would you describe as being a high-point experience in your organization, a time when you were most alive and engaged?
- Without being modest, what is it that you value most about yourself, your work, and your organization?
- What are the core factors that give life to your organization— when it is at its best, without which the organization would cease to exist?
- What three wishes do you have now to enhance the health and vitality of your organization?

Since the first edition of the *Appreciative Inquiry Handbook*, many practitioners have replaced the *three wish question* with a more imaginative series of questions:

Imagine your organization five . . . years from now, when everything is just as you always imagined it would be. What has happened? What is different? How have you contributed to this future?

Pre-selected Topic Choices

Some organizations have succeeded with preselected topic choices. For example, a midsized long-term care company located in the Midwest had been struggling with census development (attracting patients) in its nursing homes and assisted living centers. The company's centers provided a high quality of care, as evidenced by both regional and statewide awards (such as the Governor's Award for Quality of Care). But many centers were experiencing a declining census base due to increased competition. The company decided to employ an AI initiative to focus on census development.

The objective of the initiative (called the Plus 1 campaign) was to jumpstart the census development effort by designing an inquiry that would include the center's stakeholders in working toward this common goal within a six-week budget period.

In an effort to focus the census campaign, the four key topics shown in **Table 2.1** were preselected in a subgroup planning discussion based on the four original topics.

Table 2.1 Appreciative Inquiry Key Topic Choices:
"Plus 1 Campaign" Example

Original Topics	Preselected Appreciative Inquiry Topics
Center of Choice	Provider of Choice
Customer Loyalty	Resident Loyalty
Treatment of Staff and Residents	Genuine Appreciation
Teamwork	The Exceptional Team

The company embraced the idea that larger gains would be made and sustained by expanding its initial goal of census development to include these preselected AI topic choices in order to understand best how to collectively achieve its census goal.

Another example is referenced in **Table 2.2**. A large global automotive firm had a rough idea of what it would take to build the positive core of a certain division.[1] However, the company wanted to make its topics more boldly affirmative. Therefore, the AI consultant worked with the group and suggested the following preselected AI topics:

---

1 A helpful resource to assist in determining preselected topic choices is the *Encyclopedia of positive questions: Volume One.* (2002). Garfield Heights, OH: Crown Custom Publishing (http://www.crowncustompublishing.com).

Table 2.2 Appreciative Inquiry Key Topic Choices: Automotive Example

Original Topics	Preselected AI Topics
Communications	Compelling Communications
Learning and Development	Continuous Learning
Management Behaviors	Integrity in Action
	Inspirational/Irresistible Leadership
Commitment and Enthusiasm	Culture As a Strategic Advantage
	Fun at Work
	Let's Do It

Who to Involve?

Selecting an affirmative topic choice can be a rich and satisfying experience, especially when it engages large numbers of people. At a minimum, a topic selection team should consist of people who have an important stake in the organization and its future. The team comprises any level of organizational participants from line staff to board of directors in order to create a "representative" steering committee.

Ideally, the topic selection team involves a microcosm of the organization. More people is better in terms of the organization's commitment to the process. Finally, the team must contain a variety of "voices," for in diversity comes a greater richness of relationship, dialogue, and possibility. **Table 2.3** details a list of potential stakeholders to consider for the topic team.

Table 2.3 Potential Representatives for Topic Team Selection

Potential Team Members

- Senior management
- Board of directors
- Middle management
- Staff or employee groups
- Union
- Customers
- Suppliers (vendors)
- Strategic partners
- Trade and professional associations

An important criterion in selecting participants is their ability to bring viewpoints and experiences from many different levels of the organization and from many different perspectives about the organization. Therefore, the list of potential participants is not necessarily limited to employees. The broad-based participant list is also the reasoning behind the statement "more is better." The more the intervention allows the participants to capture the true spirit of development, the better. In short, greater input will yield a stronger base of dialogue.

Once participants have been identified, a qualifier about team dynamics becomes important. Every participant in the topic selection team should have an active and equal role. The organization's leaders, executives, and/or managers must not control the dialogue. The participants must use a watchful eye to prevent this from happening on either a conscious or subconscious level. All who participate must be encouraged to speak their minds and say what is in their hearts.

The ABCs of Topic Choice: How to Do It

The topic selection team meets for a one- to two-day period. (The material in **Chapter 3** provides examples that can help lead to the affirmative topic choice.) Whether a two-hour executive overview or a one-day introduction, the process begins with a brief introduction to the initiative and goes directly into "mini-interviews," given the broad categories of topics initially selected. For these interviews, team members should be assigned to partners who are different from themselves with respect to functions, management levels, gender, age, tenure, and ethnicity. The goal is to get diverse opinions and to create dialogue. The mini-interview is an opportunity to create a genuine one-to-one relationship with the partner, and that opportunity should not be wasted. A simple rule is to have someone interview someone else that he or she has not spoken to before or barely knows.

The four AI starting questions are generally used for the mini-interviews. These questions have been used in many variations. Thus, you should tailor the basic questions to suit the needs of the inquiry and the organization. The four questions are given in **Table 2.4.**

Table 2.4 The Four Appreciative Inquiry Foundational Questions

1. What was a peak experience or "high point"?
2. What are the things valued most about...
    - Yourself?
    - The nature of your work?
    - Your organization?
3. What are the core factors that "give life" to organizing?
4. What are three wishes to heighten vitality and health?

Following the mini-interviews, topic selection team members should organize into groups of six to eight members, staying with their original partners. In this smaller group, each member should introduce his or her partner, share stories and highlights, and begin to find common threads within the group. The groups must allow adequate time and space for dialogue and relationship building. They also must do whatever is necessary to prevent people from identifying themes before team members have really talked. The team must take time to dialogue, listen, and reflect. They must listen and take good notes. Next, within these groups, team members must identify key patterns and/or themes that have emerged.

When the time is right, these groups reassemble into the full group. The full group shares highlights and feedback from the small groups and discusses emerging themes and patterns. Are any of the themes related? Do any of the themes speak more loudly than another? less than another? Will any of the themes have a greater or lesser impact on the organization? Subgroups continue talking and working, if necessary, moving in and out of the large group.

The facilitator of this session also may be a participant in the process. This is acceptable because the facilitator is a member of the group. The facilitator must not monopolize; however, the facilitator can add value by sharing insights and ideas that have emerged.

On a final note, throughout this process, considerable dialogue and deliberation over particular words or phrases are not "just semantics"; they are essential. In an AI intervention, a fundamental assumption is that "words create worlds"; so the words chosen will have enormous impact on what is shared, what is learned, and where the group is headed with the inquiry. This is especially true at this stage of the inquiry. The selection of the affirmative action topic(s) drives the process from this point forward. A difference of one or several words may lead to different conclusions later in the process. Therefore, the moderator must allow for ample time and discussion over points that may seem irrelevant to some. For example, in the discussion that ensued from the topics provided in **Table 2.1**, a theme that emerged constantly was the treatment that staff and residents extended to each other and received from other stakeholders. A large group dialogue ensued, discovering that what the organizational members wanted was to better understand what "appreciation" meant and how "appreciation" was to be given and received as part of the culture and not as a specific event or award. This is how the topic choice of study moved from *treatment of staff and residents* to *genuine appreciation*.

Characteristics of Good Topics

Topics can be anything related to organizational effectiveness. Two such examples are provided in **Table 2.5**. Topics can include technical processes, human dynamics, customer relations, cultural themes, values, external trends, and market forces. Topics must be positive affirmations of the organization's strengths and the potential it seeks to discover, learn about, and become. In the end, somewhere between three and five compelling topics should be identified, all of which meet the following criteria:
  • Topics are affirmative or stated in the positive.
  • Topics are desirable. They identify the objectives people want.
  • The group is genuinely curious about them and wants to learn more.
  • The topics move in the direction the group wants to go.

The following principles apply as the group proceeds through the process:
  • Organizations move in the direction of their images of the future.
  • Their images of the future are informed by the conversations they hold and the stories they tell.
  • The stories they tell are informed by the questions asked, so . . .
  • The questions asked are **fateful** (i.e., they affect the answers given).

Table 2.5 Affirmative Topic Choice Samples

British Airways	**Other Organizational Examples**
1. Happiness at Work	1. Revolutionary Partnerships
2. Harmony and Sharing among All Employees	2. Customer Intimacy
3. Continuous People Development	3. Optimal Margins
4. Exceptional Arrival Experience	4. Lightning-Fast Consensus
	5. Transformational Cooperation
	6. Leadership at Every Level

These topics are used in sample interview guides available on the CD-ROM.

These two examples help illustrate that topics can be anything an organization considers strategically and humanly important, such as technical processes, market opportunity identification, sustainability, or social responsibility.

Table 2.6 summarizes useful guidelines to help create affirmative topic choices.

In the case of topic choice, the stated premise is still true: *human systems grow in the direction of their deepest and most frequent inquiries.* The AI process truly begins when a conscious choice is made to focus on the affirmative.

Table 2.6 Affirmative-Topic Choice Guidelines

Main Points

Topic choice is a fateful act.
Organizations move in direction of inquiry.
Vocabulary is not "just semantics"; words create worlds.
People commit to topics they have helped develop.
  • Everyone is an active participant.
  • Diversity is essential.

Critical Choice

Build a representative steering committee, or
Start with senior executive-level team, or
Involve the whole system to whatever extent is possible.

Rules of Thumb

No more than five topics are ultimately selected.
Topics are phrased in affirmative terms.
Topic is driven by curiosity—spirit of discovery.
Topic is genuinely desired. People want to see it "grow."
Topic is consistent with the overall business direction and intentions of the organization.
Topic choice involves those that have an important stake in the future.
Topic choice should take up to two days.

The *Discovery* Phase

Identify what gives life.
Appreciate the best of what is.

The primary task in the *Discovery* phase is to identify and appreciate the best of "what is." This task is accomplished by focusing on "peak times" or high-point experiences of organizational excellence—when people have experienced the organization as most alive and effective. Seeking to understand the unique factors (e.g., leadership, relationships, technologies, core processes, structures, values, learning processes, external relationships, and planning methods) that made the high points possible, people deliberately let go of analyses of deficits and systematically seek to isolate and learn from even the smallest wins. Recognizing that organizations are not always at their best, during discovery, people seek to uncover and learn from times and situations when the organization was at its best.

In the *Discovery* phase, people share stories of exceptional accomplishments, discuss the core life-giving factors of their organizations, and deliberate on the aspects of their organization's history that they most value and want to bring forward to their work in the future. In this phase, members come to know their organization's history *as positive possibility* rather than a static, eulogized, romanticized, or forgotten set of events. Empowering and hopeful conceptions of organizations frequently, if not always, emerge from stories that are grounded in the realities of the organization operating at its best. Appreciation is alive, and stakeholders throughout an organization or a community are connected in a dialogue of discovery. Hope grows and organizational capacity is enriched. *Capacity* is the ability or potential to mobilize resources and achieve objectives. It is everything necessary to construct the relationships required to achieve an organization's vision, mission, and goals.[2]

This is where the storytelling begins. The distinguishing factor of AI in this phase is that every carefully crafted question of the topic choice is unconditionally positive and seeks to inquire deeply into where the affirmative topic choice can help move the organization in the direction it wants to go.

---

2 See Stavros, J. (1998). *Capacity building using an appreciative approach: A relational process of building your organization's future.* Unpublished dissertation, Case Western Reserve University, Cleveland, OH.

The *Dream* Phase

Identify what might be.
Envision results the world is calling for.

The *Dream* phase amplifies the positive core and challenges the status quo by envisioning more valued and vital futures than those that are currently envisioned by organization members and stakeholders. The *Dream* phase asks the people whose future it is to engage with one another to create more vital and life-giving images for their own future. The primary purpose of the *Dream* phase is to expand or extend people's sense of what is possible.

Especially important today is the envisioning of potential results—the organization's contributions to the **triple bottom line** (i.e., profit, people, and planet).[3] Organizations today, be they business or social-profit, realize that financial well-being is one of three important criteria for success. The other two criteria are environmental sustainability and social well-being.

AI is uniquely suited to enhance an organization's contribution to the triple bottom line because it engages all stakeholders in envisioning their future together. When people who previously thought of themselves as adversaries, such as management and unions or corporations and environmentalists, meet and engage in dialogue through AI, they are able to create images of a future that works for all.

The *Dream* phase is practical in that it is grounded in the organization's history. It is also generative in that it seeks to expand the organization's potential, keeping in mind the voices and hopes of its stakeholders.

One aspect that differentiates AI from other visioning or planning methodologies is that images of the future emerge out of grounded examples from the organization's past strengths. These images are compelling possibilities precisely because they are based on extraordinary moments from an organization's history.[4] These types of data can be compared with benchmarking studies of other organizations. In both cases, the "good news" stories are used the same way an artist uses materials to create a portrait of possibility. Without all of the colors (red, green, blue, and yellow), the painting is less beautiful. So, too, are many visions or reengineering programs that fail to take notice of organizational history.

---

3 The triple bottom line focuses on economic prosperity, environmental quality, and (the element business has tended to overlook) social justice and people. Refer to Elkington, J. (1998). *Cannibals with forks*. Oxford: Capstone Publishing.

4 "Ground theory" is the qualitative research methodology of choice. It is inductively derived from the study of the phenomenon it represents. It is discovered, developed, and provisionally verified through a process pertaining to the phenomena explored. For more information, refer to Strauss, A., & Corbin, J. (1998). *Basics of qualitative research: Grounded theory procedures and techniques*. Newbury Park, CA: Sage Publications.

The *Dream* phase is a time for key stakeholders to collectively share their stories of the organization's past and their historical relationship with the organization. As the various stories of the organization's history are shared and illuminated, a new historical narrative emerges. This narrative engages those involved in much the same way a good mystery novel engages a reader. As participants become energetically engaged in re-creating the organization's positive history, they give life to its new, most preferred future.

During the *Dream* phase, organization stakeholders engage in conversations about the organization's position and potential in the world. Dialogue about the organization's mission (present purpose) and the unique contribution it can make to global well-being catalyzes a furtherance of images and stories of the organization's future. For example, a sustainable development organization would seek to cocreate an organization that aligns it strengths and opportunities to best deliver economic, social, and environment benefits for the society in which it does business.[5] For many organization stakeholders, this is the first time to think "great" thoughts about and create "great" possibilities for the organization. The process is both personally and organizationally invigorating.

The *Design* Phase

Identify what should be the ideal.
Coconstruct the future design.

The *Design* phase involves creation of the organization's social architecture. This new social architecture is embedded in the organization by generating *provocative propositions* (also known as *possibility statements or design principles*) that embody the organizational dream in the ongoing activities. Everything about organizing is reflected and responsive to the dream, the organization's greatest potential.

A provocative proposition is a statement of the ideal organization as it relates to some important aspect or element of organizing: leadership, decision making, communication or customer service, and so on. Successful design involves identifying the elements of organizing that need to be designed and crafting the provocative propositions that integrate discovery and dream ideals into the elements.

---

5 To learn more about how to redesign your organization's strategy to focus on the triple bottom line and create a strategic framework that moves your organization to sustainability refer to Hart, S. (2005). *Capitalism at the crossroads.* Upper Saddle River, NJ: Wharton School Publishing.

By crafting the organization's social architecture, stakeholders define the basic infrastructure. This phase requires in-depth dialogues about the best strategies, structure, staff, and processes needed to support the new system. By analogy:

> *To construct a home, one must decide to include or not to include windows, doors, a cooking space, sleeping spaces, spaces to greet visitors, fireplaces, and/or walls, and so on.*

> *To construct an organization, one must decide to include or not to include leadership, strategy, structure, human resource management, customer relations, and/or culture, and so on.*

As provocative propositions are composed, the desired qualities of organizing and organizational life are articulated. To further illustrate:

> *To construct a home, one must, after deciding to have doors, determine the number and nature of doors to build.*

> *To construct an organization, after deciding to have collaborative leadership, one must describe the quality of organizational life, relationships, and interactions that are desired enactments of collaborative leadership.*

The *Design* phase involves the collective construction of positive images of the organization's future in terms of provocative propositions based on a chosen social architecture. These designs help move the system to positive action and intended results.

The *Destiny* Phase

Identify how to empower, learn, and improvise.
Sustain what gives life.

The *Destiny* phase delivers on the new images of the future and is sustained by nurturing a collective sense of purpose and movement. It is a time of continuous learning, adjustment, and improvisation (like a jazz group)—all in the service of shared ideals. The momentum and potential for innovation and implementation are extremely high. By this stage in the process, because of the shared positive image of the future, everyone is invited to align his or her inter-actions in cocreating the future.

During this phase, stakeholders are typically invited into an open-space planning and commitment session. Individuals and groups discuss what they can and will do to contribute to the realization of the organizational dream as articulated in the provocative propositions. Relationally-woven action com-mitments then serve as the basis for ongoing activities.

The key to sustaining the momentum is to build an "appreciative eye" into all of the organization's systems, procedures, and ways of working. For exam-ple, one organization transformed its department of *e*valuation studies to val-uation studies (dropping the *e*). Others have transformed focus group methods, surveys, performance management systems, merger integration methods, lead-ership training programs, and diversity initiatives. The areas for application of AI are far-reaching. Provocative propositions may require an organization to redesign its processes and system in this phase of inquiry.

Frank Barrett's four areas of competency development are central to sus-taining appreciative organizing.[6]
1. Affirmative Competence
2. Expansive Competence
3. Generative Competence
4. Collaborative Competence

These competencies are fully discussed in Chapter 7 in the *Destiny* phase.

The *Destiny* phase is ongoing and brings the organization back full circle to the *Discovery* phase. In a systemic fashion, continued AI may result in new affirmative topic choices, continuous dialogues, and continued learning.

Chapter 2 presented a basic understanding of how AI works, but AI is best learned by doing. Something as simple as a conversation with a colleague to move an issue forward or a team building initiative to get two areas within a department communicating is enough. It could be as simple as asking these questions at the end of a staff meeting: What do we do well as a team? What do we want to do more of as an effective team? To get started with an AI ini-tiative, a major change program is not required.

One of the wonders of AI is that it can be implemented after limited expo-sure to its theory base (**Chapter 1**) and process overview (**Chapter 2**). Those who want more formal training in AI will find a Bibliography at the end of this book.

One of the first challenges in planning an AI initiative is how best to intro-duce the concept, theory, and process to an organization. **Chapter 3** provides tips, suggestions, selected AI projects, and sample agendas to help prepare for an AI initiative. A good start usually leads to a good finish. An AI initiative is

---

6 See Barrett, F. (1995). *Creating appreciative learning cultures*. Organizational Dynamics, 24, 36–49.

no exception. The way AI is introduced to the organization sets the tone for the process that follows. Getting started involves three key activities: introducing AI; defining the project, purpose, and process; and creating a project plan. This next chapter includes an overview and examples of each of these three key activities.

3

Introducing, Defining, and Planning an Appreciative Inquiry Initiative

Introducing AI

For most organizations, AI is a new approach to organizational change. If some members of an organization have heard or read about AI, they generally have many questions. For example, how does it work, how might it fit with our culture, and how can we involve our people without closing down the business? The novelty of AI requires that successful AI engagements begin through the introduction of AI to key stakeholders. Some of the best experiences of introducing AI share the following characteristics.[1]

Involve the Whole System from the Beginning

AI is a high-engagement, high-performance process. The way it is introduced to an organization should be a demonstration of the way it will be carried out should the organization decide to go forward with it. This means that from the start, all relevant and interested people—all stakeholders—should be involved. When AI is introduced, as many informal opinion leaders (influencers) as possible should be involved, along with formal leaders, holders of the purse strings, and some of the many people who will be impacted by AI. At the very least, this action will create a sense of positive anticipation in the organization. Often it will begin the long-term process of transforming the organization's inner dialogue by demonstrating that people at all levels of the organization and in all functions have a valuable contribution to make.

Experience Is an Inspiring Teacher

AI can't be "sold" without giving people an experience of AI. What kind of experience do people need to become engaged by and attached to this new way of thinking, working, and being? First, they need to experience an appreciative interview that includes some variation of the four generic AI questions presented in **Chapter 2**, as follows:

- What would you describe as being a peak experience or high point in your life—personal or professional?
- What do you value most about yourself? your work? your organization?
- What is the core factor that gives life to your organization?
- Describe your vision of the future for the organization and your world.

This interview helps people taste the power, the effect, and what some people have described as the intimacy of the AI process. The interview begins to build relationships within the team that later become the driving force for a

---

1 Adapted from Whitney, D., & Trosten-Bloom, A. (2003). *The power of appreciative inquiry: A practical guide to positive change.* San Francisco: Berrett-Koehler.

whole-system inquiry. Each person finds a partner to interview. Each partner conducts an interview of the other person for at least 20 minutes. Then after the 40-minute interview session, the whole group reconvenes to discuss the experience. Depending on the size of the group, each person may introduce his or her partner to the group.

People must hear the story of AI, and its successes should be told. The powerful stories of personal transformation, community development, organizational change, and global organizing that have emerged from the extensive work in the not-for-profit and for-profit sectors are impressive and should be shared. These stories bring a level of inspiration, of "global relevance," to the process. They touch people's hearts in ways that elevate their decision making and assessment of AI as a viable tool for their organization. The details of the AI 4-D Cycle can be explained through stories, too, including testimonials to augment the presentation. Many of these testimonials are included in this handbook. You also can visit the AI Commons at http://appreciativeinquiry.case.edu. The AI Commons is a worldwide portal with the most complete and up-to-date academic resources and practical tools on AI. This site is hosted by Case Western Reserve University's Weatherhead School of Management.

AI is a process that speaks for itself when given the chance. As such, it calls leaders of change—consultants, scholars, students, and business managers—to new levels of humility. A successful AI engagement depends less on a single person's capacities to communicate and facilitate and more on the wisdom and insight that resides within the hearts and minds of people throughout every organization and community. The power of AI comes alive in the initial discovery interviews and continues in the group dialogues during the *Dream*, *Design*, and *Destiny* phases.

Use Alternative Media Whenever Possible

Talking and stories are effective, but pictures (and other media) speak a thousand words. Videos, music, and other methods can enhance the story of AI—its assumptions and its successes. The message of AI can be supported by inspirational quotes posted on walls. Excerpts from stories and poems can be read. Video clips may help demonstrate and describe the phases of the 4-D Cycle.[2] Interviews and outcomes may be quoted. To illustrate, in one introduction to a large workforce, video clips that had been shot in the company's production plants were shown of people talking about their peak experiences with the company. Visit the AI Commons where you can download video clips for your review. People must experience and be stimulated by AI on multiple levels.

---

2 The video produced by Amanda Trosten-Bloom, *The Appreciative Inquiry Approach to Whole System Change*, which is available at Amazon.com, is but one example.

Create Cultural Sketches Consistent with the Desired Outcome

As with any good organizational change effort, each step, including the intro-duction, should be consistent with the desired outcome. For example, if an out-come is to reduce organizational hierarchies, the process leading to a "flattened" organization can be introduced. The conversation or interview guide can start with a vision of a lean organization. If another organizational outcome is to build bridges across functions, cross-functional introductions must be created.

"Surprises" in an AI introduction can be a powerful signal that there will be no more business as usual. For example, several of the most compelling introductory sessions have included field trips to production sites or other busi-ness divisions or involvement of external stakeholders in an initial AI mini-interview. In the Hunter Douglas Case Clipping in **Chapter 7**, the business development and top management team were taken on a road trip to tour and interview employees working in the plants.

Include Impact and First Steps Conversations

As AI is introduced, participants need space and opportunity to discuss and imagine implementation possibilities and impact while they are still close to the first experience. If first steps or next steps are included in discussions in the introduction, imagining what AI might offer the participants' organiza-tion can be powerful. After a brief introduction and experience with an AI inter-view, participants should discuss why AI makes sense for the organization. People should have the opportunity to share how they see AI being used in their organization and to volunteer for upcoming activities. The key is to help people make the transition from the abstract to the practical while inspiration and insights are at a fever pitch.

Inspire a Team

If a team can be inspired, activities will move faster and enjoy greater organ-ization-wide support. A small group of captivated and engaged people, even in nonleadership positions, can create a forward momentum for strength-based positive change. A cohesive group tends to be more creative, more insightful, and more enthusiastic than any one person alone.

Defining the Project Purpose, Process and Plan

In implementing an AI initiative, the authors have found it useful for organizations and consultants to be clear about the project's purpose, process, and overall plan for implementation. Each of those steps is discussed in the following paragraphs.

Purpose

AI can be used for a wide range of organizational initiatives—from transformation of a whole-system culture to strategic planning to retention to process redesign. Clarity of purpose is essential to successful large-scale AI work. The purpose of the effort usually affects the design of the AI process. For example, in the case of a merger or partnership between two organizations, the inquiry process would include cross-organization interviews, dialogues, and presentations. Once the purpose is established, the AI process is then designed. A simple statement should be articulated:

Our organization will use AI because we want to _____ in order to _____.

Process

Each AI process is designed to meet the needs and constraints of the organization(s) involved. Some organizations (as described in this handbook), such as Hunter Douglas and British Airways North America, have used AI processes that span a year and have been fully integrated into the organization. Other organizations, such as Nutrimental Foods and Roadway, have accelerated AI through a whole-system four-day summit. The following questions have been helpful in considering an AI change initiative. These questions are not intended to be comprehensive or to be used in any specific order. They are intended to prompt meaningful discussions and to remind you of people to involve and tasks to consider for leading successful positive change efforts.

Most likely you will not be able to ask or answer all of the following questions at any given time. If that is the case, consider including the unanswered questions in your discussions with the organization's or community's leaders, your core team, or others involved in the project and its success.

GETTING STARTED
Overview of the Situation
- What is the mission (purpose) of the organization or community?
- How many people are in the organization or community? Where is it located?
- Who are the organization's or community's most involved, interested, and influential stakeholder groups—internally and externally?
- Who are the people interested in AI? How much do they know about AI?
- Who are the people you hope to get interested in AI?
- Who is the change champion, sponsor, and group that will be directly impacted? What do you believe the expectations are?

Change Agenda (In asking these questions, define to whom or to what organization you are referring.)
- What change does the person or organization hope for?
- What is the person's or the organization's image of an ideal future?
- What results does the person or organization want to achieve?
- Why is the person or organization interested in AI?
- How would you *state* the person's or the organization's change agenda (or intended purpose) in inspiring language?
- Why do you believe AI is a good approach to achieving this purpose?

Leadership
- Who are the people who must be involved in leading this process? What will their role in the process be?
- Who else needs to be involved for the project to succeed? Why are they important, and what will be their role?
- How will you get them involved?
- In what ways will leadership stay involved, informed, and inspirational to others?

Core Team
- How many people need to be on your core team to ensure that the entire organization or community has a voice?
- What functions (i.e., Human Resources, Sales, Marketing, Engineering, Finance, Manufacturing, and so on.) need to be included to ensure success of the process?
- Who else would add to the creativity and effectiveness of the process?
- How will the core team be chosen?
- What will be the responsibilities of the core team? How often will the core team meet?
- How will the core team continue to communicate between meetings?

Introduction of AI to the Organization

- Is an introduction to AI needed for the leadership of the organization or community?
  Who needs to be included?
  What will you teach about AI?
  How will the leaders experience AI?
  When will you do this introduction?
- How will you introduce AI to the core team?
  What will you teach about AI?
  How will the team experience AI?
  When will you have this core team meeting?
- Will you have an organization- or community-wide kickoff for the change process?
  How will people be invited?
  Who will describe the purpose and process of the change effort?
  What will you teach about AI?
  What will be the experience of AI?
  What is the leaders' role in the kickoff?
  What is the core team's role in the kickoff?
  How will you make the kickoff a creative and fun event or series of events?
  When will the kickoff happen?
  How will you maintain momentum following the kickoff?

Form of Engagement: Design of the AI Process

- What do you think is the best form of engagement for the organization or community to achieve its change agenda? Why?
- Who will be involved in deciding on the form of engagement?
- When will the form of engagement and process design be determined? (Forms of engagement: summit, a whole systems inquiry, or a core team inquiry)

Preliminary Affirmative Topics

- Will the topics be "home-grown" or "preselected"?
- If preselected, who will select your topics?
- If preselected, given the change agenda, what topics do you think would be meaningful subjects for inquiry?
- How will you and the core team determine and finalize the selection of affirmative topics?

Interview Guide
- Who will create the draft interview guide? When?
- Who will finalize the interview guide? When?
- Will you pilot the interview guide? If not, who will do it? When?
- How will revisions and refinements be included? When?

DISCOVERY PHASE
Learning about the best of what has been and is currently being practiced

Interview Strategy
- Who will be interviewed? Who are all of the stakeholder groups—internal and external—that you will interview? Why is each group important?
- Who will do the interviews?
- How many interviews will be conducted?
- Over what period of time will the interviews be held?

Interviewer Training
- Will interviewer training be conducted?
- Who will lead it? When?
- What will the training include?

Story Collection, Sharing, and Meaning Making
- How will you collect and share stories of best practices, organizational excellence, success, and innovation? (Some ideas: reports, newspapers, videos, storyboards, books, and AI room)
- Who will be responsible for collecting and sharing stories?

Mapping of the Positive Core
- How will you gather and illustrate all of the organization's or community's strengths, resources, and abilities?
- Who will be involved in mapping the positive core?
- How will the positive core be communicated organization- or community-wide?

DREAM PHASE
Envisioning a better world, organization, or community

Envisioning of the Future
- How will you engage people in envisioning the future? When will this occur?
- What questions will you ask to stimulate bold dreaming?
- How will you inspire bold and playful dreaming?
- Who will you involve in envisioning the future?

Opportunity Mapping
- How will you collect and record opportunities embedded in the dreams?
- Who will determine which opportunities to pursue?

DESIGN PHASE
Determining the ideal organization or community

Provocative Propositions
- Who will be involved in writing the statements describing your ideal organization or community? When will this occur?
- How will these statements be shared with and validated by the organization or community? When will this occur?

DESTINY PHASE
Recognizing and sustaining positive change

Innovation Teams
- How many innovation teams will you establish and support?
- How will innovation team projects and membership be determined?
- Who will be the leadership champions for the innovation teams?
- How will you ensure the success of the innovation teams?
- What is the timeline for innovation teamwork?

Recognition of Innovation
- How will you identify and recognize creative expressions of positive change?
- How will you identify and recognize great examples of appreciative leadership?
- How will you identify and recognize people who are living the change?

Creation of an Appreciative Organization
- Are there people who can benefit by further training in AI?
  If so, who are they?
  How will they receive the training—internal workshop or public workshop?
- Will you conduct an Appreciative Leadership Development Program?
  If so, who will attend?
  When will it be held?
- Will you conduct an Appreciative Management Development Program?
  If so, who will attend?
  What topics will be covered?
  When will it be held?

- What Appreciative Human Resource Processes will you create?
  Hiring?
  New Employee Orientation?
  Performance Valuations?
  Others?
- How will you further develop an appreciative approach to customer relations?
- How will you create opportunities for appreciative team development?
- How will you ensure ongoing appreciative communication throughout the organization and/or community that has been impacted?

Plan

The plan must align with the purpose and process. In addition, a useful plan serves to order activities and to point people in a common direction. It specifies who will do what and when, providing guidance for the effort. It also must be flexible because AI is an emergent process, one that unfolds as success builds on success. As a result, organizations tend to be most successful when they combine long-term macro plans, which approximate the activities and time frame of the AI 4-D Cycle, with short-term detailed plans, which clearly specify times and outcomes for specific activities such as meetings, trainings, and interviews.

Samples

The remaining materials in this chapter are sample designs used to initiate an AI-based process. The five samples can be used independently or in combination with one another.

- **Brief Introduction to AI: One-Hour Agenda**
  This session can be used to acquaint members of the organization with the concept and value of AI. It can build interest in and demand for a more intensive session. It is typically used as a brief, yet formal presentation by the AI practitioner to a decision-making group.

- **Executive Overview to AI: Two-Hour Agenda**
  This session provides a little more time to explore the theory and process of AI as well as to engage in a set of mini-interviews.

- **Workplace Redesign Using AI: Four-Hour Agenda and Slides**
  This session reinforces concepts introduced in the Executive Overview to AI (the 2-Hour Introduction, developed in the following pages) and introduces more of the 4-D Cycle. It also includes more activities that allow participants to begin practicing AI techniques.

- **Values Project Using AI: Detailed Project Plan**
  This sample captures the same conceptual material as the other two options. In addition, it provides a concrete, detailed project plan that demonstrates the key elements of the AI process for the organization and an action plan to get the organization moving toward its destiny.

- **Two-Day AI Workshop, Agenda, Project Roles, and Interview Guide**
  This sample contains materials developed for The University of Kentucky Hospital/UK Children's Hospital. It begins with a project overview and includes a Core Team Kickoff agenda, the interview guide, an Appreciative Inquiry Workshop agenda, introductory remarks, and a summit agenda. It shows responsibilities of the core team and its organization divided into subteams focused on the interview guide, data collection and synthesis, and communication and the results.

The following materials can be modified or adapted to plan for and conduct an AI initiative for an organization.

Brief Introduction to AI: One-Hour Agenda

This outline for a brief informative introduction to AI was used for a global automotive manufacturer. The goal is to introduce the key concepts and highlight success stories appropriate for the organization. It should include a mini-experience so that people get a sense of AI's potential and its uniquely positive way of looking at the organization's future.

Agenda

1. AI—What's It All About? (10 minutes)
   - Define AI (theoretical and practitioner).
   - Introduce the Five Principles:
     - The Constructionist Principle
     - The Principle of Simultaneity
     - The Poetic Principle
     - The Anticipatory Principle
     - The Positive Principle
   - Highlight AI benchmark success stories.
   - Hand out success stories such as Roadway: AI Summit.[3]
   - Ask why we are here.

2. Opening Interviews—Using two of the four foundational questions (30 minutes)
   - Set up the process by reading the four questions:
     - What would you describe as being a peak experience or high point in your life—personal or professional?
     - What do you value most about yourself? your work? your organization?
     - What is the core factor that gives life to your organization?
     - Describe your vision of the future for the organization and your world.

   - State that time is only committed for the following two questions:
     - Think about a time when you were really engaged in and excited about your work. Tell me a story about that time. What was happening? What were you feeling? What made it a great moment? What were others doing that

---

3 See article by Hammonds, K. (July 2001). *Leaders for the long haul.* Fast Company, 56–58.

contributed to this moment? What did you contribute to creating this great moment?
  – If you had three wishes for this organization, what would they be?
- Divide participants into pairs; allow 15 minutes per person.
- Return to the group and discuss how it went (e.g., sharing descriptive adjectives).

3. Sample Interview Guide Using Client's Choice Topics (10 minutes)
    - Review traditional problem-solving topics clients provide and rework these topics into affirmative topic choices.
    - Review the newly revised topics (based on group discussion) in the new AI protocol.
    - Discuss differences from traditional problem-solving questions.

4. Wrap-up—How can it help your organization? (10 minutes)
    - Go around the room and ask the following questions: How does this sound? Is it interesting enough to explore further?
    - Ask: What applications can you imagine for your organization? What does your organization want more of?
    - Discuss multiple ways to launch AI initiatives in a large organization.
    - Next step: Think of one AI project, big or small, with which you might like to experiment.

After a formal introduction, the decision-making team will want to engage in a planning session with the AI practitioner to set up an Executive Overview and/or a half-day to two-day workshop. The AI process is flexible enough to fit the organization's desired design and time frame.

Executive Overview to AI: Two-Hour Agenda

This outline is for a typical two-hour Executive Overview to AI. In a two-hour overview, the stage is briefly set and people begin interviews as quickly as possible, typically within the first 15 minutes. The keys to the success of a brief introduction of AI are the interview experience, stories of the impact of AI in other organizations, and the opportunity for participants to discuss applications of AI for their organization.

Agenda

1. Context Setting (10 minutes)
   - State that it's time to rethink human organization and change.
   - Describe it as something hopeful and heartfelt (in facilitator's own words).
   - Ask why we are here.
   - Define AI (theoretical and practitioner).

2. Five Principles of AI (5 minutes)
   - Introduce the Five Principles:
     - The Constructionist Principle
     - The Principle of Simultaneity
     - The Poetic Principle
     - The Anticipatory Principle
     - The Positive Principle
   - Acknowledge that these are abstract principles and explain how they work together.

3. Opening Interviews—Using the four foundational questions (35 minutes)
   - Set up the process by reading the following questions:
     - What would you describe as being a peak experience or high point in your life—personal or professional?
     - What do you value most about yourself? your work? your organization?
     - What is the core factor that gives life to your organization?
     - Describe your vision of the future for the organization and your world.
   - Divide participants into pairs; allow 15 minutes per person.
   - Return to the group and process how it went (e.g., sharing descriptive adjectives).

4. Introduction to AI (30 minutes)
    - Shift from deficit change to positive change.
    - Discuss the 4-D Cycle.
    - Describe a story of the AI process and success in another organization.
    - Discuss the importance of topics and questions.

5. A Sample Interview Guide (10 minutes)
    - Hand out a concrete example to participants.
    - Review two or three of the questions.
    - Discuss differences from traditional problem-solving questions.
    - Ask participants to imagine something like this for their organization.

6. The Choice Points: (15 minutes)
    - Decide what the topics are.
    - Decide who to include on the interview team and who to interview.
    - Decide how many interviews to conduct.
    - Discuss many possibilities for Dream and Design.
    - Make this point: "Our job today is not planning!"

7. Discussion: (15 minutes)
    - Go around room and ask these questions: How does this sound? Is it interesting enough to explore further?
    - Ask: "What applications can you imagine for your organization?"
    - Ask what the next steps are.

Workplace Redesign Using AI: Four-Hour Agenda and Slides

Once the purpose of an initiative is determined, it is often necessary to introduce AI to the people who will be leading the overall effort. The following agenda is an example of a four-hour introduction of AI in such a situation.

In this example, the decision had been made to use AI to study and redesign the workplace environments worldwide throughout the company. In this meeting, 30 people from around the world learned about AI and the project. They were invited to serve on the leadership team to help create the interview guide and to chart the course of the endeavor. This meeting was both an introductory meeting and a working session to get input and to clarify the project plan.

The slides that follow the agenda were used to support the introductory presentation. They provide background information about AI and specific information about the proposed project, including the stakeholders to be interviewed, the broad timeline for the project, and specific outcomes for various meetings. The two slides of assumptions (Slide 11 and Slide 12) are especially noteworthy because they highlight the conditions for success and the constraints that influenced the ultimate design of the AI process. They are a good example of how an AI process can be tailored to the needs and constraints of a specific organization and purpose.

This four-hour meeting illustration resulted in widespread support for the use of AI for the proposed project and numerous ideas for other ways the organization could use AI. Consequently, several informal AI initiatives have begun and are spreading best practices in areas related to customer service; employee morale; and, of course, work environment and productivity.

Agenda

1. Introductions and Stage Setting (5 minutes)
   - State the purpose for this meeting.
   - Introduce AI consultant or facilitator(s).

2. Brief Introduction to AI (15 minutes)
   - Discuss what it is—philosophy and methodology.
   - Discuss definitions—Appreciate and Inquiry
   - State where it's been used and with what results.

3. Mini-interview (45 minutes)
   - Set up the process by reading the following questions:
     - What would you describe as being a peak experience or high point in your life—personal or professional?

– What do you value most about yourself? your work? your organization?

– What is the core factor that gives life to your organization?

– Describe your vision of the future for the organization and your world?

- Allow 20 minutes for each person to interview his or her partner.

4. Debrief Interviews and Dream Question (20 minutes)
    - Debrief interview experience—descriptive adjectives? What was the experience like?
    - Debrief dream question—surprises? What new things did you learn?

5. More about AI (30 minutes)
    - Introduce the Five Principles:
      – The Constructionist Principle
      – The Principle of Simultaneity
      – The Poetic Principle
      – The Anticipatory Principle
      – The Positive Principle
    - Discuss the 4D Cycle; provide examples of how it has been implemented in other organizations. Share a video clip of another organization using AI.
    - Review the interviews just conducted and discuss their relationship to Discovery.

6. Break (10 minutes)

7. Proposed Process to Use for Workplace Redesign (45 minutes)
    - Discuss assumptions.
    - Discuss preliminary project plan.

8. Discussion and Decisions (45 minutes)
    - Discuss potential revisions to process.
    - Discuss timelines, including endpoint.
    - Discuss selection of core team.
    - Close with revisit of purpose and expectations.
    - Ask whether there are other issues.

9. Wrap-up—Next Steps? (15 minutes)

The following slides were used for the session.

Workplace Redesign Using Appreciative Inquiry—PowerPoint Slides

An AI Approach for Designing
a Flexible Workplace

"XYZ" Company

Intro Slide

Agenda

- Introductions
- So, what is AI?
- Mini-interviews
- Interview debrief
- More about AI
- The process we propose to use for this pilot
- Assumptions
- Wrap-up

Slide 1

What is Appreciative Inquiry?

"Ap-pre'-ci-ate, v."	*"In-quire', v."*
". . . to value or admire highly; to judge with heightened understanding; to recognize with gratitude."	". . . to search into, investigate; to seek for information by questioning."

Slide 2

AI . . .

- Focuses organizations on their most positive qualities
- Leverages those qualities to enhance the organization

Appreciative Inquiry is the study of what works well.

Slide 3

What's *Different* About AI?

- Purposefully positive
- Builds on past successes
- "Grass roots" and "top down"
- Highly participative
- Nurtures a positive "inner dialogue"
- Stimulate vision and creativity
- Accelerates change

Slide 4

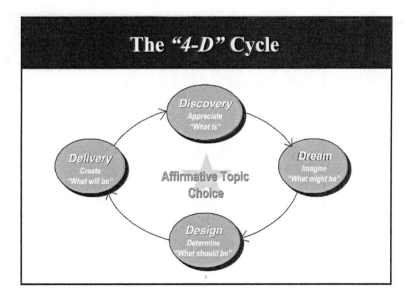

The *"4-D"* Cycle

Slide 5

AI Success Stories

- **British Airways**
    - **Customer Service and Culture Change**
- **Hunter Douglas Window Fashions Division**
    - **Culture Change and Strategic Planning**
- **GTE Telecommunications**
    - **Union/Management Relations**
- **United Religions Initiative**
    - **Organization Design**
- **Green Mountain Coffee Roasters**
    - **Business Process Improvement**

Slide 6

Questions to Start Us Thinking

- **Think back over your entire career, and all the work you've ever done – for pay, or for volunteer. Now, think about a peak experience or high point – a time when you experienced yourself as most successful and most satisfied.**

    - What was it like?

    - What were the conditions that contributed to that extraordinary level of success and satisfaction? In particular, what was it about the *physical space* that contributed to that experience?

Slide 7

Questions to Start Us Thinking cont.

- **Without being humble, what do you most value about . . .**

    - . . . yourself and your capacities to produce and contribute to your team and your organization?

    - . . . your team and its contribution to *XYZ company* and its clients?

    - What are the core factors that support your highest levels of success and satisfaction?

8

Slide 8

Questions to Start Us Thinking cont.

- **You fell asleep at work and you just woke up! You resume working and you are more successful and satisfied than you have ever been.**

    - Where are you working, and on what?

    - What is it like? (Details, please!)

    - What is it about you, the situation, and the task that makes you so successful and satisfied?

    - What type of support did *XYZ company* provide for you that contributed to this remarkable spike in your performance?

9

Slide 9

Purpose for the Inquiry

To engage XXX location stakeholders in a process of discovering "how we work at our best," in order to:

- Determine the necessary components of a *successful* and *satisfying* "new workplace."

- Generate relevant and meaningful insights related to the physical, technological, sociological, and organizational *design* of the new space(s).

- Create a *positive transition* to the new space(s) by building understanding, support, and buy-in for the change (and all that the change implies).

10

Slide 10

Assumptions

- We want the flexible workplace solution to reduce operational costs.

- We want to increase or maintain employee satisfaction and performance.

- We are limited in our ability to get blocks of committed time from employees serving clients.

- We need to be focused on the future in that the changes we make today are dynamic and flexible enough to meet future needs.

11

Slide 11

Assumptions cont.

- We have a broad population with differing needs and preferences. Not every group or individual employee wants or needs the same setting/services to be optimally productive and engaged.

- This will be a big cultural change and we need to work with other groups to make this successful.

- The flexible workplace solution will reflect the input of our stakeholders.

- The process we use for implementing the change should be inclusive.

12

Slide 12

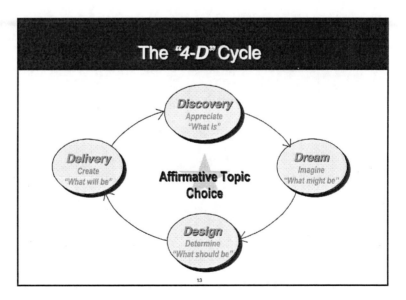

The *"4-D"* Cycle

13

Slide 13

"Discovery"

- Getting Started

- Inquiry / Interviews

  - "When we are at our best, what makes work exciting, interesting, invigorating, motivating and productive?"

- Meaning Making / Reflections

- Preparation of report or presentation

14

Slide 14

Getting Started

- Hold an Initial Meeting:

  - 2-1/2-days

  - 17-20 participants (representatives from every related stakeholder group)

  - Early January

15

Slide 15

Meeting Outcomes

- Select Affirmative Topics

- Make Critical Decisions:

  - Who will conduct interviews?

  - Who will we interview?

    - Do we interview clients? Suppliers?

    - Do we benchmark other organizations? If so, which ones?

  - What are our timelines?

16

Slide 16

"Next Steps"

- Set up Sub-Groups

  - Finalize interview guides

  - Prepare interviewers

  - Prepare interview assignments / timelines

  - Make meaning of the "data"

17

Slide 17

Inquiry Process

- Conduct one-to-one interviews with stakeholders:
  - Internal "customers"
  - Clients
  - Vendors/suppliers
  - "Benchmark" organizations
  - Outside "experts" (architectural firms, consultants, other *XYZ company* offices, etc.)
- Answer the question: "When we are at our best, what makes work exciting, interesting, invigorating, motivating and productive?"

18

Slide 18

Meaning Making / Reflections

- Hold clusters of "synthesis" meetings
  - Keep interviewers *close* to their own data
  - Imagine *implications* and *possibilities*
  - Seek *inspiration,* not "common ground"

- Meeting outcomes
  - Broad sharing of interview insights
  - Creation of a small team which will meet to create the final report / presentation of interview data

19

Slide 19

The Summit
DREAM, DESIGN and DESTINY

- 1-1/2 days
- As many stakeholders as possible
- Meeting outcomes
  - Determine a variety of *organizing possibilities* that will build upon what we've learned works (from the Inquiry).
  - Agree to a set of *design principles* around which we will organize our "new workplace."
    - These principles will ensure that we will continue to operate at the highest possible levels of customer and client satisfaction and productivity - even as we realize savings in our overall costs.
  - Organize to *implement* the "next steps" that are suggested by our Design.

Slide 20

In other organizations, this four-hour topic selection process can be expanded into a longer workshop format that allows organizations to explore other potential topic areas. The next sample is a detailed project plan for a large-scale AI initiative at the American Red Cross.

Values Project Using AI: Detailed Project Plan

Following a two-day AI workshop, the emergent American Red Cross project conducted 5,000 appreciative interviews during a two-month period to discover the values implicit in the services the organization provides nationwide. Careful and detailed planning was one of many factors that supported the success of this effort. As one might imagine with an organization of this size, commitment was unquestionable and enthusiasm was high.

At the president's national conference presentation only three months after the Values Project began, the project plan showed milestones along the way. This plan showed in great detail all that goes into a mass mobilized inquiry, from creating the interview guide to identifying interviewers to conducting interviews to collecting data and stories to synthesizing the data and preparing a report. In this case, the final report was accompanied by a highly inspirational video showing various Red Cross employees and volunteers demonstrating the values in action as they provided service to people in need. The result of this extraordinary inquiry was the identification of "living values," the values that are embedded in the day-to-day activities of the American Red Cross.

The following project plan illustrates how effective project management techniques can be used to help an AI project arrive at various milestones. The American Red Cross, for example, had important deadlines for the AI interviews. A national convention was the place where the narratives of hope, courage, and excellence were shared. More than 2,000 people from American Red Cross chapters all over the country came together for this convention. In a case like this, the details and time frames can make or break the AI momentum. AI is powerful on its own, but it is even better when the best project management and other consulting and facilitating techniques are integrated to support the positive AI intentions.

Project Plan—Major Milestones

(**V**–Vince, **H**–Harry, **D**–David, **J**–Jan, **B**–Brian, **R**–Bob, **VT**–Values Technology)

Bold = Major Milestones

Italics = Values Technology

Standard = Appreciative Inquiry, combined activity or other activity

Week	Milestone	Date	Who	Notes	Complete = X
1	Project milestones and plan defined	3/2	V, H, B, R		X
	Interviewer criteria defined identified	3/2	V, H, B, R		X
	Major resource requirements	3/2	V, H, B, R		X
	Contracting with AI and VT vendors begins	3/3	CE&T		X
	Conference rooms reserved for training	3/4	B		X
	President's communication to ARC prepared and approved	3/4	J, B		X
	Chapters, blood regions, NHQ units supplying interviewers selected	3/5	V, H, B, R		X
2	Values project plan presented to OMC	3/8	President, V		X
	President's communication re: Values Project on Cross Link and by mail to board and key leadership	3/8	Comm.		X
	Hotel arrangements completed for AI training	3/9	CE&T	Hotel info and budget numbers needed for interviewer recruitment letters	X
	Interviewer recruitment letters completed and sent to execs.	3/9	J, B	Package contains cover letter specifying exec's recruitment job and due date and letter to interviewers describing process and admin. details	X
	Budget and account number assigned	3/9	B	Finance	X
	Execs. in chapters, blood regions, NHQ who are supplying interviewers are notified	3/10		Comm.	

Week	Milestone	Date	Who	Notes	Complete = X
	Determine requirements (if any) for customizing values inventory	3/10	V, H, VT		X
2	Print values inventory forms	3/12	VT		X
	Contract process completed with vendors	3/12	Contracts Office		X
3	Determine values inventory sample range	3/16	H, VT		X
	Mailing labels and cover letters sent to VT or mailing service	3/17	H		X
	Execs. send in names of committed interviewers	3/17	Field units	Send as e-mail to CE&T	X
	Interviewers sent notice of acceptance and travel details	3/18–3/19	CE&T	Phone or e-mail to CE&T	X
	Protocol for reporting stories and interview data determined	3/19	R	Demonstrate protocol for sending AI data during training; brief VT on interview reporting process	X
4	Mail values inventories	3/22	VT	Completed 3/19	X
	Determine date for values drafting meeting	3/22	V, H	Meeting date 5/5	X
	Develop participant list for drafting values statement	3/23	V, H		X
	AI training conducted	3/23–3/24	D, CE&T	Washington Marriott	X
4–6	VT inventories completed and mailed in	3/23–4/9	HQ and field units	Completed forms sent directly to VT. Forms processed as received.	
	Appreciative Inquiry interviews scheduled	3/25–3/28	Interviewers		
	Appreciative Inquiry interview protocol developed	3/25–3/28	D	Delivered to CE&T on 3/26, if possible.	
	Interview protocol sheets delivered to interviewers	3/29	CE&T		
4–7	AI Interviews conducted	3/29–4/12	Interviewers		
	Draft letter from president inviting senior leadership to values-drafting meeting	4/5	B, J	Meeting date 5/5	

Week	Milestone	Date	Who	Notes	Complete = X
5–7	Story compilation	3/29–4/13	Interviewers	Interviewers send in story packages as completed; stories sent to VT for analysis	
5	Send invitation to senior leadership meeting to draft values statements	4/7	President, V, H	NHQ, BHQ, field representation	
	Determine convention broadcast options	4/8	V, H, Comm		
	Reserve satellite time for convention broadcast	4/30	Comm	If necessary	
6	All VT forms completed and sent in	4/9	ARC staff		
6–9	Analysis of VT forms	4/9–4/30	VT		
7	All AI stories received by CE&T	4/15	Interviewers, CE&T		
	Electronic versions of stories sent to VT	4/17	R, CE&T		
7–9	Document analysis of stories	4/23–4/30	VT		
7	Purchase (or release) satellite time for convention	5/1	V, H, Comm	Decision and purchase on same day. Might need decision sooner.	
10	Meeting to interpret data	5/3–5/4	V, H, B, R, D, VT		
	Meeting to draft preliminary values statement	6-May	V, H, D, VT	Target date; key leadership from BHQ, NHQ, and field	
10–12	Prepare convention presentation and related activities and materials	5/5–5/20	V, H, B, R, Comm, et al		
	Preliminary values statement presented to president	5/6	V, H		
	Draft values statement revised as necessary	5/7	V, H, B, R		
10	Draft values statement sent to strategic planning comm. of board and appropriate senior leaders for comment	5/11	V, H, B	Involve strategic planning committee of the board	
10–11	Comments on draft values statement received from board members and senior leaders	5/13–5/19	CE&T		

Week	Milestone	Date	Who	Notes	Complete = X
12	Presentation of Red Cross Values at National Convention	5/21–5/23	President, V, H, D		

Two-Day AI Workshop, Agenda, Project Roles, and Interview Guide

This sample contains materials developed by Susan Wood and Karen Stefaniak for an employee development project focusing on nursing excellence at The University of Kentucky Hospital. It begins with a project overview, the project scope, and sponsorship and funding. Included are the Core Team Kickoff Meeting Agenda, the AI Workshop Agenda, a Sample Introduction to use before starting a workshop, Core Team Roles, Core Team Kickoff Meeting Learnings & Results, the interview guide, brief project milestones, and an update with measurable results. The agendas show responsibilities for the core team and the organization into subteams focused on the interview guide, data collection and synthesis, and communication.

The University of Kentucky Hospital/ UK Children's Hospital

"Nursing Excellence – The UK Way"
By Karen Stefaniak and Susan Wood

Purpose and Overview

In 2001, University of Kentucky Nursing was designated a Magnet facility by the American Nurses Credentialing Center. The Magnet examination process (extensive documentation and a four-day on-site survey) validated nursing leadership's belief that the work environment facilitated autonomous professional nursing practice. However, a nurse satisfaction survey conducted in 2002 indicated the one area of nursing satisfaction that needed improvement: "professional autonomy." Although the result of this satisfaction survey was a surprise and puzzle to leadership, the staff's perception was taken very seriously. Further discussion with staff indicated frustration and powerlessness resulting from the need to solve the same or similar problems over and over again. Staff nurse councils' recommendations required far too much time to become reality, so the staff would "give up" and move on to another pressing issue. The time and commitment involved was draining the staff's energy. They needed to see their own successes and appreciate their contributions to patients, the organization, and the profession.

Two unrelated events occurred in late 2002 and early 2003. First, Karen Stefaniak, RN, PhD, the chief nursing officer (CNO), was introduced to AI by the nursing staff education director and immediately began reading everything she could find. She tested the approach with nursing leadership during an annual goal setting session. The positive approach was readily embraced as energizing and effective.

Second, Dr. Stefaniak was selected for a Robert Wood Johnson Executive

Nurse Fellows Program, which provided funding for a project. After consulting her colleagues, she began the search for an expert in AI to assist her in leading a culture change in nursing to one in which nurses appreciated themselves and each other. Further, it was hoped that the nurses would internalize their worth and appreciate the professional and autonomous work environment validated by the Magnet designation. AI was the method chosen to facilitate such a change because AI assumes that all organizations have past and present successes and encourages perpetuating those successes to create more successes. The AI 4-D Cycle would be the approach that nurses would use to share their stories, requiring reflection and self-insight.

Dr. Stefaniak conducted an online search; found the AI Commons Web site at Case; reviewed past projects of the consultants on the "Find an AI consultant" link; and located Susan Wood, who specialized in applying AI in healthcare. After a telephone conversation in which Dr. Stefaniak expressed the goals of her project and her vision of the future state of the nursing culture, Susan was interested in working with UK nursing to increase nurse and nurse manager satisfaction and retention, educate nursing leadership in the AI philosophy and methodology, and ultimately improve patient satisfaction.

Project Scope

Aim: Discover stories about nursing excellence, learn AI, and generate innovative ideas to reframe "Nursing Excellence – The UK Way." This would be communicated throughout the hospital with positive meaning for "The UK Way." Specific expectations included the following:

- Increase satisfaction of nurses and managers
- Improve problem solving skills and process improvement
- Amplify understanding of Magnet nursing
- Enhance teamwork and empathy for each other (know more about what everyone does)

"The project began 2003 and will last forevermore," stated Dr. Stefaniak. The purpose of the project was to develop nursing management and to move the nursing culture to one in which nurses at UK accepted nothing less than excellence in everything they did. The nursing department (1,600 nurses) initiated the inquiry, inviting pharmacy, nutrition, and other staff to participate in workshops and interviews.

Project Leaders

- Dr. Karen Stefaniak, RN, PhD, Associate Hospital Director/CNO, and Robert Wood Johnson Nurse Executive Fellow, UK Hospital/UK Children's Hospital

- Craig Casada, Nurse Recruiter, UK Hospital
- Susan O. Wood, Principal, Corporation for Positive Change
- Nurse Managers who taught 20 AI workshops at UK Hospital

Sponsorship and Funding

Dr. Karen Stefaniak holds a Robert Wood Johnson Executive Nurse Fellowship, a three-year program that includes a leadership project and professional development. She led "Nursing Excellence – The UK Way" with agreement and support from the UK hospital administration.

Core Team Kickoff Meeting

Forty-four staff members convened for 12 hours over two days to get the project started. What followed were meetings where nurse leaders and hospital administrators were introduced to AI and asked to support the initiative. They readily agreed, and a core team was invited to meet to select topics of inquiry and design the process. The core team was made up of 30 nurses from all units and stakeholders who work closely with nursing—pharmacy, nutrition, radiology, volunteer, rehab and respiratory, nurse recruitment, and quality improvement. Fourteen nurse managers who guided core team activities and led workshops joined these 30 people. Two-way interviews were done in 20 workshops over ten months, with a Story Collection Team gathering data.

UKH Core Team Kickoff Agenda

Purpose: Orient Steering Group to AI; plan and launch inquiry

Goals:
- Experience and understand Appreciative Inquiry
- Clarify purpose and desired outcomes of project
- Select topics for inquiry; draft interview guide
- Refine project plan, roles, and timeline

Products:
- Project plan, roles, and timeline
- Interview guide
- Workshop and interview schedule and process for interviewing
- Task teams—interview guide, communication, education, story collection, and summit planning

Day 1			
Activity	**Leader**	**Handout**	**Time**
Introductions/Purpose/Goals Introductions AI partners	Karen Stefaniak	1	5 minutes
Appreciative Interviews Pairs, quads, eights Mural (best stories/themes)	Karen	2	2 hours
BREAK – 15 minutes			
Appreciative Inquiry Briefing	Karen/Susan	3, 4	45 minutes
LUNCH – 45 minutes			

Topic Selection for Inquiry
    Debrief stories and mural
A "fateful act"
    What you want more of
	Susan/Karen		45 minutes

Topic Definition/Lead-ins
    Definition
    Ring bell for appreciative feedback
	Susan/Craig	5	1 hour

BREAK – 15 minutes			

Interview Guide Development
    Qualities of appreciative questions
    Sample guide/structure
	Susan/Craig	6	15 minutes

Round One: Subgroups Develop
Questions by Topic
    Refine lead-in
    Draft 3 or 4 questions
    Ring bell for appreciative feedback
	4 groups		1 hour

Round Two: Questions by Topic
    Improve questions
    Ring bell for appreciative feedback
    Assemble draft guide (computer for input)
	Susan/Craig		30 minutes

Review/Close/Questions	Susan/Karen/Craig		15 minutes

Day 2			
Activity	**Leader**	**Handout**	**Time**
Check In/Goals for Today	Karen/Susan		5 minutes
Brief Interviews 1/1 　　2 questions 　　Comments	Craig		10 minutes
Pilot-test Interview Guide	Craig		45 minutes
BREAK – 15 minutes			
Visioning Activity for Project Draw a Picture of Success/Best-Case Scenario Name the Project—An Exciting and Evocative Name Refine Measurable and Immeasurable Outcomes	Susan/Craig	7	45 minutes
Project Planning 　　Core team role Timeline 　　Stakeholders 　　Workshops and interviewing—review design, guidelines	Susan/Karen/ Craig	8	1 hour
Task Teams: Communication, interview guide, summit planning, story collection, and education/innovation (workshops)			
Teachable Moments—Lead with Affirmation	Susan +	9	15 minutes
Next Steps	Susan/Karen/Craig		15 minutes
Closing Comments	All		15 minutes

AI Workshops—Led by Nurse Managers

The following agenda was used by 14 nurse managers who led Appreciative Inquiry workshops. All staff and stakeholders were invited to enroll, and participation was deliberately mixed across nursing units and stakeholder groups. Interviewing partners sometimes took their conversations onto their units where they showed each other how things worked. This heightened understanding and appreciation of each other's roles. In one case, a nurse requested a transfer when she became intrigued with the work in the neonatal intensive care unit.

AI Workshop Agenda

Purpose: Illuminate the positive core of nursing through stories about nursing excellence.

Goals:
- Capture and contribute stories to the positive core of UK Hospital Nursing
- Develop expertise in Appreciative Inquiry interviewing
- Generate innovative ideas for bringing topics to life

Handouts:
- Interview guides with summary sheets (to be collected)
- 1-page summary of project
- Lead by affirmation

Materials Kit (AI bag):
- UK AI intro script, mural paper, tape, markers, graphic agenda, camera

Room Setup:
- Graphic agenda, 2 easels, blank mural posted with BESTS written at the top and WISHES at the bottom

Products from Each Workshop:
- Stories for story collection team (interview guides and summary sheets)
- List describing positive core
- List of innovative ideas
- Mural, which will be used at the summit (Take a picture and give mural to EF.)

Deliverables:
- Project timeline and plan
- Core team roster and role
- Draft interview guide
- Communication plan

This is the script the managers used to introduce the workshop:

First, introduce self: name, job title, and department

Suggested introduction: *I am here today to briefly speak with you about my experience with Appreciative Inquiry. I am part of the AI core team at UK Hospital, and we recently attended a workshop to introduce the concept to the nursing staff. Appreciative Inquiry (AI) is a process that helps participants remember and value what it is they do and why they do it. It facilitates positive change in an organization because looking for what works well is more motivating and effective than focusing on what is not working. By asking questions in a positive way, our thinking is geared more toward what works and what we want more of. Studies have shown that an organization will move in the direction of what they focus on!*

On a personal level, AI has been shown to have an overall beneficial impact on someone's life. At the AI core team meeting, we learned that from asking interview questions, we got stories. From stories, we got ideas on what works, leading to the question, What do we have that we want more of? We then brainstormed in small teams and identified our project title, the topics we believed were important and the questions that created the interview guide you will use today. So I invite you to be part of our journey, to share your stories. By doing so, you will begin the process of creating a positive change for all of us at UK Hospital!

Core Team Roles

The role of the core team (steering group) includes all of the following activities. Some have specific time frames for completion; others are ongoing for the life of the project. In addition, subteams have specific functions related to the interview guide, data collection and synthesis, and communication. It is very important to note who will complete what by when and to assign a lead coordinator to keep track of assignments/tasks.

- Articulate purpose and goals of project
- Identify and enroll stakeholders
- Select topics for inquiry
- Refine project plan
- Form necessary subgroups as specific "task teams" and assign responsibilities
- Design and test interview guide
- Invite others to interview
- Capture and document stories
- Plan and help design meetings and summit
- Track progress and outcomes during and after inquiry/measurement
- Communicate plans and progress

Task Teams

Following is a list of subteams and typical tasks.

Communication

Refine project title, purpose, and measures
Generate communication about the project to encourage involvement
Spread stories
Create a summit invitation

Interview Guide

Refine and test interview guide
Identify stakeholders and design interview guides

Story Collection

Collect stories using summary sheets from interviews
Read and organize stories, identifying key stories to share in summit
Pass interesting stories to communication team to share

Education and Innovation

Lead AI workshops
Capture ideas/innovation from workshops (via summary sheets/murals)
Prepare ideas to bring to summit

Summit Planning

Advise on whom to invite and how to invite and design of summit
Act as host at summit

Core Team Kickoff Meeting Learnings & Results

Purpose: Orient core team to AI; plan and launch inquiry to discover affirmative topic choices; write interview guide

During the core team launch, someone said, "Oh, that's just the UK way," referring to times when problems resurfaced and were not fixed. "The UK Way," with all of its negative connotations, had become a catch phrase. Nurses and stakeholders (pharmacy, nutrition, and so on.) decided right then to change the meaning of "The UK Way" from "when things go wrong" to reflect "nursing at its best." From the stories the team members told, five topics became the focus of inquiry for "Nursing Excellence – The UK Way." The topics were as follows:

1. Art of Nursing
2. The UK Quilt of Teamwork
3. UK Magnet Nursing

4. Celebrate Life as UK Nurses

5. Humor—A Vital Sign of Life

Another moment of truth occurred when the core team talked about how newly hired nurses were treated. "We eat our young," one of them said with some embarrassment. Susan asked, "What would it be if you did the affirmative opposite of eating your young?" After several moments of silence, someone said quietly, "We embrace our own." Mentoring and assimilating new staff became an important part of the inquiry.

The inquiry culminated in two one-day summits held in October 2004. In January 2005, an **Appreciative Inquiry Summit** convened to refine the vision and develop action plans to engage others in making the bold ideas come to life. Four themes emerged for action:

- Interdisciplinary Excellence
- Technology, Equipment, and Facility
- Quality of Work Life
- Our Public Image

AI Interview Guide

The following interview guide was created by the core team at the kick-off meeting:

The University of Kentucky Hospital/UK Children's Hospital
"Nursing Excellence – The UK Way"

Date: _____
Name: _____
Unit: _____ Phone: _____

Thank you for participating in this interview. I am an interviewer for this nursing project. We are inquiring and learning more about "Nursing Excellence – The UK Way." Nurses and related staff will be interviewed directly to collect the "best-case" stories on which to build the future. Your input will be an important contribution to generate meaningful ideas and actions.

Many times in the interviews, we ask questions about things that aren't working well so that we can fix them. This time we are going to approach things from a different angle. We are going to find out about your experiences of success so that we can find ways to create more of those types of experiences at UK Hospital and UK Children's Hospital.

Over the next few months, we will interview as many nurses as possible, primarily in workshops. We also will interview others who have a stake in quality nursing care. When the interviews are complete, everyone's input will be synthesized to identify qualities of nursing care that make UK Nurses unique. With those qualities as a foundation, we will create specific future steps to build on our strengths.

During our interview, we will be exploring your experiences in five areas: (List topics below)

    1. Art of Nursing
    2. The UK Quilt of Teamwork
    3. UK Magnet Nursing
    4. Celebrate life as UK Nurses
    5. Humor—A Vital Sign of Life

I want you to listen like you have never listened before. The following series of questions will be very thought-provoking. Please listen carefully about each question and allow yourself time to think about your answer. Remember, there are no right or wrong answers.

Before we begin, do you have any questions?

1. What were your initial hopes and dreams when you first joined the UK Hospital?
2. What has been your most positive experience since you've been here?
3. Without being humble, explain what you value most about:
   – Yourself?
   – The people you work with?
   – Your department? your work?

Topic One: Art of nursing

Nursing care is an art at its very best. What we do with our minds, hearts, and hands is truly beautiful. We paint with brush strokes of compassion, weave tapestries of comfort, and sculpt an environment of caring beyond technology for our patients, their families, and often for one another. At UK, this is the art of nursing.

Question 1: What does the art of nursing mean to you? Describe a time when you or someone else demonstrated the art of nursing.

Question 2: Imagine the perfect painting of nursing at UK. What does it look like? Where do you picture yourself in it?

Topic Two: Nursing, the common thread that unites a patchwork of disciplines into a quilt of teamwork

Question 1: Tell me about a time when you accomplished more than expected by working together as a team. What was it about the team that made it work?

Question 2: What three wishes do you have for fostering teamwork and collaboration at UK?

Topic Three: UK Magnet nursing—a strong force pulling out the best in people through:

Mentoring—embracing our own
Autonomy—achieved through independent Nursing Practice
Growing—always learning something new
Nurturing—focusing on patients, their families and each other
Excellence—exceeding expectations/above and beyond
Teamwork—being a good fit/always being the insider

Nursing in a Magnet-status hospital provides improved patient outcomes, offers a better working environment, supports autonomous nursing practice, and encourages professional development. The infrastructure provides avenues for nurses to fully use their knowledge and expertise to deliver exceptional patient care. We believe in the value of superior nursing care and the way it can transform lives—we recognize the power of what one nurse can do for himself or herself and the patients he or she cares for.

Question 1: Tell me about an experience you had when you knew you were having a "Magnet Moment" (high point) (e.g., a specific situation or event of nursing excellence you have been part of).

Question 2: What three wishes do you have that could make UK Hospital and UK Children's Hospital more "magnetized"?

Topic Four: Celebrate life as UK nurses
Sail the 7 Cs
Celebrate our camaraderie, compassion, caring, commitment, and collaboration through complimentary words and actions.

Question 1: Tell me about an event or a situation in which you felt appreciated as a nurse. What did you value most about that experience?

Question 2: Describe a moment or example when you recognized a colleague by words or actions that conveyed a message that indicated "I could not have gotten through this without you." What were the circumstances surrounding this experience, and how did you and others feel afterward?

Question 3: What ideas do you have for celebrating success and expressing appreciation at UK?

Topic Five: Humor is a vital sign of life. Laughter sometimes is the best medicine. Humor allows us to deal with sad situations and job stress and enables us to relax and enjoy our patients, their families, and each other.

Question 1: Describe a specific work experience in which humor eased a painful, stressful, or tense situation or enhanced a positive one.

Closing: I'd like to ask you two final questions:
1. In your opinion, what was the highlight of this interview?
2. What do you hope comes of this process?

Project Milestones (what was accomplished; what AI topics/themes emerged)

One goal was to transfer knowledge and skill in AI to staff and leaders at UK Hospital so that the positive perspective would last beyond the initial project scope. This happened in several ways:

Craig Casada and Karen Stefaniak went with Susan Wood to an AI workshop to learn the principles and to create an effective project plan.

Managers learned AI and led workshops that accelerated permeation of AI.

Beyond nursing—Stakeholders were invited to participate with nurses in workshops, which strengthened relationships and generated innovative improvements.

Environmental Services (a UK vendor) picked up on AI and used it for conversations to define customer expectations with UK Hospital!

A nursing and materials management team designed its own inquiry to improve efficiency, cleanliness, and teamwork.

Vision Statement

Here is the vision statement that came from the summits held in October 2004 and January 2005.

The vision of Nursing Services at the University of Kentucky Hospital is as follows:

> *To be the premier nationally and internationally recognized leader in professional practice, patient care, education, and research thereby advancing our institution's pursuit of achieving top 20 academic health center status.*

The participants added the following "In 2004, Nursing Services discovered its Positive Core, using Appreciative Inquiry. We selected 5 topics to study. Then we told each other stories about our best moments in patient care, what we love about our work and our colleagues, what excellence looks like, and what makes our work fun and enjoyable. We are permeating the entire hospital with positive meaning for 'The UK Way.' Through *planned osmosis*, we invite our colleagues in all disciplines to join us in a positive revolution so that UK Hospital/UK Children's Hospital will be changed forevermore, building on our strengths and what we do well."

"The UK Way" means:
- We exceed expectations.
- Safe and efficient.
- Cutting edge.
- Respectful.
- Considerate.
- Visionary.

Reflections from participants about "Nursing Excellence – The UK Way" included:
- This process helped me rediscover the joy of nursing.
- The strongest thing at UK is the teamwork.
- We have a new understanding of one another.
- It's nice to "live outside my area" for a while.
- The experience has been a big boost.
- I may now be able to deal more effectively with negative people.

– This needs to go on indefinitely.
– "Nursing Excellence –The UK Way" stimulated me to come up with new ideas to brighten my patients' days.
– Positive energy is better than negative—it's more fun to make it work.
– So many changes! Nursing is stepping forward in a positive way now— not just waiting.

Project Update

Although the introduction of AI into nursing at UK began as a solution to a perceived negative attitude among nurses and to fulfill a Robert Wood Johnson project assignment, ultimately the goal was for AI to be part of the fabric of nursing and to become integrated into nursing management. It would be employed as a strategy for process improvement, recruitment and retention, morale enhancement, and strategic planning. This has been accomplished, and examples of the goal accomplishment are regularly visible.

Quantifiable results that improved: RN vacancy rate decreased from 6.2% to 4.1%. RN turnover rate decreased from 10.35% to 8.42%. RN staff autonomy score increased from 46.93 to 50.89 over the year after implementation. Manager satisfaction was unchanged.

A more impressive outcome that speaks to the versatility and the compelling nature of AI is the frequency with which the nurses spontaneously approach a problem and/or project with a simple question: What and/or where does it work well? That question has surfaced repeatedly during the planning and designing of a new hospital. Certainly, ineffective processes and systems are not to be moved to a new building. On the other hand, those systems that work well are being used as a model for the desired operations in the new facility. During recent preparation for one of the first unannounced Joint Commission on Accreditation of Healthcare Organizations (JCAHO) surveys, those units working well were used as models for process improvement of less prepared units.

Another pressing issue at UK today is patient satisfaction. The nursing managers of those units with the best scores are actively utilized in assisting other managers with their efforts. Although not always identified as AI, the philosophy is leading positive change in the organization. AI is now a major influence in recruitment activities, creative marketing copy, exit interviews, new employee interviews, performance improvement projects, and shared governance council operations. In 2005, UK nursing received Magnet redesignation with no recommendations for improvement. In fact, AI was central to most of the written materials. During the survey, the nurses repeatedly referred to their AI work and met the surveyors with, "I want to show you and tell you what we do." The pride was overwhelming, and the entire visit was a celebration of Nursing Excellence the UK Way.

From the beginning, nurses at UK Hospital talked about how to measure change. They developed the following list at the core team launch. In every core team meeting, they talked about "what's already changing" using these measures. The following measures remain topics of focus today:

Quantitative measures
– Nurse satisfaction
– Manager satisfaction
– Patient satisfaction
– Retention and recruitment tool
– Increase occupancy/capacity (beds) by virtue of staff available
– Affirmative problem solving (solve and resolve, not repeat)
– Inclusion (how many elect to be interviewed, attend workshops, and go to summit)

Qualitative measures
– Increase in positive thinking
– More appreciative mind-set
– Shared ownership
– Increase in self-confidence, self-image
– A "blame-free" culture

Other desired results
– "The UK Way" described in positive terms
– "Benefit of the whole"
– Greater nursing leverage
– Confirm and renew articulation of values for UKH
– Market ourselves in the community and improve image
– Capitalize on providing service to all, including indigents and under-served

A Final Note

The agendas, interview protocols, and methods provided in this chapter have been successfully modified and used with hundreds of organizations (large and small; for-profit and nonprofit) and governments to accomplish their respective organizational strategies and structures. The purpose of these samples is to provide different ways to launch an AI initiative for key organizational leaders and their stakeholders.

PART 2
Application of the 4-D Cycle of Appreciative Inquiry

AI is a process for positive change. It may be applied to whole organizations, teams, or departments. It may be used for strategic planning, merger integration, culture transformation, or leadership development. Whatever the purpose or change agenda for using AI, it is most often addressed through the AI 4-D Cycle of *Discovery, Dream, Design,* and *Destiny,* introduced here as Part 2.

The AI 4-D Cycle may be as formal as a year-long, whole-system process involving hundreds of employees and other stakeholders in interviews, dialogue, and decision making. Or it may be as informal as a conversation between a manager and an associate. While the hallmark of AI is organization-wide interviews using a set of unconditionally positive questions, AI is more than crafting questions, conducting interviews, and gathering data. It is a process for engaging all relevant and interested people in positive change.

Successful change requires new relationships to be formed along with large amounts of energy, enthusiasm, and creativity. To do this, AI engages people throughout the organization in discovering, sharing, and building on inspiring accounts of peak experiences, successes, and strengths—their positive core. When individuals, organizations, or communities tap into their positive core and link it to their change agenda, personal, professional, and/or organizational transformations never thought possible can emerge.

The AI 4-D Cycle is a dynamic iterative process of positive change. The 4-D Cycle, along with supporting information, is presented in the next four chapters.

- *Discovery:* What gives life? (Chapter 4)
- *Dream:* What might be? (Chapter 5)
- *Design:* How can it be? (Chapter 6)
- *Destiny:* What will be? (Chapter 7)

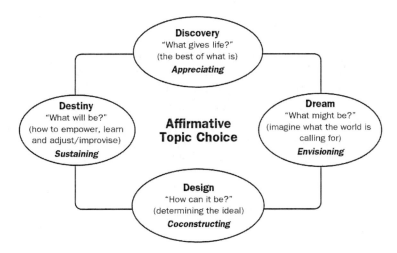

This brief overview of the 4-D Cycle provides the context for the next several chapters. During the first phase, Discovery, interviews are conducted to uncover success stories from the company's past and present. These stories include not only organizational successes but also individual successes. To capture these positive life-giving events, the interview questions will be designed intentionally to solicit positive affirming answers.

Chapter 4 provides examples of engaging AI interview questions that might surface during the *Discovery* stage. Once the interviews are completed, the stories are shared and discussed in an attempt to create a shared vision, or dream, of the future for the company. As an example of the latter, the Case Clipping at the end of Chapter 4 is an interview guide from an insurance company.

Chapter 5 illustrates the movement from discovery to the *Dream* stage through an application of AI at the Roadway Express Summit; this edition also includes an update on Roadway's continued AI applications. The chapter ends with an introduction to Design, which takes the vision of what the organization can be and creates specific action-oriented provocative propositions, also called possibility statements or design statements.

Chapter 6 contains Tendercare, Inc.'s "+1 Census Development Campaign" case study to demonstrate how an organization and its key customers move together from discovery to dream to create a set of possibility statements in the *Design* phase. This chapter includes an update of the Tendercare story and two new powerful additions to the ways the design phase can unfold to allow for creativity and enhance speed of innovation in reaching the marketplace. A new application from Fairmount Minerals demonstrates how AI can be used to create new products and business processes based on the ideal of sustainable development.

Chapter 7 concludes Part 2 with the *Destiny* phase in which organizational members can declare intended actions and ask for organization-wide support from every level. The chapter also uses the updated Case Clipping from Hunter Douglas Window Fashions (one of the longest sustained applications of AI) to describe how the company has changed and sustained its appreciative corporate culture. Hunter Douglas was awarded the honor of one of the "Top Ten Places to Work" in Denver, Colorado, in 2004 and in Colorado in 2006.

4

Discovery:
What Gives Life?

Perhaps, the most important thing we do as leaders and consultants is inquiry. We read situations; we do organizational analysis and diagnosis. It all starts with inquiry. The key point is that the way we know is fateful. The questions we ask, the things that we choose to focus on, and the topics we choose to ask questions about determine what we find. What we find becomes the data and the story out of which we dialogue about and envision the future. And so the seeds of change are implicit in the very first questions we ask. Inquiry is intervention.

—David Cooperrider

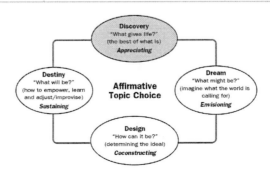

The task in the *Discovery* phase is to uncover, learn about, and appreciate the best of "what is." This is done by focusing on one's highpoint experiences and successes. In this phase, stakeholders share stories of exceptional accomplishments and explore the "life-giving" factors of the organization. Recognizing that the organization is not always at its best, AI seeks to discover rich accounts of when it is at its best and use those accounts as a foundation for the future.

During *Discovery*, interviews are conducted, stories are shared, and themes are identified that cut across the many stories and high-point experiences. The data collected during the interviews help the AI team identify, illuminate, and understand the distinctive strengths that lend the organization life and vitality when it is functioning at its best.

Data collection and narrative exploration represent the core of the inquiry process in this phase. They serve as the jumping-off point for dialogue and the application of learning to a unique theory of organizational innovation and change. In traditional research processes, data are collected as an objective reality. Such data are assumed to stand apart from the people involved and the process through which they are generated. In the AI process, collecting objective data is not the goal. It is not the goal because interviewers assume an active role in order to explore and enliven the interview process through their stories of the organization.

When data are collected, an important goal is to stimulate participants' excitement and delight as they share their values, experience, and history with the organization and their wishes for the future. In addition, thinking and dialoguing about positive possibilities are invited into the process. To lead the *Discovery* phase interview, the interviewer must actively listen and learn. Data collection and its associated narrative exploration are mutual learning processes. Both the interviewer and interviewee learn as they explore the participants' values, peak experiences, and aspirations for the organization's future. In this phase, participants are sharing and creating newly emergent strengths and possibilities.

This chapter begins by exploring the key steps in *Discovery* data collection. Considerations for data collection are presented. Instructions are provided to create the interview protocol and guidelines for effective AI questions. Tips for conducting AI interviews are included. This chapter ends with a Case Clipping of a completed interview guide from an insurance company.

Key Steps in Data Collection

Discovery: At this point, inquiry begins. Management genius rests on the ability to craft and ask the unconditional positive question—a powerful, penetrating question that mobilizes an organization-wide inquiry and draws out the best creativity and vision from all. As already stated, by transcending problem- and deficit-based approaches to change management, AI opens a new path to affirmative growth in human systems. This path begins with a person discovering who he or she is when at his or her very best.

Collecting appropriate, useful, strength-based, and future-focused data is the key to the *Discovery* phase. Data collected at this stage serve as the basis for the next stage of creating the organizational dream and possibilities in support of that dream. Table 4.1 summarizes the key steps.

Table 4.1 Key Steps in Data Collection

1. Identify stakeholders.

2. Craft an engaging appreciative question.

3. Develop the appreciative interview guide.

4. Collect and organize the data.
   - How will the findings be used?
   - How will the findings be recorded?
   - How will the team's data be compiled?
   - How will the data be reported?
   - Who will be responsible for collecting and organizing the data?

5. Decide how and when interviews will be conducted and who will conduct them.

6. Conduct interviews.

7. Make sense of inquiry data.

Step 1. Identify Stakeholders

Successful *Discovery* data collection requires identifying key stakeholders in the organization and deciding who will interview whom and when and where to conduct interviews. Stakeholders are typically people who have a vested interest in and/or a strong impact on the organization's growth and future and who can supply valuable insights into selected topic areas. These members become the core AI team or the steering group. Chapter 2, Table 2.3, Potential Representatives for Topic Team Selection, provides a list of possible stakeholders.

Once key stakeholders have been identified, this core team (sometimes referred to as the steering committee) creates the interview guide and develops the inquiry architecture. This team can be as small as four people or as large as twenty-five. Ideally, this team involves a microcosm of the whole organization and includes a variety of voices to encourage diversity. The goal is to seek out stakeholders who offer unique viewpoints and experiences from many levels and perspectives in the organization. This is why the list of potential participants is not limited just to employees; the list also can include customers, suppliers, and community representatives.

Inclusiveness also is the reasoning behind the statement that "more is better." Larger representation allows for a stronger base of dialogue. In an AI initiative with the Girl Scouts, the organization cocreated the statement "Don't do anything about me without me!" The authors' advice is to make sure to include those members (mentioned above) who may be impacted by the change initiative.

Step 2: Craft an Engaging Appreciative Question

As stated previously, the heart and spirit of the AI process starts with the crafting of engaging questions in the *Discovery* phase. The questions asked are fateful in that they ultimately determine the change of direction for the organization. The following guidelines generally produce engaging appreciative questions:

- State questions in the affirmative.
- Begin with a leading question that builds on the affirmative topic choice.
- Give a broad definition to the topic.
- Invite participants to use storytelling and narratives.
- Phrase in rapport talk, not report talk.
- Allow ambiguity because it gives room to "swim around."
- Value "what is."
- Spark the appreciative imagination by helping the person locate experiences that are worth valuing.
- Convey unconditional positive regard.
- Evoke essential values, aspirations, and inspirations.

AI is based on the premise that the *art of inquiry moves in the direction of evoking positive images that lead to positive actions.* Therefore, every question must begin with a positive preface. This plants the seed of what is to be studied. It deliberately tells the interviewee what will be learned. Each question has a Part A and a Part B.

Part A: The question must evoke a real personal experience and narrative story that helps participants see and draw on the best learnings from the past.

Part B: This part of the question allows the interviewer to go beyond the past to envision the best possibility of the future.

This premise (positive image—positive action) explains the need for engaging appreciative questions, as shown in the following question:

U.S. Navy Illustration: Organizations Developing Bold and Enlightened Leadership: Think about the best organization you have seen, heard, read about, or directly experienced outside your own organization. We are looking for exemplary, even radical, models or places that attract great people because of the positive culture or enlightened leadership at every level. Please share what you have heard or know of this organization and its approaches to leadership or leadership development. What is its story? What characteristics do you most admire about this organization and its leaders? Why? What is it doing? How is it doing it? What are the benefits? Where can we take this model? Share what you think an organization would look like if bold and enlightened leadership was at every level. What does the organizational culture and climate look like? What is happening?

Step 3: Develop the Appreciative Interview Guide

Once the stakeholders are identified, the core team must arrange, develop, and distribute an interview guide. Creating the interview guide is an exciting task. A complete **interview guide** incorporates a formal introduction to explain the project and the purpose of the interview, the desired questions to be asked, and a summary report sheet. This process includes three types of questions:

1. Opening questions:
   - Describe a "peak experience" or "high point."
   - What are the things valued most about:
     - Yourself?
     - The nature of your work?
     - Your organization?
2. Questions centering on three to five affirmative topic choices selected by the core team.

3. Concluding questions:
   - What are core factors that "give life" to organizing?
   - Operating at its "best from it strengths," where do you envision this organization five years from now? How can you and/or your team contribute to its success?
   - What are your three wishes to heighten the vitality and health of your organization?

1. Opening Questions

The first and second opening questions capture the tone, energy, and direction that set the stage for the entire inquiry. For example:

- Let's start with something about you and your work—and a larger sense of purpose. What is it that you do now and what most attracted you to your present work that you find most meaningful, valuable, challenging, or exciting?

- One could say a key task in life is for everyone to discover and define his or her life purpose. Think back over important times in your life. Can you think of a story to share about a moment or a milestone where clarity about your life purpose emerged for you? For example, perhaps you experienced an important event or the gift of a special mentor or teacher or perhaps you were given unexpected opportunities or faced difficult challenges.

2. Topic Questions

The second set of questions relate to the affirmative topic choices. They should be in the form of questions with lead-ins that assume the subject matter in the question already exists. A helpful resource for creating these questions is the *Encyclopedia of Positive Questions* (see the Bibliography).

- We have all been part of initiatives, large and small, where we joined with others to create positive change, that is, change that brought into being ideas and dreams of a better world. As you think about the years of your work, you will likely recall ups and downs, high points and low points. For the moment, we would like you to reflect on a high-point experience, a time that is memorable and stands out, a time when you felt most engaged, alive, challenged, or effective as part of a positive change initiative.

  - Please share the story of the experience. Where was it? What happened? What were your feelings and insights about change?

- Now beyond this story, let's imagine I had a conversation with people who know you quite well. I asked them to share the three best qualities they see in you and the qualities or capabilities you bring to the leadership of change. What would they say?

- As you continuously seek to develop into the best leader you can be, would you be willing to share with me how you generate your own inspiration to lead positive change initiatives? What are the personal, spiritual, and developmental practices you have found most useful?

This second set of topic questions is the heart of the inquiry and allows the participants to collect the data that are necessary to advance the human system or the organization being studied in order to achieve the desired objectives.[1]

For example, another possible topic choice is enhanced learning:

- People learn in different ways and experience the joy of learning in a variety of settings, both in and out of the classroom.

  - Describe a learning or mentoring experience that was particularly meaningful for you. When and where did it occur? Who was involved? Why was this experience so effective and memorable?

  - In your experience, what are one or two of your organization's most effective tools or techniques for enhancing student learning and success?

  - What two or three wishes do you have to further enhance learning?

Concluding Questions

The concluding question is most effective when it incorporates and follows the third and fourth foundational questions. For example:

- It is now 2015. We are able to preserve our core strengths, and we have innovatively transformed our ways of doing business to best serve our customers. We are an organization you want to be part of and others want to join. How would you describe this division's relationships with

---

1 These questions were selected from the "Business as an Agent of World Benefit (BAWB)" Interview Guide. This is a project cosponsored by The Weatherhead School of Management at Case Western Reserve University, Spirit in Business, The Society for Organizational Learning and Appreciative Inquiry Consulting, LLC.

its business partners? How does this business work to achieve strategic business objectives? What are people doing? How are you working differently in 2015? What was the key to your success and the organization's success? How did you get there?

- What was the smallest change the division made that had the most significant impact?

The following two options for a generic concluding question have often been used to good effect:

- Looking toward the future, what are we being called to become?
- What three wishes do you have for changing the organization?

Each Case Clipping in this chapter and in each of the following chapters offers complete interview guides.

At a minimum, an interview guide should contain the purpose of the inquiry (why we are coming together to complete this and what will be done with the data gathered) and instructions for preparing, conducting, and reporting the interview. Table 4.2 provides tips for creating an AI interview guide. Many complete AI interview guides are offered throughout the Handbook.

Table 4.2 Tips for Creating AI Interview Guides

AI Interview Guides should include:

- Project background and description.
- Interview instructions.
- List of questions to ask.
- Instructions to collect and record data.
- Information summary sheet.
- Demographic summary sheet if applicable.
- Interviewee/respondent consent form.
- Description of follow-up activities.
- Thank-you to the interviewee/respondent.

Step 4: Collect and Organize the Data

Designing appreciative questions requires some thought regarding how the data will be collected, organized, and used. Careful consideration is needed because the design entails the discovery of the life-giving forces. Table 4.3, Data Collection and Organizing Considerations, highlights information that must be taken into consideration in order to discover, re-create, and understand the positive core of the organization.

Table 4.3 Data Collection and Organizing Considerations

Methods of data collection	Interviews
	Participant observations
	Focus groups
Agents of data collection	Outside party
	Core team or steering committee
	Everyone—the interview chain
Information that is meaningful to collect	Best quotes and wishes
	Best stories and practices
	Exemplars
	Illustrations of the positive core
The AI Report	Rich narratives
	Exemplary stories
	Description of the positive core
	Multi-media presentations

Finally, there are some side benefits to the process of inquiry beyond the content. A typical question is, How many interviews should we conduct? The answer: Do as many interviews as possible. Why? For one thing, it is clear that inquiry and change are a simultaneous event and the changes begin at the moment of inquiry. It makes sense to involve all relevant and affected parties in any change effort. This fact has been reinforced and documented by many years of change research. Second, the methods make it easy to engage everyone.

The cascade interview approach works well. For example, 30 or so people are trained in AI and they each interview three others in their system. After their interviews, they ask the person interviewed how the interview went and whether he or she would be willing and interested in conducting three interviews. Many people instantly say yes, and the process is off and running. The first 30 people interview an additional 90 people. Those 90 then interview 270. The whole process builds momentum quickly. At the Red Cross Values Project (presented in Chapter 3), 5,000 people shared their hopes and dreams for the future within two months.[2]

Another major benefit is observed in what happens to the interviewers. As

2 Refer to Chapter 3, "Introducing, Defining, and Planning an Appreciative Inquiry Initiative," for the American Red Cross Values Project.

they sit down with people from different departments and with different functions and meet with stakeholders at every level, they often report how their own visions of possibility expand. It is often exciting for people to experience this view, and the resulting networks become major resources. These people begin to see the organization much as any CEO would—by taking in the big picture. In the early stages of AI work, the careers of people doing the interviews are often accelerated.

To illustrate, at Touche Ross, a financial services firm in Canada, John Carter conceived the *Discovery* phase as a leadership development process. Thirty or so of the high-potential junior partners conducted the interviews, first with each other as a training exercise and then with 400 senior partners of the firm. These junior partners then analyzed the themes and stories and kicked off the partnership's strategic planning process. The junior partners played a prime-time role. They learned the industry's trends and opportunities. They developed a consciousness of the whole, and they built relationships. At the same time, "the elders" were valued. The younger people showed the deepest kind of respect: listening to the best of history and recording insights, acquiring hard-won wisdom, and helping to transmit values. The elders not only felt valued but also felt like teachers. This created a positive atmosphere of trust and regard; and, of course, many of the junior partners became senior partners in due course.

Whereas many change initiatives are a threat, this kind of AI generates positive feelings. Consider Margaret Mead's observation about the intergenerational nature of societal learning. The best learning, she argued, was always intergenerational, with the young people alongside the elders and together with the middle generation adults.[3] Bringing people together in these kinds of natural ways, across the whole system, quite simply brings out the best in human behavior.

These examples illustrate a key point: there are tremendous developmental benefits for organizations in the *Discovery* phase alone. All of this is missed if one simply thinks of the data collection in scientific "sampling" terms. Again, inquiry and change are a simultaneous event and the system can benefit as much from the process as it can from the succeeding content.

---

3 To learn more about Margaret Mead and her work on intergenerational learning, visit the Mead Centennial 2001, The Institute for Intercultural Studies, at http://www.interculturalstudies.org/Mead/2001centennial.html.

Step 5: Conduct the AI Interviews

The final section provides helpful tips for conducting the AI interviews. The following tips should be reviewed before the first interview begins.[4]

1. **Explaining Appreciative Inquiry:** Like anything new, appreciative interviewing may seem different at the beginning. It may be equally awkward for the interviewee. He or she may be caught up in looking at the organization as a problem to be solved and may not immediately understand this positive, strength-based inquiry approach. Saying something like the following may help:

   Before we start, I would like to explain a little bit about what we are going to do because it may be a little different from what you are used to. This is going to be an appreciative interview. I am going to ask you questions about times when you saw things working at their best in your workplace. Many times we try to ask questions about things that aren't working well, the problems, so we can fix them. In this case, we try to learn about things at their best, the successes, so we can find out what works and find ways to infuse more of the positive core into the organization's performances. It is much like what we do with children and athletes when we affirm their smallest successes and triumphs so they will hold a positive image of themselves and envision even greater possibility. The end result of the interview will help me understand the life-giving forces that provide vitality and distinctive competence to your organization. Do you have any questions?

2. **Respecting Anonymity:** Tell the interviewees the information will be kept anonymous. The data from this interview and others will be compiled into themes. No names will be associated with the overall summary or report. Stories and quotes from interviews will not have names associated with them.

3. **Managing The Negatives:** Sometimes people work with individuals and places they don't like. An explanation like the one above can generally get a person to identify things at their best. However, people should feel free to talk about things they believe require fixing. Depending on the interviewer's empathic understanding of the interviewee, this can be managed in several different ways:

---

4 See Johnson, P. (1992). *Organizing for global social change: Toward a global integrity ethic.* Unpublished manuscript, Case Western Reserve University, Cleveland, OH.

- *Postponing:* Tell the interviewees you would like to make note of what they have said and come back to it later. The question What would you change if you could change anything about the organization? is a place to collect this "negative" data. Make sure you come back to it at the appropriate time.

- *Listening:* If someone feels real intensity about what he or she wants to say about issues, let the person say it. If it is "up close and personal," you are not going to get any appreciative data until the person speaks his or her mind. This may mean muddling through quite a bit of organizational "manure," and the biggest threat is that you will absorb it and lose your capacity to be appreciative. You must be empathic, but remember that you cannot take on that person's pain. You cannot be a healer if you take on the patient's illness. Maintain a caring and affirmative spirit.

- *Redirecting:* If you have listened sufficiently to the seemingly negative issues, find a way to redirect the interviewee back to the task at hand. "I think I understand some of the problems . . ." and paraphrase a few you've heard. "Right now, however, I would like to focus on times when things were working at their best. Can you think of a time, even the smallest moment, when you saw innovation (for example) at its best?" If the interviewer says it never happened where he or she works, before giving up, find out whether the person ever had the experience in any organization or work context.

4. **Using Negative Data:** Everything people find wrong with an organization represents an absence of something they hold in their minds as an ideal image. What organizational processes, if present (rather than absent), might create the ideal organization, which the negatives imply? Data are data. Use the information, but use it affirmatively. One could argue that there is no such thing as negative data, for every utterance is conditioned by affirmative images.

5. **Starting With Specific Stories—The Interview Rhythm:** There is a rhythm to these interviews. When you begin to address your topic, start with specifics relevant to the person interviewed. Try to get him or her to tell a story. A useful beginning might be this: Tell me a story about a time when you experienced *cooperation* (the topic) at its best. Probe deeply and intently—not like a dentist or like a pira-

nha going after the bait, but like an interested friend hanging on to every detail. *Be genuine.* Listen and learn from this experience. Try to find out "who did what when" and "what were you thinking" and "what you did then." Be an active listener. Your goal is to learn not only what the person did (behavior) but also what the person thought or felt (values) while he or she was doing it.

6. **Generalizing About "Life-giving" Forces:** After you have thoroughly heard the interviewee's story, go for the generalizations: What is it about this organization—its structure, systems, processes, policies, staff, leaders, and strategy—that creates conditions where cooperation (for example) can flourish? If your topic (e.g., *cooperation*) was a plant, you would be trying to find out what kind of soil, water, and sunlight conditions nourish it. Sometimes people will not understand what you mean by organizational conditions, factors, or forces. Give examples: Are jobs designed a certain way, for example, to foster cooperation? How does the culture or climate of the organization foster cooperation? Try to get the person to think a bit abstractly about what is present in the organization when peak experiences have occurred relative to the topic (i.e., cooperation).

7. **Listening For Themes—"Life-giving" Factors:** To get a sense of some of these factors, listen for information about what the structure was like, as well as the systems, rewards, and so on. It may not be necessary to ask systematically about the factors; the stories may contain information about them. If the stories do not, gently probe. Listen for a theme, an idea, or a concept presented or defined in the stories being told during the interview. Present these themes in the dialogue session during the *Dream* phase to see if the group thinks these are important.

8. **Keeping Track of the Time:** An interview typically has a fixed schedule, so keep track of the time. If more time is needed, ask the person if he or she has more time. It is best to pace questions appropriately to the time scheduled.

9. **Having Fun And Being Yourself: It's A Conversation:** Try not to approach the interview as a piece of drudgery; otherwise, the interview may be lost before it has begun. Welcome each interviewee as if he or she is a special person. Take time to listen and value the

best of whom he or she is. Be humble; the interviewee is the teacher. Be yourself. Do not put on an expert role or pretend that every word in the interview protocol must be exactly right. Be a learner. Realize that everyone likes to share his or her knowledge and wisdom with people who genuinely want to listen and learn. If you have an affirmative spirit going into the interview, mistakes in wording will not impede the collection of data. Finally, have fun. This is an opportunity to get to know someone new and hear some fascinating and important stories.

Following these guidelines will help ensure that the appreciative interview has the key characteristics shown in Table 4.4, Key Characteristics of the Appreciative Interview.

Table 4.4 Key Characteristics of the Appreciative Interview

- Assumption of Health and Vitality
- Connection through Empathy
- Personal Excitement, Commitment, and Caring
- Intense Focus through "Third Ear" and "Third Eye"
- Generative Questioning, Cueing, and Guiding
- From Monologue to Dialogue

Creating the interview guide, collecting the data, and locating the themes that appear in the interview stories represent the key activities of the Discovery phase. It is where the dialogue begins in the AI process.

Step 6: Sense-Making from Inquiry Data

After the interviews are completed, it is time to make sense of the data. **Sense-making** is an umbrella term used to explain how people make sense of conversations and events based on their experiences in the world. Sense-making is making sense of the themes and patterns discovered in the interviews, lifting up meaningful metaphors and stories that give momentum to organizational success. As it relates to AI, one asks, What is the best way to capture and transform the stories from the interviews in order to be able to understand the positive core of the organization? What does one want to learn more about?

In sense-making, a diversity of approaches has been used—from formal narrative analysis to narrative forms of best stories and moral tales.[5] Data can

_____

5 See A. Coffery, A., & Atkinson, P. (1996). *Making sense of qualitative data*. Newbury Park, CA: Sage Publications.

be reduced and displayed in diagrams, charts, tables, pictures, storybooks, newsletters, and other visual aids. The search for one perfect method to make sense of data is not the point. There is no single right way to analyze the data. What is important is to find creative ways to organize, listen, and understand what is being said from multiple perspectives, both during and after the interviews. Look for common threads and anomalies in the data. Specifically, what are the best stories, practices, and wishes that came out of the interviews? The goal is to identify themes to discover how to do more of what worked well in a situation. Focus on the meaning of the data. The meaning of these data forms the foundation of dialogues that inspires the dreams based on the best stories told (continuity) and the best of what will come (novelty). The *Design* and *Destiny* phases transform (transition) the data into the desired future.

AI is a method, a type of action research, that attempts to discover "the best of what is" in any organizational/human system. In completing the interviews, the objective should be to understand *when* and *why* organizations are operating at their best and *what* are the core capabilities to allow the organization to perform well. The process seeks to identify the positive core that contributed to such operation (continuity) and that can transform itself to the new vision (novelty).

In managing the information and structuring it in a meaningful analysis, the data collection step outlined earlier coincides with data interpretation and narrative reporting and writing. Code the data under key themes. It also may require recoding under new, emerging themes based on the conversations around the original themes.

A primary goal is to reduce and interpret the meanings and, through dialogue, confirm that these are the interviewees' meanings. That is why Interview Summary Sheets are helpful. An example of a generic AI Interview Summary Sheet is shown here.

Interview Summary Sheet

Please use whatever space you need to answer each question.

1. What was the most appreciative quotable quote that came out of this interview?

2. What was the most compelling story that came out of this interview? What details and examples did the interviewee share? How were the interviewee and/or others changed by the story?

3. What was the most life-giving moment of the interview for you as a listener?

4. Did a particularly intriguing "golden innovation" emerge during the interview? If so, describe what you learned about it, including who is doing it and where.

5. What three themes stood out most for you during the interview?

6. What small steps toward positive change emerged as being possible?

7. What broader steps of positive change emerged?

The *Discovery* phase is both exploratory and descriptive. It allows for an open-ended discovery of an organizational system at its best. The objective is to generate themes, descriptors, a dream, the vision, and key ingredients for dialogue and design of possibility propositions. The topics of dreaming and design will be covered in more detail in Chapter 5 and Chapter 6.

Case Clippings: Texas Insurance

The Texas Insurance Company employed an AI approach to facilitate the transformation of its information technology (IT) organization, approximately 2,000 employees, from a traditional internal IT function to a business/client-facing operating model. The goal of the transformation was threefold: (1) to create a culture of service, (2) to demonstrate the strategic value of IT, and (3) to ensure high levels of productivity and effectiveness during the transformation to the new operating model. Central to this transformation was the strategic inquiry (Discovery) into the life-giving factors of the organization and three positive transformation themes. Of primary importance were the affirmative topic choices to guide the successful design of the new operating model: Revolutionary Partnerships, Continuous Transformation, and Innovative and Adaptive Environment.

The following interview packet illustrates affirmative topic choices and meets the criteria for an engaging AI question. It includes the following:

- *Purpose of the interviews*
- *Overview of the interview process*
- *Tips for conducting interviews*
- *Interview guide*
- *Interview summary sheet*

The Discovery phase was carried out over a three-week period and included approximately 130 interviews across a broad cross section of the IT organization and key clients. The Discovery outputs were used extensively as input into the design of the three-day Dream and Design Summit that followed. In alignment with the intent of the Discovery process, the goal of the interview guide was to obtain information on the three factors that give life to organizations—continuity, novelty, and transition. (Refer to Mini-lecture VIII in Chapter 1.) The following outcomes resulted from the Discovery phase:

- *Quotable Quotes wall*
- *Texas Insurance's Positive Core (continuity)*
- *Individual visions of a best-performing IT organization (novelty)*
- *Positive Deviant Profile (novelty/transition)*
- *Positive Transformation Themes (transition)*

Purpose of the Interviews

Thank you very much for participating in this information-gathering process. The Application Services group is actively involved in a business transformation that will focus on the design and development of a business/client-facing operating model that will accelerate time and results. In this way, Application Services will better serve our internal business partners and strengthen Texas Insurance's overall competitive position. To this end, we will be gathering specialized input from colleagues across the organization. These interviews are part of an intense effort to discover our internal best practices and high points, to use this rich experience as leverage for the Application Services Transformation, and to apply this learning to the development and implementation of our future-state operating model. In addition, the results of the individual and group IT fact-finding discussions, along with information and research on external best practices, will be integrated into our design process.

As part of this process, we will look at:
- What core factors enable success in our organization.
- What we can learn from our experiences, especially when we closely examine those moments when we have been at our best.
- What our most effective practices, strengths, and best qualities are—what we need to preserve as we transform.
- What important lessons we can draw from our experiences.
- What kind of organization we want to create in the future—the organization that we and others want to be part of.
- How our positive past, the best of our experiences, can help us become more daring and innovative as we think about our true potential as an organization.
- In the context of Texas Insurance, what our specific hopes and images are for the future of Applications Services.

Application of Interview Feedback
- All interviews will be reviewed and summarized for thematic content.
- Themes will be shared and discussed based on relevance to the Application Services Transformation.
- At a three-day off-site design session, Accelerated Solutions Environment (Design Shop), in August, which multiple Texas Insurance participants will attend, these themes will be used as key input in designing the Application Services future-state operating model.

- An additional output from the Design Shop is an implementation road map, which will outline key activities and workstreams to support our new operating model. Interview themes will be applied directly to some of the resulting workstreams and indirectly to many of the other workstreams.
- All comments from the interviews will be anonymous. Names will not be attached to any of the stories, suggestions, or examples.

Overview of the Interview Process

Part I—Completing Four to Six Interviews
- You will be provided a list of the names of four to six colleagues to interview. You typically will be assigned individuals with whom you may not interact on a regular basis. This is a good opportunity to get a fresh perspective.
- The Transition Team will notify your interviewees that they have been selected as participants. Contact your interviewee to schedule the interview. Explain that each interview will take approximately one hour to complete.
- Complete your interviews and post your summary forms to the Phase I-Interviews folder in the Transition Team Folder as soon as they're completed, but no later than July 18.
- Assure your interviewees that all comments are anonymous but not confidential. In other words, stories and quotes will be shared but no names will be attached to them.
- If you're having difficulty scheduling an interview, call so we can help you by supporting scheduling of the interview or by providing an alternative interview participant.

Part II—Returning the Interview Summaries
- Please use the space after each question for taking notes during the interviews. (Note taking is usually very individualized, but we want you to be able to recall your interview to best assure your summarization.)
- It is recommended that you summarize the interview immediately after the interview session. Use the attached two-page summary template at the end of this guidebook.
- Remember to note your name, the date of the interview, and the interviewee's organizational group and service date on the summary page.

- Post the electronic summary forms to the Phase I-Interviews folder in the Transition Team Folder no later than July 18.

Try not to wait until July 18 to send all of the interview summary forms. Please post them as you complete them.

Part III—Leveraging the Interviewing Feedback: Next Steps
- All interview summaries will be reviewed and integrated. In this way, we will document major themes to better understand our internal best practices, high-point moments, and images of the future.
- These internal best practices and positive transformation themes will be shared and leveraged during the August off-site Design Shop to support the development and implementation of our Application Services operating model. In addition, the results of the individual and group IT fact-finding discussions, along with information and research on external best practices, will be integrated into our design process.
- Following the Design Shop, the new operating model, the benefits of the new model, the positive transformation themes, and the general timeline for implementation will be shared.
- We will make a special effort to share positive transformation themes with all interview participants in late July.

Tips for Conducting Interviews

Use the interview question section for script guidelines and note taking.
- Use these questions to probe further:
  - Can you tell me more?
  - Why was that important to you?
  - How did that affect you?
  - What was your contribution?
  - How did the organization/business area/team support you? (e.g., information systems, leadership, resources, and structures)
  - How has it changed you?
- Let the interviewee tell his or her story.
- Take notes and listen for great quotes and stories.
- Be genuinely curious about their experiences, thoughts, and feelings.
- Some people will take longer to think about their answers. Allow time for silence.
- If somebody doesn't want to or can't answer any of the interview questions, that's okay. Let it go.

- Use the questions as guidelines. You may choose not to use of all the questions or to adapt the questions to what works best for your interviews.
- Allow the interviewee to interpret whether the questions apply to work or to personal situations.

Interview Guide

Suggested Opening

I'm (name). Thank you for meeting with me and participating in this process of gathering information from colleagues across the organization. These interviews are part of an intense effort to discover our internal best practices in key strategic business areas. These best practices will be leveraged by our Application Services Transformation project to develop our future-state operating model. In addition to these interview findings, we will be leveraging information related to external best practices and the individual and group IT fact-finding discussions.

This interview is divided into three sections:
- Celebrating Texas Insurance's Rich Heritage and Past Successes
- Carrying Forward What We Value Most
- Wake Up. It's 2010: Your Vision of a Best-Performing Application Services

Before we start, I would like to explain what we are going to do because it may be a little different from what you are used to. I am going to ask questions about times when you were at your best in your work. You may be more familiar with interviews that ask questions about things that aren't working well—the problems—so we can fix them. In this case, we are going to find out about your work and the organization at its best—the successes—so we can find out what works and find ways to integrate what we learn into the Application Services Transformation moving forward. This positive-change approach has been widely researched and proven effective in a variety of situations; for example, transformation efforts, education, building learning organizations, parenting, athletics, increasing team and organizational effectiveness, and healthcare. The end result of the interview will help us understand those positive factors that will increase our vitality, effectiveness, and success going into the future together. Specifically, we are gathering information on what we are calling Positive Transformation Themes. To surface these themes, the interview questions focus on areas that we believe are critically important to the successful design of our new Application Services operating model:

- Continuous Transformation
- Revolutionary Partnerships
- Innovative and Adaptive Environment

What questions do you have?

OK. Let's begin.

I. **Celebrating Texas Insurance's Rich Heritage and Past Successes**
    To start, I'd like to learn about your beginnings at Texas Insurance. When did you come to the organization, and what attracted you to Texas Insurance? What keeps you at Texas Insurance? What sets us apart and makes the difference for you?

    In your work at Texas Insurance, you have probably experienced ups and downs, twists and turns. For a moment, I would like you to think of a time that stands out to you as a high point at Texas Insurance—a time when you felt energized, passionate about your work, and most effective and a time when you were able to accomplish more than you imagined.

    Please describe in detail the situation and the people involved and what made it a high-point experience for you. What actions did you and others take? How did those actions translate into business results?

    Let's talk about some things you value most—specifically, about yourself and Texas Insurance as an organization.
    - Without being humble, what do you value most about yourself as a human being? What are the most important qualities or strengths you bring to Texas Insurance?
    - What is it about the nature of the work that you do here that you value most? What is most interesting or meaningful?

    Continuous Transformation:
    Organizations today must continually change and evolve to remain ahead of the competition and to thrive in this rapidly changing

economy and business environment. Organizations that have passion and energy for continual transformation display business excellence and are distinguished from their peers—leading the way and creating their future instead of reacting to it.

Tell me about a time when you were involved with a significant transformation or change effort, a time when you positively influenced the results. What was exciting about the transformation? What did you and others do to make it effective?

Revolutionary Partnerships:

The mark of a revolutionary partnership is doing things together radically different—not only different, but quicker, with a common focus, leveraging each other's diverse strengths. It is also establishing new ways of doing business that are based on trust, mutual respect, and a shared vision.

Think of a time when you were part of a revolutionary partnership, a time in your life (at work or in your personal or community life) when you not only met another person or other people halfway but also met and exceeded needs on both sides. Describe the situation in detail. What made it feel radically different? Who was involved? How did you interact differently? What were the outcomes and benefits you experienced?

Innovative and Adaptive Environment:

"Nature has been learning to adapt for four billion years; maybe we need to pay attention." – Stuart Kauffman, molecular biologist

As this is true in nature, it is also true in the business world. An effective environment enables risk taking, empowers leadership throughout the organization, is agile, and thrives on change. These powerful environments can balance speed and discipline, are liberating yet standards-based, and support growth and innovation.

Think of a time when you were in an innovative and adaptive environment. Describe how the environment supported your success—that is, leadership, creativity, tools, recognition, and/or resources. How did it feel? What were the keys to success? What were some of the significant breakthroughs you achieved? Again, this could be personal, community-oriented, or work life-based.

II. **Carrying Forward What We Value Most**

Good organizations know how to "preserve the core" of what they do best and are able to let go of things that are no longer needed. In transforming Application Services, what are three things—core strengths, values, qualities, ways of working—you want to see preserved and leveraged moving into the future?

III. **Wake Up. It's 2010: Your Vision of a Best-Performing Application Services**

Fast-forward. It is now 2010, and we were able to preserve our core strengths and transform Application Services. Revolutionary partnerships, continual transformation, innovation, and adaptability are how we do business. It is an organization you want to be part of and others want to join.

- How would you describe Application Services' relationships with business customers? How do they work together differently in 2010 to achieve Texas Insurance's business objectives?

- What are people doing? How are you working together differently in 2010? What was the key to your success and the organization's success? How did you get there?

- What was the smallest change Applications Services made that had the most significant impact?

This is the end of the interview. Thank you very much for your time. Your input will be summarized and used to design the Application Services Operating Model.

Interview Summary Sheet

Complete and post by Wednesday, July 18, to the Application Services Transition Team shared drive in the Phase I-Interviews folder. Save the document using the filename Interviewerlastname-interview#.doc (e.g., Smith-interview3.doc).

Name of Interviewer (your name): _____

Date of Interview: _____

Interviewee's Organizational Division: _____

Interviewee's Service Date (year is optional):_____

What was the most quotable quote that came out of this interview?

What was the most compelling story that came out of this interview? (Use as much space as you need.)

Overall, what was your sense of what was most important to this individual?

What three positive themes related to each of the following stood out most to you during the interview?

Revolutionary Partnerships	Continuous Transformation	Innovative and Adaptive Environment
1. _____	1. _____	1. _____
2. _____	2. _____	2. _____
3. _____	3. _____	3. _____

Carrying Forward What We Value Most

- _____

- _____

- _____

Vision of the Future

1. _____

2. _____

3. _____

5

Dream:
What Might Be?

"One of the basic theorems of the theory of image is that it is the image which in fact determines what might be called the current behavior of any organization. The image acts as a field. The behavior consists of gravitating toward the most highly valued part of the field."

—Kenneth Boulding

Once an organization discovers its positive core, the next step is to imagine and envision its future. The *Dream* phase of the AI 4-D Cycle accomplishes this step.

The *Dream* phase is an invitation for an organization to amplify its positive core by imagining the possibilities for the future that have been generated through the Discovery phase. During the *Dream* phase, the participants are encouraged to talk about (and dream about) not what is, but what might be a better organization and a better world. The *Dream* phase is practical in that it is grounded in the organization's history and generative in that it seeks to expand the organization's true potential. It is the time to challenge the status quo of the organization. It is intended to create synergy and excitement. Once the group gets into the spirit and acknowledges the possibility of greatness, the positive core can be channeled, focused, and used to design how it will be and create the destiny of the envisioned dream.

The primary goal of the *Dream* phase is twofold. First, it is to facilitate a dialogue among stakeholders in which they begin to share positive stories in a way that creates energy and enthusiasm. This is accomplished by asking those who participated in the Discovery phase to share their stories with the entire group. These stories are the vehicles for bringing out the positive core of the organization. Therefore, those who are telling the stories must be encouraged to share the essence of the stories, not a bullet point description of events. Giving the storyteller the latitude to share the story in full and rich detail generates more data for theme building. Therefore, the job of the facilitator is to gently probe for details in order to continue identifying themes. One tool used to encourage these conversations is dream dialogues. The dream dialogue is often integrated into appreciative interviews with questions about wishes, hopes, and dreams for a better organization and world. Some interview guides probe for best practices and peak experiences from outside the organization in question. Thus, interviewers might learn through discovery of positive possibilities that have existed elsewhere and that might be transported into their system.

The second goal of the *Dream* phase is to allow participants to begin to see common themes. At this point, it is important to encourage the group to observe and value the stories rather than critique, judge, or analyze them. Unlike other organizational change methodologies, AI does not focus on solving a problem. Dreaming is a journey of mutual discovery, not an analytical journey. Therefore, dreaming does not emphasize identifying one best idea. Instead, participants look for broad themes or **life-giving forces** that contribute to the organization's success. Those positive themes are the building blocks for the rest of the AI process. They are the short answers to the question What do people describe in the interviews as the "life-giving" forces of this organization?[1]

---

[1] See Watkins, J., & Mohr, B. (2001). *Appreciative inquiry: Change at the speed of imagination.* San Francisco: Jossey-Bass/Pfeiffer.

Accomplishing those two goals helps participants imagine the organization as they would like it to be. By building energy, excitement, and synergy and by extracting the common themes or life-giving forces, participants can begin to envision an organization of the future; an organization that embodies the images, hopes, dreams, and visions of its people.

The remainder of this chapter deals with creating the *Dream* activity, introduces the concept of dialogue that creates vision consensus, and provides an example of the Roadway Express AI Summit. A complete project plan for the Roadway Express AI Application is available at the end of this chapter.

Creating the Dream Activity

Organizations tend to move in the direction of what they study. The crafting and asking of questions and activities during the *Discovery* and *Dream* phases possesses strategic significance to eliciting the information needed to identify the themes that will become the starting point for the next phase of the 4-D Cycle.

Many of the best Dream activities share common components:[2]

- They take place on the heels of some sort of brief Discovery process, one that brings the spirit of the original inquiry into the room in personal and creative ways.

- They often involve large groups of people—anywhere from a couple dozen to hundreds at a time.

- They begin with some kind of energizing activity (e.g., guided visualization, a walk, a high-energy activity, or yoga).

- They use a focal question that "primes the pump" for rich, creative dream dialogues. (Facilitators select the question, along with an appropriate time frame for individual and group discussions.)

- As participants complete their individual dreaming reflections, they move into groups (ideally, no more than 12 people per group) to talk about what they've seen, heard, and experienced in this world of the future during the Discovery interviews. This dream dialogue takes up to an hour. The dialogue is finished when people have had a chance to

2 See Whitney, D., & Trosten-Bloom, A. (2003). *The power of appreciative inquiry: A practical guide to positive change.* San Francisco: Berrett-Koehler.

share fully what they have seen and imagined and to create a collective verbal picture of the desired future.

- The group creatively depicts what they have seen. The more playful the depictions, the better. The facilitator (whose role was introduced in the organizational overview) can offer a variety of ways in which to depict the dream. Some examples include a picture, a story, a skit, a commercial, a newspaper, a song, or a poem. The facilitator should be ready with a variety of supplies and props to aid in this creative process.

- Each dream team prepares a brief Appreciative Report from its dream session (often less than five minutes each). Although each team has a spokesperson, everyone on the team is included in the presentation. All presentations are made to the entire group.

- Small-group discussions of common themes and common threads often follow these presentations.

The *Dream* phase is the time to push the creative edges of positive possibilities and to **wonder** about the organization's greatest potential. To illustrate, an AI initiative was launched with Roadway Express at the Akron, Ohio, terminal. Roadway is one of the largest trucking companies in America, with about 30,000 employees. The company is unionized, and the relationship between Roadway and the Teamsters is strong. Roadway's goal is to create an organization with leaders developing leaders at every level, a "high-engagement organization." The inquiry started with this opening question:

When did you feel most alive, most engaged, in your job at Roadway?

The *Dream* phase began on Day 2 when participants were divided into small groups (teams) to envision the organization's potential for positive impact. The next foundational question was asked:

Imagine you've awakened after being asleep for five years. What does Roadway look like? What will be happening in the world outside? What is the best outcome you can imagine?

The *Discovery* was about the positive core and valuing the best in Roadway's history. The *Dream* phase, about the future and the possibilities, includes two activities. The first activity is a collective conversation on "images of the future." The second activity is the creation of possibilities. Roadway did this in the form of an "opportunity map." In moving from *Discovery* to *Dream*, employees at the Akron terminal focused on the following purpose:

"To begin to build a future you want, an Akron Roadway team that is truly dedicated to "maximizing throughput with unsurpassed speed, driven by employee pride and involvement."

Roadway's dream dialogue focused on the following three statements:

- Share your wishes and dreams from the interviews you did yesterday morning (Question 3). Add any ideas or thoughts about changes or improvements you think will have a major impact on improving our throughput.

- Brainstorm a list of opportunities to improve throughput at the Akron complex.

- As a group, choose the three to five opportunities your team believes will have the greatest impact on throughput.

From this opportunity map, each team created aspirations and visions of the future. For example:

Roadway Aspiration Statement
Measurement, Technology, Procedures, and Equipment Team

"Roadway is #1 because employees take pride and are engaged in ensuring that customers are receiving unsurpassed service and error-free delivery that is unequaled by any other carrier.

Employees know and understand cost impacts of all decisions and information is shared through technology so all employees are empowered to make customer-focused and profitable decisions."

The *Dream* activity gave team members the opportunity to summarize key success factors collectively and preserve the past. Together they mapped the highest impact opportunities. More details on the *Dream* activity are available at the end of this chapter.

Dreaming is a strategically significant activity that leads to higher levels of creativity, commitment, and enthusiasm for the organization and its future. It is this new level of enthusiasm and images embedded in the dreams that facilitate the creation of specific actions and propositions for the future (*Design* phase).

Evolution of Dialogue to Create Vision Consensus

A vision is a direction for an organization. It is what the organization wants to be. It expresses a desire by the organization to be more than what it is. It is strategic in providing a focal point for direction and movement. It is fateful in defining what an organization holds dear and creating excitement for ways to move forward and achieve it.

Sometimes a vision is a statement created by senior management that is passed down to employees. If so, it is at best a sneak preview of what the leaders of the company believe is important, providing some indication as to why decisions are made. At its worst, it is ink on paper without significance or meaning for or without connection to stakeholders. The power of AI lies in its ability to collectively breathe life into a vision; to make it speak to all stakeholders; and to provide some value, consequence, and direction in stakeholders' daily lives.

Through the *Discovery* and *Dream* phases, participants have been asked to share times and events during which they operated at their peak, felt most alive, and were inspired to push beyond the mundane. Now, while riding on the enthusiasm and energy created by sharing these high points, the group should be asked to imagine an organization in which these sporadic glimpses at brilliance are the norm. What would this organization look like?

Once the group begins to create a shared vision of the new and improved organization, the power of AI becomes apparent. Unlike other visioning exercises, AI creates a shared vision for the future that is grounded in examples from the organization's past. It is the greatness demonstrated in the past that allows stakeholders to achieve their vision for the future. In short, there is no question as to whether the new vision is achievable; the participants have already demonstrated their desire, willingness, and ability to make it possible. This most preferred future, along with the accompanying energy and synergy, is what will carry the group to the *Design* phase. The *Design* phase is where the key stakeholders regroup and work to transfer the dreams into a concrete plan of action.

Sample Dream Questions

The following Dream questions may prove helpful in shaping the dialogue to achieve the vision for the future of the organization.

- It is the year 2015, and you have just awakened from a long sleep. As you look around, you see the world just as you always wished and dreamed it would be.

- What is happening? How is the world different? How is your organization contributing to this new world? What are you doing that makes a difference?

- As you reflect on the industry and business environment in which your organization works, what do you see as the two or three most significant macro trends emerging? How might they change the way your industry and business operate? In your opinion, what are the most exciting strategic opportunities on the horizon for your organization?

- Imagine that it is 2015 and your organization has just won an award as the outstanding socially responsible business of the year. What is said about your organization as the award is dedicated? What are customers saying? What are employees saying? What did it take to win the award?

AI Summit: Using Large Groups to Mobilize Positive Change

The **AI Summit** is a large-scale meeting process that focuses on discovering and developing the organization's positive change core and designing it into the organization's strategic business processes, systems, and culture.[3]

Participation is diverse by design and includes all of the organization's stakeholders. The duration is generally three to four days and involves 50 to 2,000 participants or more. AI serves as the framework for an AI Summit. The AI Summit can be used to conduct the *Dream* and *Design* phase if data are available from the *Discovery* phase. Many variations are possible; therefore, planning, creativity, and flexibility are required.[4]

---

3 We want to acknowledge the important role Marvin Weisbord and Sandra Janoff played. Their pioneering work with Future Search impressed us most with the principle of the whole system in the room as well as the clarity of worksheets and some of the exercises in a typical Future Search. For more on Future Search, refer to *Future Search: An Action Guide to Finding Common Ground in Organizations and Communities*, 2d ed. (San Francisco: Berrett-Koehler, 2000).

4 Material contributed and adapted from *The Appreciative Inquiry Summit: A Practitioner's Guide for Leading Positive Large-Group Change*. The book details the strategies for whole system participation and activities before, during, and after an effective summit. (Available from Berrett-Koehler, Spring 2003, by Ludema, Mohr, Whitney, and Griffin.)

The AI Summit is designed to flow through the AI 4-D Cycle of Discovery, Dream, Design, and Destiny in real time. Figure 5.1 illustrates the Akron Roadway Summit AI 4-D Cycle.

Figure 5.1 Akron Roadway Summit's 4-D Cycle

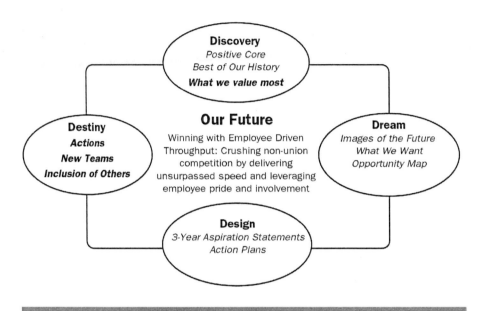

Day 1—*Discovery*: Participants discuss the organization's positive core, which was discovered in earlier interviews. Participants look at characteristics of which they are most proud and discuss those characteristics that create success and build a competitive future for Roadway. They are asked the questions Who are we? Whom do we represent? As a group, they dialogue about why they are here and what they hope for.

Key activities include defining the context and purpose of the summit, conducting more AI interviews, highlighting stories from prior AI interviews, mapping out the positive core, and launching a continuity search. A **continuity search** is seeking out and preserving what the organization does best. For example, Roadway wanted to build optimal margins; therefore, it first wanted to learn what things Roadway did best organizationally.

Day 2—*Dream*: This phase builds on the outcomes of the *Discovery* phase. Participants break into small groups and envision their organization's potential for positive influence and impact. The discussion is centered around developing ideas of what the future can be. What will the company look like in 2015? What is happening? What is better? What positive things are the stakeholders saying? After the small breakout discussions, the groups report back to the entire summit to share their stories.

Key activities include sharing of dreams; enlivening the dreams; and enacting, imaging, and defining the dreams.

Day 3—*Design*: Participants focus on cocreating an organization (that includes the positive core and dreams in every element possible). The design results for Roadway were called "Aspiration Statements," describing the organization participants hoped Roadway would become, and "Action Plans," describing how the organization would function.

Key activities include creating the organization's architecture, selecting high-impact organization design elements, and crafting possibility propositions (possibility or aspiration statements without conditions).

Day 4—*Destiny*: This is where the energy is channeled into action planning to understand what needs to happen to deliver on the possibility statements defined in the Design phase. Participants craft the newly created organizational design into a list of inspired action-oriented tasks. Task groups emerge around each Aspiration Statement. Then each group establishes principles for working together after the AI Summit and agrees on immediate steps they will take next.

Key activities include generating possible action steps, selecting possible action tasks, forming task teams, and closing the large-group summit.

Little, if any, AI training occurs during a summit; the summit is about enacting AI. After a summit, organizations may decide to develop their capacity in AI by conducting a training program for key employees in leading organizational change. In this situation, AI is taught as a process for management, leadership, and organizational development and change. The result is sustainability of AI beyond the initial initiative into the everyday actions of members.

From start to finish, the AI Summit process invites the whole organization to participate. A successful summit takes time, careful planning, and attention. The task must be clear. The summit is usually a three- or four-day event that can include from 50 to 2,000 participants, as stated. The typical results from a summit are:

- More informed and ultimately more effective change efforts.
- A critical mass of people making changes in which they all believe.
- A total organization mind-set.
- Simultaneous change.
- A perception of change as "real work."
- A fast-change organizational network.

The following example from Roadway illustrates an AI Summit, the results, and an update on how AI has been sustained in Roadway's culture.

Case Clippings: Roadway Express[5]

The work at Roadway has been very powerful. Again, Roadway's goal was to create an organization with leaders developing leaders at every level, a high-engagement organization. An important part of this goal was building a strong financial literacy at every level, where everyone was thinking and acting as owners of a business. As a result, the main topic in one of the early AI statements at Roadway had to do with "optimizing margins." While topics on AI interventions can concern human, technical, environmental, or financial issues, nonetheless, the same principle still holds true: human systems move in the direction of what they most persistently, actively, and deeply ask questions about. When reviewing the questions below on optimizing margins, think about potential changes that might take place in the future.

In this case, something remarkable did happen at the Akron terminal of Roadway. In 2002, a few years after the start of the AI work at Roadway, one of the AI teams came up with a $10 million-per-year-cost savings idea. When this happened, the excitement was understandably quite high. This illustrates the principle that the seeds of change are implicit in the first questions asked. Keep that in mind while reading the interview questions that follow.

The Case Clipping includes the following:

- *Interview Guide*
- *Summit Preworksheets*
- *Summit Working Agenda*
- *Summit Agenda Overview*
- *AI Organizational Summit*
- *Discovery Worksheet #1*
- *Discovery Worksheet #2*
- *Discovery Worksheet #3*
- *Dream Worksheet #1*
- *Dream Worksheet #2*
- *Dream Worksheet #3*
- *Design Worksheet*

---

5 http://appreciativeinquiry.case.edu/practice/toolsFilmDetail.cfm?coid=585

The following resulted from the Dream phase:
- *An Opportunity Map of needs and priorities*
- *Identification of which needs and priorities were most pressing*
- *Action teams formed to address organizational trust, drivers as strategic sales representatives, employee communications, performance measurements, and monitoring and education.*

The most surprising learning was that it did not matter what your job was; everyone wanted the same thing—to win.[6] Shared goals included sustained growth, happy customers, and job security. Within two years, stock rose from $14 to more than $40 per share, resulting in a sale to an even larger firm, Yellow Trucking. Other measures have steadily improved: operating ratios, throughput, overtime changes, increased morale and levels of trust, clarity in mission and vision, and job functions.

Sustainability

Over time, Roadway has conducted more than 60 AI Interventions with more than 10,000 employees. During this time period, Roadway has improved its performance and union-management relationships. Measurable results: improvement in throughput increased 47% to 64%, average transit speed was reduced from 2.3 days to 2.1 days, average production efficiency increased 59% to 64%, and more.[7]

Today Roadway is one of the largest carriers in the nation and is one of the most stable LTL employers, one that offers seamless service in 50 states. It merged with Yellow to form Yellow Roadway Corporation. As a testimony to the perceived value of the AI change process, the AI Summit was selected as the approach to bring the two organizations together. The synergistic savings from this merger are estimated at $300 million.[8]

---

6 For more information on this story, see Hammond, K. (July 2001). Leaders for the long haul. *Fast Company*, 56–58.

7 For more detailed information on how Roadway applied the 4-D Cycle and results, see Barrett, F., & Fry, R. (2005). *Appreciative inquiry: A positive approach to building cooperative capacity.* Chagrin Falls, OH: Taos Institute Publishing.

8 For more information on this continued success of Roadway, see Cooperrider, D., & Whitney, D. (2005). *Appreciative inquiry: A positive revolution in change.* San Francisco: Berrett-Koehler.

Interview Guide

A Roadway Inquiry into Optimal Margin
Opening Dialogue

(In diverse pairs complete an interview. [across functions and levels])

- **Results you want:** With revenues, tonnage, and sales at record levels, one of the most important opportunities we face is to engage everyone in increasing positive margins now. To do so will call on discovery of new strengths, build on old strengths, and carry us to higher levels financially.

  A. As you look at Roadway from the perspective of our capabilities and as you think about the business context and opportunities, how do you define "optimal margin" for us? What is the positive margin you want and believe we have the capability to create right now? What is a moderate time frame looking at the long term?

  B. What results do you want from this meeting? What would make this day a good one for you?

- **Insights from your work:** We all pride ourselves on the things we do that add the most value in terms of creating margin. Some of our work activities add a great deal of value, while others do not. Likewise, some things we do as leaders—our style, our approaches to managing people—engage everyone else in increasing margins. Let's reflect using the essential things you do that you believe add the most value.

  A. When you think of your precious time and how you spend it, what are the things you do that, in your view, add the most value in terms of creating margin? Any examples?

  B. In the ideal, if you were able to recraft what you do, what parts of your work (from the perspective of creating margin) would you want to keep doing, let go of, or do new and differently?
     - Keep doing?
     - Let go of (things that are not really needed)?
     - Do new or differently?

C. As you reflect on your leadership role here at Roadway—times when you have mobilized or helped develop others—there have been high points and low points and successes and failures. Please describe one situation or change initiative you are proud of, an achievement in which you believe you had an impact in realizing better margins. What happened? What were the challenges? What was it about you or your leadership style? What lessons were learned?

D. Let's think about other leaders or successful stories of change—situations you have heard about or seen here at Roadway as they relate to engaging people to achieve good margins. Is there a story or an example that stands out for you—something that exemplifies the kind of leadership approaches we should aim for more often? Can you describe the leadership and insights?

- **Continuity search:** Good organizations know how to preserve the core of what they do best and are able work out or let go of things that have built up or are no longer needed. Preserving the right things is key. Letting go of other things is the next step.

    A. In relationship to building optimal margins, what are the things we do best organizationally—for example, measurement systems, leadership systems, ways of developing others, accountability systems, ways of delegating and building trust, and technologies—things that should be preserved even as we change in the future?

    B. Assuming that things do build up, there is a need to "work out" and streamline. There is a need to let go of things that, given precious time constraints, are not needed. Assuming that very few things are sacred, what things (small or large) do you think we should consider letting go of?

- **Novelty:** Novelty is imagining new possibilities for optimal margins. If anything imaginable were possible, if there were no constraints whatsoever, what would the ideal Roadway organization look like if we were delivering optimal margins? Imagine that you had a magic wand to use. Describe what we would be doing new, better, or different? Envision it happening. What do you see happening that is new, different, or better?

- **Transition:** Transition is moving from A to B, asking how we get from here to there.
  A. What is the smallest step (an action, a decision, an initiative) we could take that would have the largest impact?
  B. What is one thing we have not even thought of yet—something that could have a payoff?

Summit Preworksheets

During the summit meeting, we will be creating a shared history of Roadway's strengths and best past experiences to help in deciding the future we all want to be part of. It is important that all of the different participants are heard and appreciated so we truly work from a shared sense of what we already do well and why.

Please take 5–10 minutes to fill out the two attached sheets. Bring them with you to the summit. We will use them on the first day.

Preworksheet #1

> *How Are Our Industry and Company Changing?*
> *What is Our Story? Our Competitive Strengths?*
> *Key Moments In Our History?*

Purpose: To develop a collective picture of our changing world, the industry, and the core of our history (strengths, achievements, challenges, changes, and so on).

- Make notes below about memorable industry events and changes in society that have had an impact on Roadway—things you believe are notable milestones, trends, and/or turning points. (At the summit meeting, you will use a magic marker to add your notes or pictures to timelines on the wall.)

INDUSTRY/SOCIETAL Events, Changes, and Trends
What happened in the trucking and transportation business? (Why was it important?)

1930s–1950s _____

1960s _____

1970s _____

1980s _____

1990s _____

2000– _____

The future you think is coming:

Preworksheet #2

How Are Our Industry and Company Changing?
What is Our Story? Our Competitive Strengths?
Key Moments In Our History?

- Make notes below on notable achievements, changes, events, trends, or turning points here at the Akron complex. (At the summit meeting, you will use a magic marker to add your notes or pictures to timelines on the wall.)

COMPANY Changes, Events, Trends, and Accomplishments
What happened at Akron Roadway?

1930s–1950s _____

1960s _____

1970s _____

1980s _____

1990s _____

2000_ _____

Where is our company going (the future changes you see coming)?

Summit Working Agenda

Day 1	DISCOVERY	PRESENTERS
8:00–8:15	Welcomes and comments on topic	Mark O. & Jim B.
8:15–8:45	Why doing this/using AI	Terry G.
8:45–9:00	Intro facilitators and topic more	Pete & Ed
9:00–9:20	Community-building activity	Ed
9:20–10:00	AI Introduction (Time to rethink. What is a summit? Prep for 1:1 interviews)	Dave & Ron
10:00–11:00	AI interviews (including break)	
11:00–11:45	Max-mix subgroups: Themes and Expectations	Pete
11:45–12:30	Group reports (only some tables)	Pete
12:30–1:30	Lunch (customer panel)	
1:30–2:00	Map timelines on walls and convene in stakeholder groups	Cindy & Ed
2:00–2:45	Stakeholders: Proudest Moments and Key Success Factors	Cindy & Ed
2:45–3:00	Break	
3:00–3:45	Group reports: Story and Factors to Keep	Cindy & Ed
3:45–4:45	Positive Image $\rightarrow$ Positive Action	Dave & Ron
4:45–5:00	Summary of day and close	Dave & Ron

Summit Working Agenda

Day 2	DREAM	PRESENTERS
8:00–8:30	Community activity: Labeling Positive Core Freight to be shipped to the future….(stakeholder groups)	Pete
8:30–9:30	Mix/max groups: Generating Opportunities for Improving Throughput	Dave
9:30–10:15	Opportunity mapping (and dot voting)	Ed & Pete
10:15–10:30	Break (facilitators cluster and label action groups)	
10:30–10:45	Self selection into opportunity groups	Ron
10:45–12:00	Dream: 3-year aspiration draft and skits	Ed
12:00–12:45	Working lunch	
12:45–2:15	Presentations of aspirations and visions	Ed
2:15–2:30	Gallery Aspiration Statements for feedback	Ed
2:30–2:45	Break	
2:45–3:00	Task for new groups: 3-year and 1-year statements	Pete
3:00–4:30	Group work: new opportunity groups	Pete
4:30–5:00	Community: Loading our aspirations for shipping	Pete

Summit Working Agenda

Day 3	DESIGN AND DESTINY	PRESENTERS
8:00–8:30	Community: Naming the Destination for our Positive Core and Aspirations	Pete
8:30–10:30	Design and action planning (ready for reports)	Pete
10:30–10:45	Break	
10:45–12:00	Presentations (3 x 15 minutes: 10 min to present + 5 min discussion)	Ron & Dave
12:00–1:00	Lunch (prep/coach for closing comments in community session)	
1:00–2:30	Continue presentations	Ron & Dave
2:30–3:00	Teams reconvene for last minute detail and next steps	Ron & Dave
3:00–3:15	Break	
3:15–3:45	Community: 1:1 interviews re personal commitments – One message I'd take back... – One thing I can do on my own... – My commitment to my team, going ahead	Ron
3:45–end	Community: Open microphone forum	Dave + all

Summit Agenda Overview

Akron Roadway

Winning with Employee-Driven Throughput: Crushing nonunion competition by delivering unsurpassed speed and leveraging employee pride and involvement.

Day 1
- Welcomes and overview
- Introduction to topic
- Community-building exercise

Discovery: 1:1 appreciative interviews
Mixed groups of pairs search for themes and factors
that "give life" to our topic

Lunch (customer panel)

Creating our shared-history stakeholder groups:
Identifying proudest moments and what we want to keep

Input: Where does positive change come from?
- Summary and closing

Day 2
- Summarizing key success factors and practices to preserve

Dreaming: Mixed groups: Improvement possibilities for our topic
Mapping highest impact opportunities
Images of our future around opportunities of most interest
(New self-selected groups)

Lunch

Presentations of images
Declaring aspirations for the future: five-year, goal and one-year steps

- Summary reflections and closing

Day 3
  • Summarizing our five-year aspirations

Design: Work on one-year, targets and action steps
                 Prepare presentation of "yes-able proposals for action"
                 Community forum:
                 Presentations from 3 or 4 action groups

                 Lunch

                 Presentations from 3 or 4 action groups

Delivery: Team formation: Action groups convene to agree on
                 (immediate next steps the will take next.)

  • Personal commitments to act on after this Summit
  • "Open microphone" to entire community for comments/reflections
  • Closing

NOTE: All sessions will begin and end on time. There will be breaks with refreshments each morning and afternoon. All sessions will be videotaped so a summary of deliberations and action plans can be communicated (if we want) to the whole organization.

AI Organizational Summit

ROADWAY
What is an "AI" Organizational Summit?
This is not your typical planning meeting!

- The **WHOLE SYSTEM** participates—a cross section of as many interested parties as is practical. That means more diversity and less hierarchy than is usual in a working meeting and a chance for each person to be heard and to learn new ways of looking at the task at hand.

- Future scenarios—for an organization, a community, or an issue—are put into HISTORICAL and GLOBAL perspective. That means thinking globally together before acting locally. This feature enhances shared understanding and greater commitment to act. It also increases range of potential actions.

- People **SELF-MANAGE** their work and use **DIALOGUE**—not problem solving—as the main tool. That means helping others do the tasks and taking responsibility for our perceptions and actions.

- **COMMON GROUND**, rather than conflict management, is the frame of reference. That means honoring our differences rather than having to reconcile them.

- **APPRECIATIVE INQUIRY (AI)** is a combination of the following: to appreciate means to value—to understand those things worth valuing. To inquire means to study, to ask questions, to search. Therefore, AI is a collaborative search to identify and understand the organization's strengths, its potentials, the greatest opportunities, and people's hopes for the future.

- **COMMITMENT TO ACTION** involves the whole system, allowing for more rapid decision making and committing to action in a public way—in an open way that everyone can support and help implement.

SELF-MANAGEMENT and GROUP LEADERSHIP ROLES

Each small group manages its own discussion, data, time, and reports. Here are useful roles for self-managing this work. Leadership roles can be rotated. Divide up the work as you choose.

- **DISCUSSION LEADER**—Assures that each person who wants to speak is heard within the time available. Keeps the group on track to finish on time.

- **TIMEKEEPER**—Keeps the group aware of the time remaining. Monitors report-outs and signals the time remaining to the person talking.

- **RECORDER**—Writes the group's output on flip charts, using the speaker's words. Asks a person to restate long ideas briefly.

- **REPORTER**—Delivers a report to the large group in the time allotted.

Discovery Worksheet #1

Interview Conversations
(Turn to person next to you.... Complete by _____ o'clock)

Our Current Reality

Today's transportation environment is characterized by fierce competition in the one- and two-day regional markets. Every day we lose market share as current and former Roadway customers give more and more freight to nontraditional nonunion carriers who beat us at the game we "invented"—service! Why? How? Because they get the freight to its destination faster than we do. We are better at rating bills and building "high-'n-tight" claim-free loads. We have better computer systems and more dock doors. We have the best-trained and most-skilled employees. On price, our base rates are better than the regionals. Yet they still beat us out of market share because they get the goods delivered quicker. But by leveraging the pride and involvement of our people, we can respond and recapture lost business as well as establish new business. Our key to success in this arena is as follows:

Throughput

Throughput is the measure we use to monitor how quickly we can process the freight through our facility. We win the battle for the one- and two-day market when we accelerate the processing of freight from pick-up, through the 211 gate, across the dock, and down the road. System speed—that's our need. If we achieve maximum throughput, we can crush the nonunion regionals and dominate the market.

Question 1:

Think back to a time at work that you recall as a high point, an experience, or a moment you remember as having left you with an intense sense of pride, excitement, or involvement in having been a part of something that was meaningful, a time when you truly believed you had contributed to the betterment of a fellow employee, the customer, or the organization.

Describe that experience. What was going on, who was involved, and what made it so memorable?

Question 2:

Tell me about a time when you thought throughput (speed) was at its best at 211 or when you were involved in moving a shipment quickly through the facility to a final destination in order to meet a customer requirement.

- Tell the story of what was going on, who was involved, and what happened.
- What did you do? What did you value most about your involvement in that story?
- What do you value most about the contribution of others in that story?

Question 3:

Tomorrow's reality. Imagine that you have awakened from a deep sleep and three years have passed. It is 2010, and the landscape of regional LTL is different. Roadway dominates the nonunion regional carriers in the marketplace! Wall Street is buzzing over the dramatic success Roadway has had in the regional markets! Articles in Transport Topics describe how Roadway—by tapping into the pride and involvement of its employees—has leveraged a dramatic improvement in speed at the 211 complex! This muscular yet agile system has catapulted Roadway Akron to the forefront in reducing costs while establishing unparalleled levels of customer service and employee satisfaction. For customers, it's now imperative that they do their one- or two-day regional business with 211/Akron! For employees, 211 is the preferred location over other Roadway locations!

- What happened to allow for this kind of success?
- What part did you play in this success?
- What three wishes do you have to help Akron Roadway reach and sustain this success?

Discovery Worksheet #2

Discovery at Roadway:
Discovering the Resources and Strengths in This Community
Group reports will begin at _____ o'clock.

Purpose: To appreciate and welcome each other and to learn about the special experiences, commitments, capabilities, and resources people bring to this conference.

Self-Manage: Select a recorder, reporter, timekeeper and discussion leader.
- **Introduce the person you interviewed.** Go around the table. Introduce your interview partner to the group and share one highlight from your interview (high-point story and vision of Roadway).

- As a group, talk about (each person shares):
  - What interests or excites you about being here? What results are you hoping for?
  - From the stories you have heard, what stands out as key factors or themes that cause effective throughput with unsurpassed speed that is driven by employee involvement here at the Akron complex?

- Recorder/reporter listens for and prepares a two-minute summary on:
  - Hopes we have for this meeting and results we want.
    - Three to five key factors that give life to throughput with unsurpassed speed that is driven by employee pride and involvement.

Discovery Worksheet #3

Discovery at Roadway:Root Causes of Success:
When Are We Most Effective and Why?
Reports are due at _____ *o'clock.*

Purpose: To look at the things we are doing of which we are most proud and to understand the things that create success and build competitive advantage.

Self-manage: Select a reporter, recorder, timekeeper and discussion leader.
- On a flip chart, list what you and this stakeholder group are doing (or have done) of which you are most proud in relationship to the task—Achieving Maximum Throughput with Unsurpassed Speed, Driven by Employee Involvement and Pride: "We are most proud of . . ." (Use the historical timelines to remind the group of significant moments, turning points, achievements, and so on.)
- Select your "proudest prouds" and come up with two examples/stories of successful "high-throughput moments."

   NOTE: These might be stories you told or heard in your opening interviews in pairs this morning.

- Now do an analysis of the two stories. Have someone tell the story and listen for patterns. What were the root causes of success? What happened that was new or different? What was it about the people and customers that stood out? What was it about the work group that led toward positive outcomes? What was it about the organization (e.g., procedures, resources, equipment, leadership, communications, and/or training) that seemed to elevate the whole enterprise of positive question asking?

- Recorder: List 5–10 root causes of success, things we want to keep doing or do even better no matter what else changes.

- Reporter: Prepare a three-minute summary. Choose one story to tell to the whole group and review the list of the root causes of success.

Dream Worksheet #1

Roadway Moving from Discovery to Dream
Mapping the Opportunities for Improvement
Summaries are due at _____ o'clock.

Self-Manage: Select a discussion leader, recorder, and timekeeper.

Purpose: To begin to build a future you want—an Akron Roadway team that is truly dedicated to "Maximizing Throughput with Unsurpassed Speed, Driven by Employee Pride and Involvement."

1. Share your wishes and dreams from the interviews you did yesterday morning (Question 3). Add any ideas or thoughts about changes or improvements you think will have a major impact on improving our throughput.

2. Brainstorm a list of opportunities for improving throughput at the Akron complex.

3. As a group, choose 3–5 opportunities you all believe will have the greatest impact on throughput.

Dream Worksheet #2

Dreaming the Future Roadway Wants
Ideal Future Scenarios
Presentations are due at _____ o'clock.

Self-Manage: Select a discussion leader, recorder and timekeeper.

Purpose: To imagine and define the future you want to work toward—an Akron Roadway team that is truly dedicated to "Crushing the Nonunion Competition by Maximizing Throughput with Unsurpassed Speed, Driven by Employee Pride and Involvement."

- Put yourselves three years into the future. It is 2010. Visualize the Akron complex you want from the perspective of the opportunity area you have chosen. What is happening?
    - How did this come about? What helped it happen?
    - What are the things that support this vision— leadership, structures, training, procedures, and so on?
    - What makes this vision exciting to you?
    - How does this vision maximize throughput with unsurpassed speed?

- Capture this dream in a three-year aspiration statement draft on one flip-chart page: "By 2010, what we most aspire to in terms of (your chosen opportunity area) is . . ."
    (See two examples on next page.)
    - Use vivid language.
    - Be positive.
    - Be bold and provocative. Make your statement a stretch that will attract others.

- Choose a creative way to present your vision to the rest of us in a five-minute "portrayal," as if your vision existed now. Use as many members of your group as possible in the presentation.
    Examples: * A TV News Report * A Song or Poem * A Day in the Life * A Skit * A Hiring Interview *

Dream Worksheet #3

Dreaming the Future Roadway Wants
Ideal Future Scenarios

Example Aspiration Statements:

Opportunity Area: Delegation and Trust

> "Roadway 2010: Roadway is an organization that is world-class in terms of its leaders developing leaders at all levels. We are known throughout the industry for our core competency of delegation. People want to work at Roadway because all employees are trusted and empowered to create value."

Opportunity Area: Career Opportunity/Training/Mentoring

> "Roadway is a proactive organization that enables employees to achieve their personal career goals by taking advantage of career opportunities, centrally administered and personally initiated training/education, and mentoring."

> "Career opportunities are provided by vehicles such as internal job fairs, intranet job postings, use of a skills database, career assessment inventories, and a formalized mentoring process—with a key emphasis on promoting from within. All employees are provided time for various training where tuition reimbursement for continuing education is "boundary-less" (i.e., all departments, job levels, and interest levels), fully supported, budgeted, and funded."

> "Training includes soft skills for all employees, leadership training, and advanced and technical training using experienced personnel as a training asset."

Design Worksheet

Designing for Optimal Throughput at Roadway

Self-Manage: Select a discussion leader, recorder, and timekeeper.

Purpose: To begin translating your three-year aspiration statement into one-year goals and steps to be taken in the next 6–12 months.

- Using the feedback and comments from other groups, take 10–15 minutes to revise, edit, or improve your aspiration statement.

- Begin formulating one-year targets or goals that can be achieved and demonstrated showing we are on our way to your three-year aspiration.
    - Brainstorm ideas about specific things that can occur or be changed in the upcoming year that will put us on a course to realize your vision for 2010.
    - Agree on key targets and scenarios for how to get there. Who would need to do what by when?

Guidelines for Action Steps:
- Is it a "yes-able" idea (likely to get support)?
- Does it address/reflect the underlying principles in our aspiration statement?
- What are we already doing (key success factors from yesterday) that can be continued or enhanced?
- What new actions would create an impact?

6

Design:
How Can It Be?

"*Organizational transformation is much more than the critical mass of personal transformation. It requires macro level changes in the very fabric of organizing, the social architecture.*"

—Diana Whitney

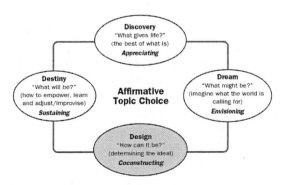

The *Dream* phase articulates the strategic focus, such as a vision of a better world, a powerful purpose, and a compelling statement of a strategic intent. In the *Design* phase, attention turns to creating the ideal organization so that it might achieve its dream. Future images emerge through grounded examples from an organization's positive core. Good-news stories are used to craft **provocative propositions**[1] that bridge the best of "what gives life" with a collective aspiration of "what might be." This is where the organization's social architecture is designed.

The *Design* phase of the 4-D process is the crucial stage in sustaining positive change and responding to the organization's positive past. Grounded in the best of what has been, good appreciative designs address all three of the elements necessary for effective organizational change—continuity, novelty, and transition—discussed in Mini-lecture VII in Chapter 1. The positive core identified and expounded in the first two phases begins to take form.

The design starts by crafting provocative propositions. Sometimes referred to as *possibility propositions*, they bridge "the best of what is" (identified in Discovery) with "what might be" (imagined in Dream). They are written in the present tense. They re-create the organization's image of itself by presenting clear, compelling pictures of how things will be when the positive core is fully effective in all of its strategies, processes, systems, decisions, and collaborations. In this way, provocative propositions redirect daily actions and create future possibilities and a shared vision for the organization and its members. It is important that the design fully integrate the "best of past and possibility" and that it be consistent with the intended outcome of the inquiry.

The following pages present the concept of social architecture and its relationship to AI-based design. The elements of a good provocative proposition are defined. This chapter includes additional provocative propositions to stimulate imagination and creativity. The Case Clippings at the end of this chapter are from a long-term healthcare organization, Tendercare, Inc. They illustrate how this organization incorporated AI into its "+1 Census Development Campaign" at an assisted-living center. The clippings demonstrate how Tendercare's Core Care Team moved from Discovery to Dream and through the *Design* phase. This second edition describes what's new and institutionalized at Tendercare, leading to sustainable organizational development and a revamped corporate culture.

In the context of moving forward to present new developments in the AI *Design* phase, this chapter offers some concluding thoughts on the social architectural approach by looking at the related fields of fashion design, graphic design, art and architectural design, and product design. These correlative disciplines contain lessons about the spirit of AI design. The authors' colleagues

---

1 Provocative propositions also have been referred to as possibility propositions, possibility statements, and design statements. The different wording depends on the language preferred by the organization.

Richard Boland and Fred Collopy have written a separate text on what they call the "design attitude," which will be highlighted later in this chapter.

IDEO, one of the top design firms in the world, has teamed up with leading AI practitioners to combine the AI Summit methods with its unique product design methods for sparking innovation. IDEO helps organizations create and innovate through design.

After a complete overview of the social architecture approach to organization design, this chapter will point to several more advanced variations, including an example of Fairmount Minerals, one of the fastest growing companies in America. Fairmont is a leader in the field of sustainable ecological design focused on "doing good and doing well." Fairmount Minerals has been using AI as an organizational development tool for more than ten years.

Social Architecture for Organizing

When creating a building, an architect considers many elements in the design, as previously stated. A building requires certain key elements: foundation, roof, walls, windows, doors, and floors. But within the constraints of those necessary elements, the architect and client have a number of choices, ways in which to accommodate their unique preferences. For example, they may choose a brick or adobe exterior, a flat roof or a roof with a pitch, a glass or solid wall, and a traditional or cathedral ceiling.

In many ways, a set of provocative propositions is a kind of social architecture for the ideal organization. The **social architecture** is the basic infrastructure that allows the organization to make the dream a reality (from concept to action). It addresses the **design elements** critical to an organization (e.g., leadership/management structure, systems, structures, and strategies) for supporting the positive core. For example, "socio" refers to the following social system components:

- The set of job functions and reporting (formal) and building (informal) relationships
- The management systems, processes, and policies

The design steps are outlined in **Table 6.1**.

Table 6.1 Four Design Steps

- Select design elements.
- Identify internal and external relationships.
- Identify themes and engage in dialogue.
- Write provocative propositions.

Step 1: Select Design Elements

The first step in AI Design is to select design elements. Organization members may choose to articulate their own social architecture; or they may choose to write provocative propositions based on other common models, such as Marvin Weisbord's Six Box Model, Watkins and Mohr's process, or McKinsey's 7-S model.[2] In Tendercare's situation, the Core Care Team selected those elements that best fit the organization's architecture for each affirmative topic choice, as illustrated in Table 6.2.

The *Design* phase defines the basic structure that will allow the dream (or vision) to become a reality. Like the other phases, the *Design* phase requires widespread dialogue about the nature of the structure and processes. This is what is meant by coconstructing the organization's future.

Table 6.2 Design Elements

Design elements to Consider When Designing a Social Architecture

Alliances and Partnerships	Market Opportunities
Beliefs about Power and Authority	New Products
Brand Identity	Policies
Business Models	Practices and Principles
Business Processes	Relationships
Communication	Results
Competencies	Shared Values
Culture	Social Responsibility
Customer Relations	Societal Purposes
Distribution of Wealth	Staff/People
Ecological/Environmental	Stakeholder Relations
Education (Training)	Strategy
Governance Structure	Structure
Knowledge of Management System	Systems
Leadership	Technology
Management Practices	Vision and Purpose

For example, if "leadership" is the element selected, cogent questions might be as follows: What kind of leadership structure is needed? What is the preferred behavior of the leaders?

---

2 For more alternative approaches on whole-system design, see McKinsey's 7-S framework in DeKluyver, C. (2006). *Strategic thinking: An executive perspective.* Upper Saddle River, NJ: Prentice Hall; Weisbord, M., & Janoff, S. (1994). *Collaborating for change: Future Search.* San Francisco: Berrett-Koehler; Weisbord, M. (1994). *Discovering common ground.* San Francisco: Berrett-Koehler; and Mohr B., & Watkins, J. (2001). *Appreciative inquiry: Change at the speed of imagination.* San Francisco: Jossey-Bass/Pfeiffer.

In the Tendercare example ("+1 Census Development Campaign" project), the Core Care Team created a unique business operating environment and culture based on an image of three rings (Figure 6.1). Tendercare's architecture placed the residents in the center ring, the stakeholders in the second ring, and the design elements in the outermost ring.

Step 2: Identify Internal and External Relationships

In the second step, staff and residents worked from the inside out to identify those relationships that helped build the positive core. They listed those key relationships that affected "resident loyalty," as shown in the two boxes labeled "Internal" and "External" in Figure 6.1. Therefore, when designing the provocative proposition, these key relationships had to be considered.

Figure 6.1 Tendercare's Business and Social Architecture

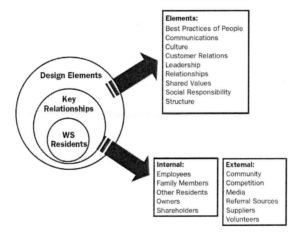

Step 3: Identify Themes and Engage in Dialogue

The third step was to go back to the AI analysis report and the Interview Summary Sheets to identify those key themes that supported resident loyalty. The Core Care Team called those themes "the key ingredients needed to build and sustain resident loyalty." These key ingredients were listed on a large sheet of newsprint. During this step, a great deal of open dialogue took place and stories were told about what contributed to resident loyalty.

Looking through the data and listening to the conversations, the team attempted to pick out statements and/or stories that seemed to exemplify the essence of resident loyalty. The following examples were included:

- Building relationships between staff and residents, staff and family, staff and community, and residents and community
- Providing caring and consistent follow-through on residents' requests
- Showing genuine interest and compassion toward the residents (staff acted like an extended family)
- Knowing each resident by name and knowing something special about him or her
- Taking time to do something helpful for a resident, such as tying his shoe or putting on her makeup
- Developing trust through the managing of a resident's finances, such as monthly budgeting for amenities or balancing a checkbook
- Keeping the physical grounds looking nice
- Helping residents keep their dignity and independence

From those statements, the team selected the best words and created new concepts they believed captured their meaning of resident loyalty. Words such as *positive relationships, nurturing, listening, understanding, trust, compassion, quality care, service,* and *independence* were listed. Then the group took time to reflect on the list and make changes, additions, and alterations. At this point, a deeper conversation took place, ensuring that just the right words were listed. For instance, the word *communication*, which was initially listed, was changed to *understanding* because the group believed *understanding* better captured what the staff and residents wanted in their relationship in order to enhance resident loyalty.

Step 4: Write Provocative Propositions

Next, each member of the Core Care Team worked independently to write a preferred possibility statement about resident loyalty.[3] At this point, the group was quiet and reflective as each member attempted to use the words the group identified as significant. The themes and key ingredients were posted to capture resident loyalty in their version of a possibility statement. The participants were instructed to incorporate these ingredients into the possibility statements, as well as to include the key relationships that were identified earlier. After adequate time was allotted, each team member read his or her statement aloud. As each statement was read, it was transcribed and posted for everyone to see.

This resulted in ten affirmative possibility statements for further dialogue. Many statements were similar, yet each had a unique offering. For example, several statements helped develop the framework of the possibility statement.

---

3 For this Case Clipping, Tendercare used the term *possibility statements* instead of *possibility propositions*

Other statements provided key ingredients to make the dreams a reality. Another possibility statement provided the concluding sentence that captured the essence of resident loyalty.

Resident Loyalty Possibility Statement:

At Wayne Seniors, residents are our lifeline. We maintain this lifeline by building relationships with our residents and their families to ensure a caring, consistent, and positive living experience.

We strive to nurture relationships by creating an environment of listening, understanding, and trust.

Residents trust us with their lives—a responsibility we hold sacred. We earn trust through unwavering commitment to superior care tempered with compassion and respect.

To provide superior care, we provide knowledge to residents, staff, and families to ensure consistent and compassionate service delivery.

With dedication to these ideals, our center for seniors nurtures resident loyalty, thereby effectively serving the community.

Typically, the core team or steering group coordinates this effort; but it is important to incorporate the feedback of all affected stakeholders. Once the design elements and stakeholders have been selected and most stakeholders identify with the dream, the provocative propositions can be written. The next section covers suggested criteria for writing a provocative proposition. These propositions articulate the desired organizational qualities, processes, and systems (created in the *Dream* phase) to help guide the organization to its higher purpose.

To get buy-in from the entire organization, a process must allow everyone affected to make a contribution. In the Tendercare example, a dietary aide later suggested creating a dining committee made up of residents and staff to explore how to improve the residents' dining experience. This suggestion resulted in a flexible meal program with more menu choices and different meal times, while also providing the residents with a greater sense of independence and control over their surroundings. This fostered greater resident loyalty. Such contributions move the provocative propositions forward to implementation of the dream in the *Destiny* phase.

Criteria for Good Provocative Propositions

A provocative proposition is a statement that bridges the best of "what is" and "what might be." It is provocative to the extent that it stretches the realm of the status quo, challenges common assumptions or routines, and helps suggest desired possibilities for the organization and its people. At the same time, it is grounded in what has worked in the past. It conveys the positive images (from the Dream phase) of the ideal organization.

The following questions serve as a guideline or checklist for crafting engaging provocative propositions:

- Is it *provocative*? Does it stretch, challenge, or interrupt the status quo?

- Is it *grounded*? Are examples available that illustrate the ideal as a real possibility? Is it grounded in the organization's collective history?

- Is it *desired*? Do *you* want it as a preferred future?

- Is it stated in *affirmative* and bold terms?

- Does it follow a *social architecture* approach?

- Does it expand the *"zone of proximal development"*?[4]

    – Used with a third party (outside appreciative eye)

    – Complemented with benchmarking data

- Is it a *participative* process?

- Is it used to stimulate *intergenerational learning*?

- Is there balanced management of *continuity, novelty, and transition*?

Provocative propositions provide a clear, shared vision for the organization's destiny. The following samples of provocative propositions focus on a specific design element and theme or topic of the organization's social architecture.

---

4 The Zone of Proximal Development (ZPD) was developed by Lev Semenovich Vygotsky (1896–1934). He suggested that the mind is not fixed in its capacity, but provides a range of potential possibilities. For more information on ZPD and how it relates to AI, refer to Stavros, J. (1998). *Capacity building using an appreciative approach: A relational process of building your organization's future*. Unpublished dissertation, Case Western University, Cleveland, OH.

Sample Provocative Propositions

DESIGN ELEMENT: Culture

THEME/TOPIC: Recognition and Celebration

The AI Advocates Standing Committee understands and honors the pivotal role of recognition and celebration within the formation of a true "appreciative organization." Therefore, frequent and visible recognition and celebration of the value of life, people, and ideas are an integral part of the AI Advocates' philosophy and practice.

We value diversity of people and ideas. We nurture and support people to express who and what they are. We begin all meetings and gatherings with positive storytelling and recognition. Whenever we are engaged in a discussion or decision-making process, we consciously use "appreciative feedback" with one another and with coworkers outside the team. We collect and publicly disseminate stories that communicate the richness of individual and collective contributions within the community. We purposefully recognize and celebrate those individuals in the community who regularly recognize and celebrate other people, ideas, and accomplishments.

DESIGN ELEMENT: Human Resources Management System

THEME/TOPIC: Performance Appraisal

Our organization acts on its value of high-level trust in the belief that people are committed to personal accountability by using appreciative performance appraisals. It focuses on employee competence and exemplary service to our stakeholders. Our employees are valued.

DESIGN ELEMENT: Shared Values

THEME/TOPIC: Authenticity

Authenticity in human relationships is a key foundation for true organizational transformation and excellence. When we are authentic, we recognize and share our thoughts, feelings, and experiences with others in the spirit of deepening relationships and in service of collaborative achievement. This dialogue allows us to:

- Unleash the best of who we are.
- Become energized and unite around our heartfelt focus.
- Meet the goals of the business.
- Contribute to the greater good.

Being authentic is a shared individual, interpersonal, and organizational responsibility. In practical terms, we:

- Each commit to reflecting and contributing openly.
- Seek out other's viewpoints so we can get the best of everyone's thinking.
- Build in pauses to allow people to know their own thoughts.
- Embrace the philosophy of slowing down so we can finish sooner.

DESIGN ELEMENT: Organizational Purpose

THEME/TOPIC: Shared Vision

Partners in all regions share a basic common vision of the firm's core mission, intent, and direction. It is an exciting, challenging, and meaningful direction, which helps give all partners a feeling of significance, purpose, pride, and unity. The firm uses whatever time and resources are needed to bring everyone on board, thus continuously cultivating the thrill of having "a one-firm feeling," of being a valued member of one outstanding national partnership.

DESIGN ELEMENT: Structure

THEME/TOPIC: Ownership

We have created an organization where everyone experiences himself or herself as an owner of the business. People at all levels believe the organization is theirs to improve, change, and help in order to reach its potential. We recognize that there is a big difference between owners and hired hands. Ownership happens in three ways: (1) on an economic level, where everyone is a shareholder and shares in the profit; (2) on a psychological level, wherein people are authentically involved; and (3) on a business level, when the big-picture purpose is shared by all and all take part at the strategic level of business planning.

The Spirit of Designing: Recent Developments

Finally, mentioned at the outset of this chapter is the goal of addressing the "spirit of designing" and several exciting additions to the ways the *Design* phase can unfold—building on and going beyond the basic social architectural approach. In terms of the spirit of designing, this chapter looks to the fields of fashion design, graphic design, art and architectural design, and product design for new lessons about the AI *Design* phase.

First, as previously mentioned, the authors' colleagues Richard Boland and Fred Collopy have written a book on what they call the "design attitude." In brief, their book is about approaching the world like an artist—with a great deal of improvising, iterating, sketching and mapping visually, creating connections and cross-pollinations across seemingly disparate domains, and moving iteratively between liquid (very open) and more crystallized (convergent) stages in the design process. Designing in this view is often visual, taking concepts—for example, verbal or descriptive elements of the ideal organization—and giving them three-dimensional form or making them into "prototype" models or storyboards.[5]

Secondly, in their work at Appreciative Inquiry Consulting (AIC), David Cooperrider and his colleagues teamed up with one of the top design firms in the world, IDEO, to combine their large group AI Summit methods with IDEO's unique product design method for sparking innovation. IDEO employs design thinking to help clients navigate the speed, complexity, and opportunity areas of today's world. IDEO calls its method the "deep dive," and it involves a powerful brainstormer method and a process of rapid prototyping.[6]

Sustainability: The Triple Bottom Line

On the CD-ROM that accompanies this edition, you will find the participant workbook for an exemplary AI Summit design session, one that utilizes these new design options. Held at Fairmount Minerals in 2005, the focus of the summit was on designing new products and business processes based on the sustainable development and triple bottom line concepts. Chuck Fowler, the CEO and president of Fairmount Minerals, and Bill Conway, Fairmount's founder and chair, had introduced the approach of AI to the company in 1991. From 1991 to 2005, the company's revenues increased dramatically—from $48 million to more than $250 million. During this period, Fairmount became the second largest sand mining operation in America.

Next on the OD agenda was to become a "**sustainable enterprise**"[7] focused on the **triple bottom line** of people (social), prosperity (economic), and planet (environment).[8] Once again, the AI Summit was selected as the way to bring the entire company as well as external stakeholders such as environmental NGOs, watchdog groups, and community citizens into the strategic planning process to advance the company as a sustainable value creator.

Three hundred people came together for three full days, and one goal was

---

5 See Boland, R., & Collopy, F. (2004). *Managing as designing*. Palo Alto, CA: Stanford University Press.

6 For a good, simple overview of IDEOS brainstormer and rapid prototyping methods see Nussbaum, B. (2004, May 17). The power of design. Business Week. Also see the IDEO Web site at http://www.ideo.com.

7 Hart, S. (2005). *Capitalism at the crossroads*. Upper Saddle River, NJ: Pearson Education, Inc.

8 Elkington, J. (1998). *Cannibals with forks*. Gabriola Island, BC: New Society Publishing.

to come away with actual prototypes of new products and "green design" business opportunities that would allow the organization to take account of the "entire life cycle from the sourcing of raw materials and energy from the earth to the reuse, remanufacture, or return of materials to the earth." In her opening talk at the AI Summit, the chief financial officer of the company spoke to the tremendous opportunity:

Not since the days of the Great Depression has there been such a severe decline of public trust in business and in our economic system—nor has there been a better opportunity to build a new era of business-led excellence and leadership in our industry and beyond. We believe that doing good and doing well go hand in hand and that economic prosperity, environmental stewardship, and empowerment of people can, in an integrated way, become a source of innovation and competitive advantage for the long term.

The *Design* phase was broken down into two parts. Following the *Dream* phase, "opportunity areas" were identified and people were asked to vote with their feet by moving to the opportunity area named on flip charts located around the room. Opportunity areas, unlike many OD summits, were focused largely on new product opportunities (socially responsible and green design). For example, one dream was to create a new business using recycled or "spent" sand; another dream was to create a low-cost sand filter product that could be used to purify contaminated drinking water in parts of the world where billions of people survive on less than $2 per day and where many childhood diseases and deaths could be averted with clean water.

In each case, the goal was to come out of the summit with more than an aspiration statement or possibility proposition and action plan for creating something later; indeed, the goal was to prototype and model the product design on the spot—even in the case of the group that was working on a less tangible piece. (They were working on a draft of the corporate sustainability principles or "constitutional beliefs," as in "We hold these truths to be self-evident."). This group was asked to create a prototype of the new corporate principles, complete with symbolism and the visual effects of the complete packaging of the principles.

Can you imagine 300 people designing new sustainable, green products—progressing from discovery of strengths and dreams to actual market opportunities and product designing? After the focus or "possibility proposition" was created, Part One of the design session involved a "deep dive brainstormer" process, an intense idea-generating session (with sticky notes going up on large blank walls). The following IDEO tips were included:

- Defer judgment.
- Encourage wild ideas.
- Be visual.
- Go for quantity.
- Hold one conversation at a time.

It was exciting to see the "hot teams" and the energy, with each opportunity group averaging more than 150 ideas in the hour-long brainstormer session.

Part Two of the design phase included a five-hour "rapid prototyping" session. Here the best of the best of the brainstormer ideas were selected for mock-ups to be brought into visual existence as 3-D models, storyboards, or skits of the emerging products or processes. The idea is that once a person starts drawing or making things, he or she opens up new possibilities of discovery, like trial balloons. Effective, rapidly created prototypes also do something more: they persuade and they help move the ball forward for real-life experimentation. In that sense, they provide a business edge, a jump start. What is going to be more effective—a five-page wordy report of a possible new sand filter for cleaning water or a cardboard mock-up of the water purifier together with a skit demonstrating its use in a part of the world where many children suffer from lack of clean water? There is something inspiringly tangible about a prototype. Ending the group meeting or summit with this kind of visual mock-up, instead of just descriptive words, gives the project added impetus.

"Takeaways" from the Summit

As a result of the three-day Fairmount Minerals Sustainable Development Summit of 2005 and the methodologies that were employed, the following "takeaways" emerged:

- More than 850 stakeholders identified and surveyed on the subject of sustainability
- Increased emphasis on reclamation projects in areas where Fairmount was mining resources, resulting in, for instance, efforts to increase diversity of flora and fauna in those areas
- Initiatives toward the recovery, recycling, and reuse of resources utilized in the mining process, including use of biodiesel fuels and the "cradle-to-cradle" use of natural resources such as "spent" sand
- Increased philanthropic sponsorship of community development programs with school districts and Habitat for Humanity, for example
- Development of a low-cost sand and water filter (producing clean drinking water), embodying "doing good and doing well"
- An overall increased awareness of the importance of sustainable development throughout the company and with stakeholders

For more information on this initiative in addition to quotations from the company officials and employees/stakeholders involved, go to http://media.mindgrabmedia.com/fairmount/Minerals/Fairmount%20Minerals.html.

Summary

You are learning that the *Design* phase can be taken beyond organizational design work into the innovative design of new products and other tangible prototypes for action. Another related point is instilling the spirit of design—the design attitude—into the establishment of the new organization, which is what AI is all about. AI is not a process that throws all of its attention and energy at yesterday's problematic patterns. It is a process of creating positive change, which, in turn, is about establishing the "new"—that is, focusing on what people want instead of what they don't want. That is also what design is and why change, in this approach, can be so much fun and so easy to facilitate.

The following Case Clippings illustrate the more commonly used foundational and fundamental ways of carrying out the *Design* phase within the traditional AI framework. At the same time, you are encouraged to consider investigating and applying some of the new design options presented previously.

Case Clippings: Tendercare

This AI project was designed and adapted to discover the positive core of one of Tendercare, Inc.'s assisted-living centers to enable the staff to focus on projects, process improvements, and rewards that were aligned to increase the residents' occupancy (census).[9] At the same time, it was designed to build a team spirit, thereby creating a better environment for the residents and staff.

Since 1990, Tendercare, Inc., has become Michigan's largest provider of long-term care services. It has 39 health centers located throughout the state and more than 3,400 employees. In an effort to build census, the marketing department created the "+1 Census Development Campaign" and invited the center's staff and residents to participate in this project. This campaign had three primary goals:

---

9 Assisted-living organizations generate their revenue by increasing resident occupancy levels. As another company works to increase sales, long-term care providers work to increase census.

- *To educate the entire staff as to the importance of increasing occupancy and how having more residents positively impacts them on a daily basis*
- *To educate the staff as to how they can help with the census development efforts*
- *To establish a census goal and create an environment of energy and excitement toward the center's census goal*

An AI intervention was designed and combined with the "+1 Census Development Campaign" to enhance the education and participation of the staff, while identifying and sustaining the positive core of the center.

Four topics were selected as the focus of this project: Provider of Choice, Resident Loyalty (stated earlier in this chapter), The Excellent Team, and Appreciation. The other three possibility statements created by the Core Care Team with the input of the entire staff and residents were as follows:

Provider of Choice

We are the provider of choice because we have a high-quality, trained, experienced, and caring staff to meet the needs of our residents. We create a positive culture that radiates energy and life through a superior dining experience and activities that encourage participation and increase the quality of our residents' lives. We offer a fun, clean, and friendly community that caters to the individual's needs.

The Exceptional Team

We are proud to be an exceptional team. Our team is driven by our commitment and ability to communicate with those we are privileged to work with and care for.

Our respect for each other is a value that is carried to every aspect of service delivery. Through appreciation, we build strong connections that result in a fun, high-energy work environment that supports friendship and loyalty to our Wayne Seniors community.

Appreciation

At Wayne Seniors, EVERYONE is appreciated. We take the time to make our residents, families, staff, and community feel welcome. We listen, care for, and support each other by:

- Greeting each other.
- Remembering special moments.
- Celebrating holidays.
- Getting to know residents.
- Sending gifts and cards.
- Sharing time.
- Valuing daily contributions.
- Recognizing accomplishments.
- Seeking out the best in one another.
- Asking if anyone needs help.
- Giving heartfelt thank-yous.
- Taking care of our environment.

Appreciation is a gift we give each other every day.

Outcomes of the Tendercare Project

The center used these possibility statements as guiding philosophies to make the center the provider of choice by building an excellent team through appreciation and development of resident loyalty, thereby creating a better environment for the residents and staff. The Case Clippings for this initiative include:

- *Project Proposal*
- *Interview Guide and Summary Sheet*
- *Project Summary*
- *Sample Master Wish List*
- *Agenda: AI Discovery and Dream*
- *AI: Discovery and Dream Minutes*
- *Agenda: AI Design and Destiny*
- *AI: Dream and Design Minutes*

The AI approach was favorably received by the staff and residents, and it yielded highly insightful information about how the staff related to each other and to the residents and how the residents related to each other. Later four managers at Tendercare remarked how drastically the culture had changed. They observed that the culture had gone from negative to very hopeful and positive in a matter of weeks. Three individuals who were reported to be skeptical and to have the most negative of the employees' attitudes shifted during their AI interviews and offered excellent ideas for improvement. They felt respected and hopeful that someone would care enough to ask what they thought could happen to turn this facility around.

The Master Wish List became an action plan that management and employees used to implement the ideas for improving the overall quality of work life and living conditions. The positive core of the staff lies within the genuine compassion and sincere caring for the residents and for each other.

The center experienced several noticeable outcomes. First, within a six-week period, the center experienced an increase in census of 12%. Second, monthly in-service meetings for the staff were reinstated. Third, the staff worked with management to develop an ongoing marketing action plan. Six months after the intervention took place, the staff voted to remove the union that had represented them to management for many years. Finally, and in perhaps the most significant demonstration of the new spirit of cooperation, 18 months after the AI intervention, government reimbursement for this type of health center changed—making it no longer financially profitable to operate this facility. Management and staff again used the AI principles and approach to develop a closing plan that included the relocation of all residents and the placement of the staff at other centers. Not one employee left the facility during this time to pursue outside employment interests until the residents were safely placed somewhere else. To this day, the company considers the closing of the center to be a model of cooperation, participation, and efficiency.

The following outcomes resulted from the *Design* phase:
- Creation of the social-technical architecture
- Crafting of the possibility propositions
- Dream becoming a reality in these statements

The original Project Proposal is outlined in the following section.

Project Proposal

Tendercare Assisted Living
"Discovering the Positive Core to Best Achieve Census Growth"

Purpose and Overview
Our vision is "to be the provider of choice for both our residents and our staff." Our team is committed to our residents and to each other.
"Caring people, caring for people"

The "+1 Census Development Campaign" is a six-week census development program designed to accomplish three goals. The first goal is to educate the entire staff as to the importance of census and the way it impacts them on a daily basis. The second goal of the campaign is to educate the staff on how they can help with the census development efforts. The third goal is to create an environment of energy and excitement toward the center's census goal. It is expected that by creating this air of enthusiasm, teamwork, and synergy and by educating the staff as to the importance of census and the way they can help increase the center's census, that census (and revenue) goals will be greatly enhanced.

This campaign will be combined and enhanced by integrating it within an Appreciative Inquiry (AI) intervention. The project will consist of completing an AI interview at the assisted-living center to identify and sustain the positive core of the center. This positive core will help to achieve census growth while placing the resident in the center of the circle of quality care. This change process will incorporate the entire staff. The results of the AI intervention will be specific actions targeting elements that help increase census.

Identifying these attributes will enable the staff to focus on projects, process improvements, and rewards that are aligned to increase census while building a team spirit.

Expected outcomes include:

- An increase in average daily census of 8 (from 92 to 100).
- Qualitative findings that articulate elements of the positive core.
- Identification of specific tactics that will enhance teamwork and cooperation.

Evaluation

It is anticipated that the AI process will generate positive feedback and goodwill as measured by the Interview Guide. Other evaluation measurements will include turnover levels, customer satisfaction scores, and identification of what is working well within the center, as well as strategies designed to repeat and amplify success.

Primary Participants
Champions—Census Care Team (CCT):
- Vice President of Marketing
- Marketing Development Consultant
- Administrator
- Director of Care

- Community Relations Representative
- Dietary Manager
- Activities Coordinator
- AI Coordinator and AI Facilitator
- Direct Care Staff (5)
- MBA Student Interns (2)

Project Scope

The scope of this project is to learn about and use an AI process to discover and sustain the qualitative elements of the positive core, identify specific tactics that will enhance teamwork, and report findings to all participants for the purpose of increasing the daily average census. A series of meetings to train a core team of participants on the AI techniques will be conducted, as will interviews and additional meetings to collect, theme, analyze, and interpret the data sets (or outcomes) of the interviews. The final deliverable will be a report of the key findings and outcomes of this project.

The AI process will be integrated with the "+1 Census Development Campaign." It will begin with the *Discovery* phase to learn about the positive core of the group. The following key topic issues/themes will be addressed:

- Provider of Choice—"Best in Care"
- Resident Loyalty
- The Exceptional Team: Working and Winning Together
- Appreciation

An AI Interview Guide will be designed around these core topics, and each team member will be interviewed to help determine the positive care core and identify what is most valued. The *Dream* phase begins with a visioning dialogue among the team members to identify the key themes. As a team, we will create images of the future, relating to what everyone wants and requires.

These themes will be designed into possibility statements based on the center's organizational architecture. The final phase will be creating the Destiny in the form of census action plans to implement these design elements to ensure continued success of the campaign. In addition, the Census Care Team (CCT) will learn about a change process called AI to use throughout their work at the center.

Interview Guide and Summary Sheet

Tendercare Assisted Living
Discovering the Positive Core to Best Build Census
Interview Guide

Thank you for participating in this interview. I am an interviewer for "Discovering the Positive Core" in our "+1 Census Development Campaign." We will be asking questions to learn more about why we choose to work here and why residents choose to live here. We want to learn about the positive core of our people and identify ways to increase the positive aspects of the work life.

Staff and residents will be interviewed to collect the "best-case" stories on which to build the future. The goal is to move forward in achieving the vision "to be the provider of choice for both staff and residents." Your input will be an important contribution to generate meaningful ideas and actions.

Many times in interviews, we ask questions about why things don't work well. This time we are going to approach things from a different angle. We are going to find out about your experiences of success at Tendercare so we can build on those experiences.

We will interview everyone who works and lives here. When the interviews are complete, everyone's input will be reviewed to identify the positive core that makes us unique. With those qualities as a foundation, we will create specific steps to build on our strengths and to build census.

The conversation will take an hour or so. I'm going to take notes as we talk. During our interview, we will be exploring your experiences in several areas:
• Provider of Choice—Best in Care
• Resident Loyalty
• The Exceptional Team—Working and Winning Together
• Appreciation

Shall we begin?

Introduction: The Privilege of Caring
Our profession is based on caring with compassion and understanding. The privilege to participate in the aging and healing relationship is what creates and maintains the passion for healthcare providers. We would like to acknowledge that passion and explore with you how to acknowledge and develop this in all of the people who work here.

First, I would like to know what attracted you to our center? What were your initial excitements and impressions when you joined this center?

Can you recall a high point when you felt most alive, most involved about your work at the center? What made it exciting? Who was involved? Please tell me the story.

- What were your hopes and dreams when you chose to work here?
- What is it about caring for others today that keeps you involved?

Before we get into our interview topics today, can you tell me what is it that you value about yourself, the nature of your work, and the center?

Topic 1: Provider of Choice

Provider of choice means that we are the place where residents want to live and employees want to work. We can be the provider of choice by identifying and nurturing the "best-in-class" qualities within our departments and job responsibilities.

The provider of choice means that we demonstrate levels of caring and excellence that are beyond the reach of other "good" assisted-living centers. It consists of the way we need to do things to allow us to accomplish exceptional results, along with high levels of care and employee satisfaction.

Please tell me what it is about you and the way you do your job that's "best in class"? What effect do those skills or behaviors have on you and your sense of belonging to the team? What effect do they have on your coworkers and the residents?

Topic 2: Resident Loyalty

Today's best companies create and maintain exceptional levels of customer loyalty. Loyal customers are great customers. They provide information, which, in time, helps us give them what they need. They share great ideas. They invite new customers.

Resident loyalty is something we must earn. We can earn it by listening to what our residents and their families or referral sources tell us they want. If possible, we can exceed our residents' expectations by treating them with genuine respect and care and by creatively anticipating ways we can provide the services they want more of in order to be happy, safe, and cared for.

By earning resident loyalty, we build ourselves a caring, competitive edge that puts each of us in a position of being the provider of choice for our residents.

1. Think of a time when you were a very loyal customer (to a large organization or, for example, to a neighborhood babysitter).
   - What were the most significant things this company or person did to earn your loyalty in the first place?
   - How did this company or person learn about what was important to you? How did this company or person stay current with what you needed?
   - Describe a time when this loyalty was tested. What did your "provider" do to keep you as a loyal customer and, if necessary, rebuild the relationship?

2. Put yourself in the place of one our most loyal residents or referral sources.
   - How would this person describe us to a new resident?
   - Why would this person say he or she is so committed to our center?

3. Suppose we could choose just three things to do more of or do differently to dramatically enhance our resident loyalty. What would they be?

Topic 3: The Exceptional Team—Working and Winning Together
An exceptional team is built on individual expertise and excellent cooperation. Cooperative teamwork, clear communication, and wisdom are essential elements in delivering superior patient care.
1. Describe a time when you participated as a team member where your expertise truly made a difference to the team.
2. Imagine that you are working with an exceptional team. Describe the team.
3. What do you value most about this team?

Topic 4: Appreciation
All of us want fulfillment through meaningful work. The most gratifying appreciation is that which is expressed from the heart by active communication, a kind gesture, or written words.
1. Describe a time when you felt extremely appreciated.
2. What is the most meaningful way your contribution is recognized and appreciated?

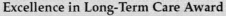

Excellence in Long-Term Care Award
Imagine that you are representing our center in accepting a national award for "Excellence in Care" in 2010.
1. Describe what you admire about working here.
2. What makes caring for our residents unique?

Three Wishes
What three wishes do you have to make our center the best place to give care and the best place to receive care?

Reflections on This Interview
In closing, I would like to ask you two questions about this interview:
1. What did you like most about this interview?
2. Would you be interested in conducting this interview with one of your residents?

Appreciative Interview Summary Sheet

Interviewer: _____

Interviewee: _____

Years of Experience in Caring _____

Years Employed _____

What are the best quotes that came out of this interview?

What were the best stories that came out of this interview?

What were the best wishes that you heard in your interview?

What were the best practices or specific recommendations that you heard reflected in your conversation?

What contributes to the positive core?

What do residents and staff want more of?

Length of Interview _____

Project Summary

A "+1 Census Development Campaign" kick-off meeting was held at the assisted-living center with the following three goals as its focus:
1. To educate the entire staff as to the importance of census and the way it impacts them on a daily basis
2. To educate the staff as to how they can help with the census development efforts
3. To establish a census goal and create an environment of energy and excitement toward the center's census goal

This AI project coincided with the "+1 Census Development Campaign" in an effort to build on momentum and to discover and sustain the positive core of the group to enable the staff to focus on projects, process improvements, and rewards that are aligned to increase census while building a team spirit, thereby creating a better world for our residents and staff.

Four topics were chosen as our project focus: Provider of Choice, Resident Loyalty, The Excellent Team, and Appreciation. Our main goal in using AI was to obtain constructive information as to what is working well today and to learn what we can do to improve with regard to the four focus topics.

Outcomes
The following key objectives were met:
- Learned and used AI to discover the qualitative elements of the positive core at the center
- Identified specific tactics that will enhance teamwork
- Conducted a series of meetings to train a core team of participants on AI
- Conducted interviews with the staff and residents
- Collected, themed, analyzed, and interpreted the data sets (or outcomes) of the interviews
- Reported findings to all participants for the purpose of increasing the daily average census

The initial training of AI with the core team (identified as the Census Care Team (CCT) in the proposal process) was conducted on April 29. The significant outcome of this meeting was 11 AI staff interviews and an introduction of the Discovery, Dream, Design, and Destiny concepts of AI to the CCT team.

The next meeting on May 6 discussed the common themes of the 11 interviews and provided an in-depth overview of the *Dream* and *Design* phases. The significant outcome was the development of possibility statements for the Resident Loyalty and Provider of Choice topics. At this point, each member of the CCT was given a list of staff and resident names to interview. The next two weeks were spent conducting interviews.

Method

A combination of qualitative and quantitative methods was used in the process of data collection and data interpretation. A comprehensive survey relating to the four focus topics was designed to identify attributes of as many staff and resident respondents as possible. The survey information was collected over a two-week period using a face-to-face interview format with the individuals. This method was used to build an environment of trust and openness and received very favorable feedback, as it gave each individual an opportunity to talk about what was important to him or her.

The total number of AI interviews conducted was 74 (24 staff and 50 residents). All staff and resident interviews were collected, themed, and summarized. From this information, a Master Wish List was created.

Sample Master Wish List

Master Wish List:

Wish	Ideas/Solutions	Time frame	Resource	Cost
More Activities: Give everyone a chance to do more around here. They just want to have more options and do and go places. Get out more—more activities instead of just smoking. Group activities outside. You're only as old as you feel; activities schedule keep their minds going. More outings. Have more family-oriented activities. Get staff more involved in resident activities. More field trips for the residents. Have more games. More outings. More family-oriented activities that involve the families. Should have the most awesome activities in the world. More entertainment. More outings for residents. To have more family-oriented events. More functions with residents and staff.	Exercise Program 1. Square dancing or some kind of dancing 2. Resident picnic 3. Go to a ball game 4. "Ask" program—Volunteers: recruit agencies, churches, and schools 5. Tabletop bowling 6. Vegas Night, Black Jack Night, Roulette 7. Shopping: dollar store or mall walking 8. Call day camps to have children come in, do activities at WS 9. Create Resident Recreation Committee: need buttons			
Facility: When someone walks in the front door, the facility should smell clean, look and feel cozy and inviting. Just make it a nice place for the residents and us. Pride in physical plan—building itself. More private areas.	1. Fresh flowers from weddings, churches 2. Put air-conditioning in the halls; some are very hot 3. Why isn't our bathroom as nice as their bathroom up front? Air freshener in employee's bathroom 4. What about new lockers? 5. Photographs of staff and residents in halls 6. A more comfortable place to sit outside (lawn chair) 7. Call landscape companies, funerals, flower shops to send overflow to center 8. Create a gardening club 9. Create Historical Room or Century Wall			
Appreciation: More appreciation from each other and corporate office	1. Send letters or certificates based on corporate calendar. Give facilities funds to recognize their employees (e.g., employee of the month)			
More training/communication	1. New employee orientation 2. Customer service 3. White board to communicate supplies needed			
Food: Do something with the menu; give a choice or two. Get a list of things residents like to eat.	1. Survey residents on food preferences 2. Coffee all day 3. Create Food Committee: Have residents volunteer to cook their specialties with the staff 4. Presentation and serving of food			

Agenda: AI Discovery and Dream

AI Discovery and Dream Meeting
9:30 a.m. – 1:30 p.m.

Facilitators: Jackie Stavros and Anne Meda
Purpose: Orient CCT to AI, plan and launch inquiry

Goals:
- Understand AI as an integral foundation of this project
- Complete AI interviews
- Explain Project Plan and Timelines

Deliverables:
- Complete the *Discovery* and *Dream* phases
- CCT group roster and role

Project Stakeholders:
- Tendercare
- Residents
- Marketing Team

Activity	Leader	Time
Introductions/purpose How we got here? Why AI?	VP Marketing	10 minutes
Agenda/roles	Jackie	15 minutes
Appreciative Interviews Mural (best stories/themes)	Jackie	1.5 hours
Discovery and Dreaming (Working lunch)	Jackie/Anne	1 hour
Report-Outs	Jackie/Anne	30 minutes
Interview Plan – Define – Rotate subgroups/refine – Need a list of employee shifts for the interviews and how to best set up interviews with the residents	Jackie/Anne	15 minutes
Review/Close	VP Marketing/Jackie	15 minutes

AI: Discovery and Dream Minutes

10 a.m.— Introductions: "If I owned the company, I would...."
Ideas:
- Hold classes for new employees (new employee orientation)
- Invite family of residents and family of workers to functions
- Hold monthly in-services with each department; mandatory staff meetings
- Hold an Appreciation Day
- Pay overtime
- Keep employees
- Ensure accountability among staff
- Change budget, build census, make sure residents are well cared for
- Add staff—lighten workload and provide better care
- Move into the twenty-first century and have more technology (would like to see residents using e-mail to stay in contact with family members living far away)
- Provide more social activities for employees and residents
- Build teamwork

96% full to break even

10:15 a.m. — Handout: Develop an Appreciative, Caring Environment "What do we do really well?"

Core Team—Whole-System Representation

Focus on common ground.

Interview Guide—Intro (question walk participants through the Interview Guide)

10:15 a.m. – 12:15 p.m.— Interviews

Debrief:

Fun, informative, more commonality—we're after the same thing; we need to know the person better; it's nice to be listened to.

12:15 p.m. – 12:30 p.m.— The Unconditional Positive Question

1. Discovery ⇒ 2. Dream ⇒ 3. Design ⇒ 4. Destiny

Today we covered the *Discovery* phase wherein we interviewed each other. The next step is to dream. Based on the stories you heard in your initial interviews, select 3–5 positive topics. We will discuss them in our next meeting. We also will cover the *Design* and *Destiny* phases in our next meeting.

12:30 p.m.— "How are the rest of the folks going to be interviewed?"
- Try talking about things from the other side; for example, What works well here?
- Create a shared dialogue, stop and listen to people, create positive intent to trust each other.
- Make a difference in the attitude of people you work with; build self-esteem.
- Create a course of action—capture the rich, thick dialogue of what people say.
- During interviews, listen and TAKE GOOD NOTES!
- CCT is responsible for its interviews.

12:55 p.m.— Read first question and state the answer that was given.
Common themes:
- Tendercare cares about employees
- Culture
- Family feeling
- Elderly care and support
- Acceptance
- Rapport with residents
- Staff (care group)
- Activities
- Appreciation
- Tenure of staff
- Likes to solve problems and impart knowledge
- Likes to help seniors, especially those who don't have family
- Extended family—residents ask employees about their weekends
- Likes to listen to residents
- Likes to be treated as his or her family is treated

Focus on what is good, not on what is wrong. What will give life to your center, what should it be, what energizes you about your well-being? Next meeting is Monday, May 6, 9:30 a.m. – 2:30 p.m.

Agenda: AI Design and Destiny

AI Design and Destiny Meeting
9:30 a.m. – 2:00 p.m.

Facilitators: Jackie Stavros and Anne Meda
Purpose: Create Possibility Statements

Goals:
- To make "dream" themes a reality
- To learn how to create an appreciative learning culture

Deliverable:
- Defined Possibility Statements

Project Stakeholders:
- Staff
- Residents
- Marketing Team

Activity	Leader	Time
Welcome Back	VP Marketing	5 minutes
Explain Design Phase	Jackie	30 minutes
Theme Selection	Anne	15 minutes
Design Team Activity	Jackie/Anne	2 hours
Destiny Discussion (Working lunch)	Jackie	1 hour
Report-outs	Jackie/Anne	30 minutes
Review/Close	VP Marketing/Jackie	10 minutes

AI: Dream and Design Minutes

9:40 a.m.— Debrief from last week's meeting

+1 Blitz went very well, heard nothing negative, made a good connection; eight people got pins that day. Picnic appears popular. Hard to choose a good time that people will attend. Just purchased a grill, can make a lunch for employees. Did you notice/get feedback from last week?

Nothing in particular, other meetings were scheduled all week, ratifying contract today. Marketing consultant is getting together with group on Thursday to brainstorm, has received great ideas. The attention from corporate has been great. Have always felt neglected; impressed to meet upper management.

9:48 a.m.— Question posed to the group by VP Marketing: If you had one superpower, what would it be?

BC: Photographic memory
BS: The ability to mind-read and know what other people are thinking
DC: Five minutes to ponder the impact of the decision you just made (see into the future)
LJ: The ability to see into the future
TF: Time travel—observe and get actual/real perspective
TS: Wants a magic wand
JP: Wants super energy
JS: The power to be in two places at the same time
AM: Wisdom
PS: The ability to control other people's minds
MH: To also be in two places at the same time
FG: To have perfect employees
JH: To control time: stop and have enough time to do everything and then start time back up again

9:54 a.m.— Agenda overview

Handed out schedule of all interviewers/interviewees. Everyone is to call Terry or Mabel to obtain information about assigned interviewee's schedule and availability.

Shift hours run: 7 a.m. – 3 p.m., days
                     3 p.m. – 11 p.m., afternoons
                     11 p.m. – 7 a.m., midnights

Copies of the Staff and Resident Interview Guide will be provided, and a master copy of both was given to Tony.

10 a.m.— Handed out meeting notes from 4/29 meeting
    Reviewed notes

A table of "wish list" items will be created and quantified so we can see each wished-for item and the number of times it was mentioned in the interviews.

DESIGN PHASE
A handout was given to the group. We are trying to do a positive revolution of change. There are things we can do now that do not cost money. When we hit census, a $200 census incentive will be added to the monthly budget. When we exceed census, we will be able to do more things. Looking at the data, (JS) came up with eight things—four can be implemented next week, and four will need help.

DISCOVERY
Appreciating—critical to people. We have chosen four topics that we discovered and turned into possibility statements. Take an idea and turn it into a possibility statement. The four topics are as follows:
1. Resident Loyalty
2. Provider of Choice
3. The Exception Team—Teamwork
4. Appreciation

Making everyone understood—take time to be an active listener.

Design ⇒ What should be the ideal? Construct possibilities.

Destiny ⇒ After we leave, how do you continue to keep this going? Cycle—every six months conduct another discovery/inquiry, find consensus.

Getting to transformational topics:

Ideas: Extra care, shoe untied, customer service: What specifically
is this? Define and demonstrate. How do you change mind-set?
Develop happier employees (via appreciation programs) to change
culture. By doing things for the employees, leading by example.
Change starts one step at a time. Have policy for employees to use.

10:30 a.m.— Two ways to deal with things (after we finish):

1. Focus on problem
2. Ask what possibilities exist that we haven't thought about yet.
   The smallest change makes the biggest impact.

Four Fundamental Questions (from handout):

Discover optimal margins—census.

DESIGN PHASE
The social-technological architecture:

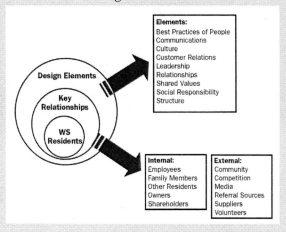

Ingredients: The themes from the interviews.

Key Relationships—Who's affected? How does it affect the center?

You design what you want and then make it happen in *Destiny*
phase, creating a grand possibility statement.

Department heads are part of the core team, must extend to a larger group and get rid of the "us versus them."

**Idea: Stress Call: pick up page—"meet me in the dining room," play the Hustle.

11:15 a.m. – Noon— Theme Exercise

Topic: Provider of Choice

As a group we:
1. Identified the inner circle: family, residents, responsible party (guardian, lawyer, and so on), and staff. This is whom we are providing care for.

2. Identified the next outer circle: Key Relationships: community, corporate office, referral sources, FIA and hospitals, transportation (taxis, bus pickups), and volunteers.

3. Identified outer circle components: Elements that affect the center and being a provider of choice: training (i.e., CPR, new-employee orientation, consistent care), culture, leadership, strategy (continuous), energy/life, activities, stability, and so on.

What makes our center the provider of choice? What is it that people would say makes us the best provider of care? What does our "ideal" center consist of?

We brainstormed the following list to answer the last question. Each team member got to vote for the four top elements on the list that he or she thought most significantly impacted the center's ability to become the provider of choice. The chart illustrates the number of votes each item received. (Items in bold were the top picks.)

Ideal Environment	Team Members				
Physical Plant					
Clean	•	•	•		
Fun	•	•	•	•	
Friendly	•				
Services (i.e., medical, nonmedical)	•				
Security/Comfort	•				
Delicious food	•	•	•		
Highly Trained Staff	•	•	•	•	•
Empathetic Staff					
Mentor System					
Concierge/Amenities (i.e., massage therapy, cable TV, and so on)	•				
Energy/Life	•				
Activities	•	•			

We also brainstormed what makes the "ideal" food environment so great. We came up with the following:
- Taste
- Quality and quantity
- Variety and choice
- Presentation
- Ambience/atmosphere
- Special meals/themes
- Salad bar

We then constructed the possibility statement using the elements that were the most frequently selected.

Provider of Choice Possibility Statement:
... We are the provider of choice because we have a high-quality, trained, experienced, and caring staff to meet the needs of our residents. We create a positive culture that radiates energy and life through a superior dining experience and activities that encourage participation and increase the quality of our residents' lives. We offer a fun, clean, and friendly community that caters to the individual's needs ...

Topic: Resident Loyalty
- Identified the inner circle: Wayne Seniors residents
- Identified the components of the next outer circle: Key Relationships: referral sources, guardians, families, staff (food), volunteers, and RA
- Identified the outer circle components: social responsibility, follow-up, follow-through, culture, systems, customer relations, education, and community

The following was the result of a brainstorm session on the definition of resident loyalty: What makes a resident loyal?

Resident Loyalty:
- Relation building, show loyalty to family members, referrals
- Consistency—same-grade service (temp/resident), what? Follow-up and through
- Genuine vested interest, how? Know thy resident, know what is important (by listening)
- Compassion—staff residents (extended family)
- Knowledge—(staff), why? In what they do (e.g., tie shoe, mash potatoes); level of service
- Finance—(trust), at ease; What are we doing with their money? Budgeting, amenities, balance checkbooks, manage money, keep independence; demonstrate by staff being members
- Physical plant

Common Parts among the Group
- Trust
- Compassion
- Interest
- Knowledge
- Dedication
- Listening
- Relationships (effective)
- Respect

Each member of the group wrote an individual possibility statement based on the definition brainstorm elements of resident loyalty. The combined possibility statement is as follows:

Resident Loyalty Possibility Statement:

At Wayne Seniors, residents are our lifeline. We maintain this lifeline by building relationships with our residents and their families to ensure a caring, consistent, and positive living experience.

We always strive to nurture relationships by creating an environment of listening, understanding, and trust.

Residents trust us with their lives—a responsibility we hold sacred. We earn trust through unwavering commitment to superior care, tempered with compassion and respect.

To provide superior care, we provide knowledge to residents, staff, and families to ensure consistent and compassionate service delivery.

With dedication to these ideals, Wayne Center for Seniors nurtures resident loyalty, thereby effectively serving the community.

7

Destiny:
What Will Be?

"Allow yourself to dream and you will discover that destiny is yours to design."

—Jackie Stavros

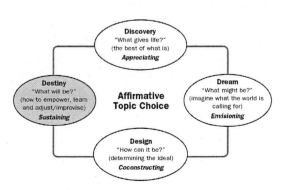

The final phase of the 4-D Cycle is known as *Destiny* (sometimes called Delivery). The goal of the *Destiny* phase is to ensure that the dream can be realized. The AI perspective looks at the role of improvisation in building appreciative management into the fabric of organizational culture. The design team publicly declares intended actions and asks for organization-wide support from every level. Self-selected groups plan the next steps for institutionalization and continued vitality. This is where the dream becomes reality.

Like the other phases, *Destiny* is systematic in terms of accommodating and continuing dialogue. Provocative propositions can be revised and updated. Additional AI interviewing may take place with new members in the organization and/or new questions posed for existing members.

The *Destiny* phase represents the conclusion of the *Discovery*, *Dream*, and *Design* phases and the beginning of the evolving creation of an "appreciative learning culture." This chapter explores both aspects of the *Destiny* phase:

- Aligning the actual organization with the provocative propositions created in the Design phase
- Building AI learning competencies into the culture

The techniques associated with the final phase of the 4-D Cycle spring from self-organized groups. They often resemble Open Space processes. Individuals and small groups self-organize to implement the Design statements (provocative propositions). This approach involves neither prioritization of needs nor an imposed sequence of concerns. Instead, people who are passionate about implementing a particular aspect of the design step forward and join with like-spirited collaborators. It is a time of continuous organizational learning, adjustment, and improvisation.

As a result of the extensive involvement of large numbers of people in the *Discovery*, *Dream*, and *Design* phases, collective focus is centered on actions to be taken. The often massive number of people engaged in interviews, large-group meetings, and critical decision making help participants get a strong sense of what the organization is about and how they can contribute to the future through their personal actions. It is a time of continuous innovation and inquiry, which continues on to the implementation stage within the newly created social architecture.

The chapter begins with the rationale of this phase's name change—from *Delivery* to *Destiny*. Following this, a summarization of Frank Barrett's material on appreciative learning cultures helps organizations and change leaders learn how to build AI-based learning competencies. The chapter also highlights GTE in its Destiny phase and concludes with *Destiny*-phase Case Clippings from the Hunter Douglas story. Excerpts from this study illustrate the outcomes that were experienced upon completion of the initial *Destiny* phase of inquiry and illustrate how the organization continues to use AI concepts and applications ten years later. The connections between the four phases, along with the outcomes that such an approach can deliver, are quite apparent and are sustainable over time.

Rethinking Destiny

In the early years of AI work, the fourth *D* was called *Delivery*. This phase emphasizes planning for continuous learning, adjustment, and improvisation in the service of shared ideals. It was viewed as a time for action planning, developing implementation strategies, and dealing with conventional challenges of sustainability. But the word *delivery* did not go far enough. It did not convey the sense of liberation that AI practitioners were experiencing. A perfect example is the well-documented hotel case *The Medic Inn*, where an organization transformed itself from a one-star to a four-star hotel by using AI and literally putting a moratorium on all the traditional problem-solving efforts it had been using.

AI practitioners soon discovered that momentum for change and long-term sustainability increased as traditional "delivery" ideas of action planning, monitoring progress, and building implementation strategies were abandoned. In several of the most exciting cases, the substitution was to focus on giving AI away to everyone and then stepping back.

The GTE (now Verizon) story told in the Introduction of this handbook (refer to the AI Insight) is still unfolding. It shows that organizational change needs to look more like an inspired movement than a neatly packaged or engineered product. Dan Young, the head of organizational development at GTE, and his colleagues Maureen Garrison and Jean Moore call it "organizing for change from the grassroots to the frontline." It can be considered the path of positive protest or a strategy for positive subversion. Whatever it is called, it is virtually unstoppable once it is up and running.

GTE calls it the Positive Change Network (PCN). GTE trained 2,000 people in AI so anyone could use it anywhere in the organization to launch a positive change initiative. One especially dramatic moment gives the sense of improvisation.[1]

> The headline article in GTE Together described what was spreading as a grassroots movement to build the new GTE. Initiated as a pilot training to see what would happen if the tools and theories of Appreciative Inquiry were made available to frontline employees, things started taking off. All of a sudden, without any

---

1 See Cooperrider, D., & Whitney, D. (2000). *Collaborating for change: Appreciative inquiry.* San Francisco: Berrett-Koehler.

permission, frontline employees are launching interview studies into positive topics like innovation, inspired leadership, revolutionary customer responsiveness, labor-management partnerships, and "fun." Fresh out of a training session on AI, one employee, for example, does 200 interviews into the positive core of a major call center. Who is going to say "no" to a complimentary request like, "Would you help me out? I'm really trying to find out more about the best innovations developing in your area, and I see you as someone who could really give me new insight into creating settings where innovation can happen. It is part of my leadership development. Do you have time for an interview? I would be glad to share my learnings with you later!"

Soon the topics are finding their way into meetings, corridor conversations, and senior planning sessions. In other words the questions, enthusiastically received, are changing corporate attention, language, agendas, and learnings. Many start brainstorming applications for AI. Lists are endless. Ever done focus groups with the 100% satisfied customer? How about changing call center measures? What would happen if we replaced the entire deficit measures with equally powerful measures of the positive? How can we revitalize the TQM groups, demoralized by one fishbone analysis after another? What would happen if we augmented variance analysis with depth studies that help people to dream and define the very visions of quality standards? How about a star stories program to generate a narrative-rich environment where customers are asked to share stories of encounters with exceptional employees? How about a gathering with senior executives so we can celebrate our learnings with them, share with them how seeing the positive has changed our work and family lives, and even recruit them to join the PCN?

The pilot had acquired a momentum all its own. The immediate response, an avalanche of requests for participation, confirmed that large numbers of people at GTE were ready to be called to the task of positive change. To grow the network by the hundreds, even thousands, GTE decided to do a ten-region training session, all linked and downloaded by satellite conferencing. A successful pilot of three sites confirmed that the same kind of energy and response could happen through distance technologies. Quite suddenly, the power of a thousand-person network caught people's attention. Very rapidly, by connecting and consistently noticing breakthroughs, new patterns of organizing could become commonplace knowledge. Changes could happen not by organized confrontation, diagnosis, burning platforms, or piecemeal reform, but through irresistibly vibrant and real visions. PCN was becoming a lightning rod for energy and enthusiasm that was previously underestimated.

Then the unions raised questions. There were serious concerns, including the fact that they were not consulted in the early stages. The employees were told the initiative was over. There was to be a meeting of the unions and GTE at the Federal Mediation Offices in Washington, DC, to put the whole thing to rest.

But at the meeting, leaders from both groups recognized something fresh and unique about AI. They agreed to bring 200 union leaders together for a two-day introduction. Their purpose was to evaluate AI to see if it should have any place in GTE's future. A month later as the session began, the room was full of tension and overt hostility. During the course of the two-day session, the group of 250 went from polarized hostility to appreciative dialogue. Then there was the moment of decision. Thirty tables of eight were instructed to evaluate the ideas and cast a vote as a group: "Yes, we endorse moving forward with AI" or "No, we withhold endorsement." For 30 minutes the groups deliberated. Tensions were high. The vote was called:

> Table 1, how do you vote? The response was ready: We vote 100% for moving forward with AI and believe this is a historic opportunity for the whole organization.
>
> Then the next table: We vote 100% with a caveat that every person at GTE have the opportunity to get the AI training and that all projects going forward be done in partnership with the unions and the company.

On and on the vote went. Thirty tables spoke. Then thirty tables voted. Every one voted to move forward. The outcome was stunning. Eight months later AI was combined with the "conflictive partnership" model of the Federal Mediation Services at the kickoff session announcing a new era of partnership. The historic Statement of Partnership stated:

> The company and the unions realize that traditional adversarial labor-management relations must change in order to adapt to the new global telecommunications marketplace. It is difficult to move to cooperation in one quantum leap. However, the company and the unions have agreed to move in a new direction. This new direction emphasizes partnership.

This story boldly illustrates how AI can accelerate the nonlinear interaction of organizational breakthroughs. Putting historic, positive traditions together with strengths creates a "convergence zone," facilitating the collective repatterning of human systems. At some point, apparently minor positive discoveries connect in an accelerating manner. Suddenly, quantum change, a jump from one state to the next that cannot be achieved through incremental change alone, becomes possible.

The *Destiny* phase of AI suggests what is needed: the networklike structures that liberate not only the daily search into qualities and elements of an organization's positive core but also the establishment of a convergence zone for people to empower one another to connect, cooperate, and cocreate. Changes never thought possible are suddenly and democratically mobilized when people constructively appropriate the power of the positive core and simply "let go" of accounts of the negative.

Creating Appreciative Learning Cultures

An important task for an organizational leader is to create cultures in which members can explore, experiment, extend capabilities, improvise, and anticipate customers' unspoken needs. Frank Barrett has called such cultures **appreciative learning cultures**.

Organizations need to innovate and strive to create new ideas and new products. The push for innovation requires a different kind of learning, one that goes beyond adapting to challenges and solving problems. Instead, such learning focuses on imagining possibilities and on generating new ways of looking at the world. Innovation requires willingness to think outside the box. It involves an appreciative approach, an ability to see radical possibilities, and a willingness to go beyond the boundaries of problems.

The challenge in the *Destiny* phase is to do just that. Whether trying to create a radically new, innovative organization or tweaking an already well-run organization, appreciative learning cultures nurture innovative thinking by creating a positive focus, a sense of meaning, and systems that encourage collaboration.

To review: AI begins with the assumption that something in the organization is working well. When engaged in appreciative learning, managers attempt to discover, describe, and explain those exceptional moments in which the system functioned well, those moments when members were highly motivated and their competencies and skills activated. The art of appreciation is the art of discovering and valuing those things that give life to the organization, of identifying what works well in the current organization. This positive approach creates what Peter Senge calls "generative conversations" as the dialogue expands from valuing the best of "what is" to envisioning "what might be." While problem solving emphasizes a dispassionate separation between observer and observed, appreciation is a passionate, absorbing endeavor. Appreciation involves the investment of emotional and cognitive energy to create a positive image of a desired future.

Likewise, appreciative learning cultures accentuate the successes of the past, evoke images of possible futures, and create a spirit of ongoing inquiry that empowers members to new levels of activity.

Destiny: An Improvisational Capacity

AI has achieved remarkable results in the areas of productivity improvement, efficiency, and performance. However, the "goal" of the process is to create highly improvisational organizations. These are organizations that, according to Frank Barrett, demonstrate consistent strength in four key kinds of competence: affirmative, expansive, generative, and collaborative.[2] In the end, these four areas of competence are expanded through ongoing application of the skills applied during *Discovery, Dream, Design,* and *Destiny.*

- *Affirmative Competence.* The organization draws on the human capacity to appreciate positive possibilities by selectively focusing on current and past strengths, successes, and potentials. In nurturing affirmative competence, leaders of a high-performing organization celebrate members' achievements, directing attention to members' strengths as the source of the organization's vitality.
- *Expansive Competence.* The organization challenges habits and conventional practices, provoking members to experiment in the margins. It makes expansive promises that challenge members to stretch in new directions, and it evokes a set of higher values and ideals that inspire members to passionate engagement. High-performing organizations create a vision that challenges members by encouraging them to go beyond familiar ways of thinking; these organizations provoke members to stretch beyond what have seemed to be reasonable limits.
- *Generative Competence.* The organization constructs integrative systems that allow members to see the results of their actions, to recognize that they are making a meaningful contribution, and to experience a sense of progress. High-performing organizations inspire members' best efforts. These systems include elaborate and timely feedback so mem-

---

2 Refer to Barrett, F. (1998). Creativity and improvisation in jazz and organizations: Implications for organizational learning. *Organization Science,* 9(5), 605–622.

bers sense that they are contributing to a meaningful purpose. In particular, it is important for people to experience progress, to see that their day-to-day tasks make a difference. When members perceive that their efforts are contributing toward a desired goal, they are more likely to feel a sense of hope and empowerment.

- *Collaborative Competence.* The organization creates forums in which members engage in ongoing dialogue and exchange diverse perspectives to transform systems. Collaborative systems that allow for dialogue promote the articulation of multiple perspectives and encourage continuous, active debate. The high-performing organization creates the environment that fosters participation and highly committed work arrangements.

Injecting appreciation and inquiry into the way work is completed requires some of the same "design elements" that were central to the original crafting of provocative propositions. High-impact systems into which AI can be integrated can make this way of working "everyday and ordinary" rather than a distinct cultural or change program that fades away. Table 7.1 identifies areas in which AI and the 4-D Cycle can be integrated into business operations.

Table 7.1 Areas for Integrating AI into Business Operations

Organization Design	Employee Satisfaction	Process Improvement	Learning & Development	Measure-ment	Customer Satisfaction	Planning
Communication Architecture	Employee Orientation	Work Process Redesign	Supervisory Development	Performance Management	Focus Groups & Surveys	Strategic
Joint Ventures	Staffing & Development	Continuous Quality Improvement	Leadership & Management Development	Metric Standards	Customer Feedback	Business
Strategic Alliances	Coaching	Benchmarking	Team Development	Reward & Recognition	Supplier Feedback Systems	Operations
	Diversity Initiatives	Innovations	Training	Surveys	Public Relations	Marketing

There is no one best way to carry out the *Destiny* phase. Each organization has chosen a different approach to implementing and sustaining the design from the dream that it discovered. One example is still unfolding in the *Destiny* phase of the Hunter Douglas story. In 1993, Hunter Douglas Window Fashions Division (HDWFD) embarked on a whole-system AI process. Branded "Focus 2000," the purpose of the process was to enhance employee engagement in creating the future of the organization. In addition, it aimed to build leadership bench strength needed for the fast-growing, highly successful organization. The entire workforce of 950 people was involved in discovering best practices and creating the future. They interviewed employees, customers, vendors, and members of their local community. They hosted a 100-person AI Summit. From the *Design* to *Destiny* phase of this event, 14 action teams were launched as "innovation teams" to coconstruct their future. The results were **transformative** for the organization and its employees.

The following Case Clipping is a snapshot of the Hunter Douglas sustained and continuous applications of AI—delivering its destiny. This is a seminal case that undeniably demonstrates the power of AI to mobilize a system in an ongoing process of sustainable positive change. Many years after the company's original exposure to AI, Hunter Douglas's stakeholders recognize and continue to acknowledge its "unique" approach to organizing—that it has at its foundation the affirmative, relational, and inspirational core of the AI 4-D Cycle. Hunter Douglas's extraordinary ten-year commitment to the AI philosophy is described in depth in the *The Power of Appreciative Inquiry* (Berrett-Koehler, 2005) by Diana Whitney and Amanda Trosten-Bloom.

Case Clippings:
Hunter Douglas Window Fashions Division[3]

Hunter Douglas Window Fashions Division is the largest and most profitable division of the Hunter Douglas Group. Innovating, manufacturing, and fabricating high-end window covering products, the division experienced a ten-year period of off-the-chart growth and leadership transitions during the late eighties and early nineties, before the "growth pains" set in. On the heels of so many changes, people were suddenly challenged with a multitude of directions and conflicting priorities when attempting to define the future. Communication gaps between leadership and the general workforce, between business units, and across functions made it difficult for people to act in service of overall organizational goals. Not surprisingly, employee satisfaction scores began to drop, turnover increased, and employees felt overloaded to a level that reduced their initiative and ability to contribute.

*Hunter Douglas leaders were looking for a change, which led to the launch of an AI process they branded "Focus 2000." Targeting **whole-system culture transformation**, they designed a process where the intended outcomes were to:*

  • *Create a collective vision that could engage and excite the entire organization and its stakeholders.*

3 Special thanks to Rick Pellet, president of Hunter Douglas Windows Fashion Division, and Mike Burns, vice president of Human Resources, for embracing AI and to Diana Sadighi, director of Human Resources, for carrying its legacy forward.

- *Re-instill a sense of creativity, flexibility, intimacy, and community throughout the organization.*
- *Enhance the skills of existing leadership and build bench strength by identifying and training future leaders.*
- *Build communication and collaboration between management and the general workforce, across business units, and between operations and support functions.*
- *Create a company culture based on values that challenged the organization and the employees to achieve higher levels of involvement, responsibility, and community.*

In the first wave of AI work (1998), more than half of the 1,000-person workforce participated in a six-month discovery that was transformational. For example, a line employee discovered a best practice in a sister business unit that he felt empowered to transport into his own organization. The practice, when adapted, eliminated the need to purchase three new fabric printing machines, which dropped $350,000 from the company bottom line. Similarly, a third-shift fabricator positively affected relationships with a group of third-shift immigrant employees and ultimately volunteered to coordinate an English as a second language (ESL) program that would enable her colleagues to gain the tools needed to access personal and professional advancement opportunities.

The Window Fashions Division's initial period of Discovery concluded with a 100-person summit involving employees, customers, suppliers, and community members. The immediate outcome of this summit was the initiation of 14 action groups, including a group that eventually created one of the most comprehensive and accessible corporate universities in Colorado. Indeed, a number of culture- and employee-focused initiatives birthed at the first Focus 2000 summit reduced turnover from 42% to 29% over a two-year period and ultimately contributed to the Window Fashions Division being named one of the top ten places to work in Denver for 2004 and in Colorado for 2006.

But Hunter Douglas leaders weren't yet satisfied. They chose to move beyond their original culture transformation objectives and apply the AI process to the business of the business. Six months after the original summit, they organized a whole-system strategic planning conference, engaging large segments of the workforce in discovering the organization's core capabilities and strategic opportunities and crafting a ten-year vision for the company's future. As a direct result of this conference, the company leveraged its core technology into a new arena, eventually spinning off a sister organization specializing in an acoustical product for commercial establishments.

And then, beginning in 2000, they combined AI with a more traditional approach to process improvement, engaging the entire workforce in quality improvement initiatives that helped fulfill the promise of one of their original provocative propositions: "Customers eagerly do business with us because we are easy to do business with." Six years later these improvement projects have increased productivity, improved product quality, dramatically reduced workplace injuries, and yielded more than $25 million dollars in cost savings and waste reduction between 1996 and 2006.

The following pages demonstrate how the 4-D Cycle unfolds by showing how a single topic (education) evolves from the initial topic selection through action. In addition, samples are provided for the Leadership and Employee Introductory meetings that demonstrate how to build whole-system commitment to an AI process from start to finish. This case study shows how affirmative topic choices led to discovery, organizational learning, dream, design, and innovative actions.

The Case Clippings include:
- *Initial Topic Selection from Concept to Design*
- *Employee Interview Guide*
- *Interview Summary Sheet*
- *Design Statements*

Initial Topic Selection: From Discovery to Destiny: AI Full Cycle

Topic Selection—Education: Given that Hunter Douglas was seeking to build the informal leadership capacities of its workforce, education was of prime interest to the 90-person topic selection team. It was selected as one of five affirmative topics.

Appreciative Interview Question: Two weeks after the selection of the topics, a ten-person subgroup finalized the interview guide and published the following question related to the topic of education.

Education: Knowledge empowers people, and people power Hunter Douglas. We each contribute to Hunter Douglas's position of market leadership through personal knowledge of our jobs and equipment, other functions in the company, our customers, our competition, and the industry.

To maintain our position as market leaders, we must continue to invest in each employee's training and education through individual coaching, challenging work assignments, cross training, tuition assistance, on- and off-site classes, and family scholarships for our children.

1. If knowledge empowers people and people power Hunter Douglas, what kind of learning opportunities would turbo-charge Hunter Douglas?
2. If you could learn more about our customers, our competitors, the industry, and all functions of our company, how would that information help you take ownership in your role for continued success at Hunter Douglas?
3. What is the best training you ever experienced? Why? How did it influence your development as a professional? How did it influence the training you passed on to others?
4. Reflecting on your past and where you are today, what types of training have proven most beneficial to you?
5. Robert Fulghum wrote a book entitled *All I Really Need to Know I Learned in Kindergarten*. If this were kindergarten, what would you like to learn for the future?

Sense-Making: Three months and 500 interviews later, hundreds of people had responded to this and four other questions. A group of 30 people gathered for two days of sense-making. Sticky notes were everywhere, and conversations were energetic.

The Report: Two weeks later a written report went to press, the Inquirer 2000 Special Edition. It was a newspaper-like report distributed to the entire workforce, including 100 people who would attend the upcoming three-day summit.

Dream: The following excerpts from the Inquirer 2000 reflect the dreams shared in the interview process.

HD WFD Supports People Through Training and Education

In a series of discussions, Synthesis team members exploring the topic of education made two important discoveries:

First, Hunter Douglas employees, customers, suppliers, and community members are committed to enhancing their work performance, career potential, and relationship with Hunter Douglas through job-related training.

Second, and perhaps more striking, employees look to the company to support their development as human beings. Some of the richest comments, stories, and dreams referred to people's desire for education, for skills that will help them not only live their lives better but also become stronger on the job. Many interviewees shared a dream that HD would help educate them for higher levels of personal as well as professional success.

Those who gave details suggested classes and programs that would help them in their personal lives as well as at work. These offerings would include a wellness program on how health is essential to a good attitude and good performance. Others asked for classes in stress and money management. Still others shared dreams for access to experts in career and life counseling, including an on-campus career guidance center or counselor. They believed this resource would help people understand the steps needed to better themselves at work and at home.

Possibility Design Statement: Turn the clock forward again by a month. It's the second day of the summit. Participants are self-organizing into "design teams." Not surprisingly, one of the seven design statements is on the topic of education. Here is the Education Design Statement:

> Education and training are cornerstones of Hunter Douglas. Individuals partner with the company to achieve a sense of inner purpose, direction, and continuous growth. This, in turn, nurtures the strength and confidence people need to achieve their full personal and professional potential.
>
> Hunter Douglas sponsors a learning center, Hunter Douglas University (HDU), which provides such things as mentoring, customer training, career counseling, and skills development.

The *Design* phase interprets the organization's dreams about the future. It is the collective commitments, principles, processes, actions, programs, structure, and tasks necessary to make the dream come alive.

Destiny: It is now the third day of the summit. All 100 participants have self-organized into groups that have been inspired by the seven Design Statements. Several of the 14 groups deal with issues of education, training, and development.

Fast-forward now in the still-unfolding *Destiny* phase. Beginning six months later, the following are implemented within the HDWFD:

- **A formal mentorship program.** With an advisory team consisting of both leaders and floor staff, this program solicits mentors and matches them with people requesting mentoring. It offers formal "accreditation" for people's personnel files. More than 30 people completed the program within the first year.

- **Appointment of a half-time career planning professional.** This person—a latecomer to the AI effort—bids for and is awarded a job transfer. He or she goes through formal training in career planning and moves to spending half of his or her time at this activity, with the other half dedicated to internal communication (in response to one of the other Design Statements).
- **Establishment of an "English as a Second Language" program.** One of the original third-shift employees conducted interviews during the original inquiry with some of the Laotian refugees who were employed on her shift, people she had seen but had never spoken to. Shocked and saddened by some of what she learned in her conversations, she informally committed herself to teaching English on her lunch hour in order to "make right" on the wrong that fate had done to her colleagues.

   She approached the vice president of Human Resources about her intention. He talked her into serving as on-site coordinator for the local community college's professionally developed ESL classes. Human Resources had been trying to get these classes under way for more than two years, having been unable to get a critical mass of non-English speaking employees to sign up for the classes.
- **Initiation of a state-of-the-art "new-hire orientation" program.** This is yet another program that the Human Resources Department had tried unsuccessfully to design for more three years. Following the summit, it becomes a regular monthly event. A year or so after its initial implementation, long-time employees begin rotating through the program. The innovation team that designs this program commits that every employee will develop a sense of his or her relationship to the entire business.
- **Establishment of a Hunter Douglas University.** Initially launched as a virtual university, it becomes the clearinghouse for all on- and off-campus classes available to HD employees. A year later the company breaks ground on an on-site learning center, dubbed Hunter Douglas University (HDU). A year after that, HDU contains two classrooms (each seating up to 50 people and fully equipped with sound and visual equipment and a breakdown wall between rooms), two conference rooms, a computer laboratory, and a library. It has a kitchen and a serving area for on-site training programs.

   In its first two years of existence, HDU hosted hundreds of training and planning meetings, several of which included 100 or more people. Its regular schedule now includes training classes in focus on excellence (continuous improvement), English as a second language, interaction management for supervisors, Dale Carnegie, personal financial planning, and Toastmasters training for presenters.

Results: A year after the initial inquiry, HDWFD conducted a mini AI interview. The first question in the inquiry solicited people's input on what is best within the division ... most worthy of holding on to ... with the greatest capacity to influence the organization positively as it grew. Almost to a person, the response was "this company's commitment to employee and customer training and education is second to none."

This story is a clear reminder that organizations move in the direction of the things they study. Therefore, it is necessary to continue to seek ways to gain a deeper understanding of those things that give life to an organization and its people. Finding ways to tell the stories, to build the conversations, and to enhance the relationships and dialogue will bring the best to life.

Employee Interview Guide

Hunter Douglas Window Fashions Division
Interview Guide

Name: _____ Phone Ext. (if available):_____

Position: _____

Business Unit/Function: _____

Years of Service: _____ Date: _____

Interviewed by: _____

OPENING

Thank you for participating. I'm looking forward to what I'll be learning from this conversation, and I hope it will be a rewarding experience for you as well. As Rick Pellett explained in his letter to you, these interviews are critical to the future of our company.

Many times in interviews, we try to ask questions about things that aren't working well so we can fix them. This time we are going to approach things from a different angle. We are going to find out about your experiences of success here at Hunter Douglas or in other parts of your life so we can find ways to create more of these types of experiences in our organization.

Later in the summer, everyone in the Window Fashions Division will have been interviewed. At that time, everybody's input will be compiled to identify the qualities that make Hunter Douglas a rewarding place to work. With those qualities as a foundation, we will dream about our vision for the year 2000 and beyond.

There are just a few more things you'll want to know about this process. Our conversation will last between 1-1/2 and 2 hours. I'm going to take notes as we talk. Sometimes if you tell a really great story or say something in a way that's especially striking, I might write down what you say word for word. But the information I collect will still be confidential and anonymous unless you ask to have your name attached to it. I am the only person who will see the detailed notes from this interview. A summary of our conversation will be turned into an independent consultant, who will work with a group of people later in the summer to pull together all of our results.

Now before we begin, do you have any questions? Okay, then. Let's get started.

1. What were your initial excitements and impressions when you first joined the company?

2. What has been your most positive or pleasurable experience since you've been here?

3. Without being humble, explain what you value most about:
   - Yourself.
   - The people you work with.
   - Your business unit or functional area here at Hunter Douglas.

PEOPLE

The foundation of any great organization lies in the strengths of its people. The experiences and diverse backgrounds are assets that any organization must utilize to be successful. When we look at Hunter Douglas, it is obvious why it has been so successful. Looking back, we have grown from a small company to a worldwide market leader. How have the people contributed to this success? Hunter Douglas has fostered personal growth through teamwork, two-way respect, communication, and creativity.

When employees have the freedom to express themselves openly and to be involved in the decisions that affect their future, they gain confidence and authority to perform at their best.

1. Describe the most memorable event that illustrates your contribution to the success of a team or an organization. What strengths did you bring to that success?
2. Reflect on someone in your life you have admired and describe his or her qualities. How do you feel those qualities have influenced your growth?
3. If you could look into a crystal ball and see the haute of Hunter Douglas and its employees, what would you like to see? How do you think we can get there?

EDUCATION

Knowledge empowers people, and people power Hunter Douglas. We each contribute to Hunter Douglas's position of market leadership through personal knowledge of our jobs and equipment, other functions in the company, our customers, our competition, and the industry. To maintain our position as market leaders, we must continue to invest in each employee's training and education through:

- Individual coaching.
- Challenging work assignments.
- Job cross training.
- Tuition assistance.
- On- and off-site classes.
- Family scholarships for our children.

1. If knowledge empowers people and people power Hunter Douglas, what kind of learning opportunities would turbo-charge Hunter Douglas?

2. If you could learn more about our customers, our competitors, the industry, and all functions of our company, how would that information help you take ownership in your role for continued success at Hunter Douglas?

3. What is the best training you have ever experienced? Why?
   - How did this influence your development as a professional?
   - How did it influence the training you passed on to others?

4. Reflecting on your past and where you are today, what types of training have proven most beneficial to you?

5. Robert Fulghum wrote a book entitled *All I Really Need to Know I Learned in Kindergarten*. If this were kindergarten, what would you like to learn for the future?

QUALITY OF LIFE

Quality of life is achieved, in part, through a balance of work and family. By ensuring personal and professional well-being, employees can reach their highest level of performance and self-satisfaction.

Throughout the past, Hunter Douglas has been sensitive to its employees' changing personal and professional needs through flexibility and awareness. We can ensure success today and in the future by continuing to acknowledge this need for balance.

1. Describe your definition of what a perfectly balanced personal and professional life is.

2. Envision a time when you were able to balance the personal and professional aspects of your life.
   - Describe how this balance was achieved.
   - What was it about the experience that made you feel this balance?

3. If you could travel over the rainbow, what do you think the quality of life would be like there?

COMMUNICATION

An ongoing and productive exchange of information and creative ideas is vital to the success of Hunter Douglas. Information about how our business is doing, our customers and competition, our plans for the future, and business processes in other parts of the company allows each of us to make the most effective decisions possible. As we grow, this kind of complete communication ensures our continued success in delivering innovative and quality products to our customers.

By exercising active listening and two-way communication, we secure our future as a fair and open organization where every voice is heard.

1. Describe the best example you have experienced of open two-way communication?
   - What did you learn from that experience?
   - How have you applied this to your daily interactions (for example, with your supervisor, coworkers, other business units, customers, and suppliers)?

2. What do you believe would be the ideal situation in which your questions, concerns, or ideas could be heard and responded to?

3. What do you foresee as the most effective process of receiving Hunter Douglas information concerning products, employees, competitors, and the Window Fashions industry?

MORALE

We, as a company, appreciate the importance of each individual's contributions to our success. Recognition, commitment to excellence, and a sense of being stretched or challenged provided the motivation to do our best and go beyond our realm of responsibility. This, in turn, creates:
- Job satisfaction.
- Self-worth.
- A sense of value.
- Ownership.

Continuous focus on positive morale ensures a fun and appreciative work environment.

1. When you reflect on your own experiences, tell me about a high point in your life that gave you a sense of ownership and value.
2. Think of someone who brings a sense of value and pride to his or her job and how he or she projects this level of ownership toward his or her peers. Tell me about it.
3. How do you think receiving recognition from your leadership and others and having the resources and equipment needed to get the job done would contribute to morale?
4. How can we continue to improve morale, build camaraderie, and have fun in the workplace?

CLOSING

In conclusion, I'd like to ask you just a few final questions.

1. What direction would you like to see yourself going with Hunter Douglas in the future?
2. Five years from now, your best friend wants to work for Hunter Douglas. What would you like to be able to tell him or her?
3. If you had three blank memos signed by Rick Pellett, the general manager of Window Fashions, that would become company policy, how would you use them?

4. In your opinion, what was the highlight of this interview? What do you hope comes out of this process?

5. Would you like to become a future Focus 2000 interviewer? If so, it will involve meeting with between two and five people over the next month or so using the same process you and I just used.

   (Interviewer Note: Fill out the Future Interviewer Notice at the end of this packet for those who say yes to this question.)

Interview Summary Sheet

Information requested from each interviewer

- Complete in full after each interview.
- Be sure to gather information from *each section* of the Interview Guide.
- If possible, review your notes with your interviewee before submitting.

What were the best quotes that came out of this interview?

What were the best stories that came out of this interview?

What were the best practices or specific recommendations that you heard reflected in your conversation?

Interviewer Name _____

Interviewee Name (optional) _____

Date of Interview _____

Please complete this summary sheet within 30 minutes of your interview and send it promptly to the Focus 2000 mailbox in Building One.

Design Statements

Hunter Douglas Design Statements
Possibility Propositions

CREATIVITY

Hunter Douglas thrives on creativity. It is the source for new ideas, the lifeblood of the company, and the catalyst for positive change. It is the basis for leadership in products and processes that are both proprietary and innovative.

Hunter Douglas leads the industry in creative ideas that involve all of the company's stakeholders, including employees, customers, and suppliers. We vigorously promote a creative culture to help reinvent and improve products, services, and organizational and business processes. We actively solicit, implement, and reward ideas generated by all people.

We foster an environment that inspires unique ideas, and we provide resources and opportunities for people to develop their creativity and bring their ideas to fruition. Decision makers actively listen to all ideas to enhance creativity and enable people to realize their dreams.

LEADERSHIP

Visionary leadership permeates Hunter Douglas and is the catalyst for our success. Leadership exists in three areas: individual, managerial, and industry. We seek out and develop leadership qualities among our employees. Leadership strongly supports hands-on involvement and mentoring; defines leadership opportunities; and actively listens to all voices, all opinions, and all ideas with fairness and impartiality.

PEOPLE

HDWFD's success as a company is built on the ideas, dreams, and diversity of our people and business partners.

We encourage, challenge, and support people in the pursuit of their ideas, dreams, and aspirations through (1) utilizing and participating in the AI process, (2) enhancing the quality of life through the balance of work and personal life, (3) providing opportunities and resources for continuous personal and professional growth and, (4) providing a safe and open work environment while honoring and rewarding individual and team accomplishments.

The future of the company is dependent upon employees' participation, ownership, integrity, and respect for others. Commitment to people and their ideas ensures continued success, enhanced profitability, and product quality for Hunter Douglas and its partners, while resulting in happier, more productive people.

EDUCATION

Education and training are cornerstones of Hunter Douglas. Individuals partner with the company to achieve a sense of inner purpose, direction, and continuous growth. This, in turn, nurtures the strength and confidence people need to achieve their full personal and professional potential.

Hunter Douglas sponsors a learning center, Hunter Douglas University (HDU), which provides such things as:
- Mentoring.
- Customer training.
- Career counseling.
- Skills development.

COMMUNICATION

Hunter Douglas demands open, honest, high-quality, and ongoing communication among its employees, business partners, and communities. We provide all stakeholders the opportunity to express and be actively listened to on all ideas and opinions.

The organization:
- Promotes continuous two-way exchange of information and ideas across all cultures and languages.
- Actively shares the big picture through open access to all appropriate information about the company, its history, and its business environment.
- Maximizes use of the most effective communication tools.
- Expects individual ownership of and responsibility for effective communication.

CUSTOMERS

Customers are Hunter Douglas's lifeblood and future. We delight customers (fabricators, dealers, consumers, suppliers, employees, and the community) by understanding and exceeding their expectations in the areas of:
- Product quality and innovation.
- Customer service and technical support.
- Customer relations.
- Training and education.

- Community involvement.
- Promises kept.

We provide professional and seamless service, create strong partnerships, and significantly contribute to customer success. The Hunter Douglas family embraces customers through commitment to excellence, innovation, imagination, dreams, and "small company values." Our culture demands an atmosphere of respect, trust, integrity, honesty, reliability, and responsibility. We expand our customer base by nurturing current and new relationships. Customers eagerly do business with us because "we are easy to do business with." We set the benchmark for others to follow!

PRODUCTS

HDWFD's market leadership is built on the strong foundation of its products. Critical driving forces behind our market leadership are product innovation, improvements, quality, and marketing. We create high-fashion, high-function, and reliable branded products. In addition, we are committed to:

- Continually reinvent our business through the creation of profitable, new, proprietary products.
- Extend, defend, and continuously improve our existing products.

Our challenge is to develop and deliver "whole" products that provide total satisfaction for our fabricators, dealers, and consumers through:

- Creation of new products that are imaginative, fashionable, and robust.
- Thoughtfully designed and engineered products, with processes that have high yields, zero defects, and minimal return rates—and that are easy to install and fabricate.
- Products that are positioned and marketed effectively so their place in the market is easily understood by dealers and consumers.
- Supportive sampling and sales efforts that effectively communicate product features and benefits.
- Low-maintenance products that require minimal care and cleaning.

This results in products that consumers display with pride and enthusiasm.

Hunter Douglas Today

Ten years after the first AI initiative was launched, Hunter Douglas Window Fashions Division remains the largest, most profitable division in Hunter Douglas worldwide—and the leading window coverings innovator and manufacturer in the world. Now this division manufactures six different products (up from one in 1985), increasing revenues by 40 percent, yet with only a 13 percent increase in head count over the past ten years. How? The company continues to reap the benefits of the positive culture, strategic gains, and efficiencies imagined and implemented in the early years of its work with AI.

In the 1998 strategic planning summit, employees' vision was to leverage the proprietary technology in a new market: interior design. The company achieved this goal in 2003 when it developed and launched TechStyle Acoustical Ceilings. According to plan, it maintained focus on its "positive core" by spinning that business off and continuing to do what it does best—window coverings. Hunter Douglas Specialty Products currently manufactures and distributes innovative acoustic ceilings for the commercial market from a new Hunter Douglas campus in Thornton, Colorado.

If you wandered into a Hunter Douglas Window Fashions Division production facility today, what would you see or hear of Appreciative Inquiry? You would see or hear very little of the phrase itself. But of the essence, you would see and hear a great deal. The *Hunter Douglas Way*, as it's sometimes known, is to regularly engage mixed groups of people in studying what has worked in the past, imagining what might happen, and creating from there . . . in leveraging strengths, in changing the world through conversation. These AI-based patterns are permanently imprinted on the hearts and minds of Window Fashions Division employees—even those who were hired after the first several years of Appreciative Inquiry-based transformation and training.

Appreciative Inquiry has enabled Hunter Douglas to build on its positive core and to maintain its leadership through a decade of industry changes. It will continue to do so in the years to come.

Appreciative Inquiry Bibliography
(includes references cited within the handbook)

Adamson, J., Samuels, N., & Willoughby, G. (2002, March). Changing the way we change at Heathside School. *Managing Schools Today*.

AI Practitioner Collection CD 1998–2004. (2005, December 10). *AI Practitioner Journal*.

Anderson, H., Cooperrider D., Gergen, K., Gergen, M., McNamee, S., & Whitney, D. (2001). *The appreciative organization*. Chagrin Falls, OH: Taos Institute Publications.

Aram, J. D. (1990). Appreciative interchange: The force that makes cooperation possible. In S. Srivastva & D. L. Cooperrider (Eds.), *Appreciative management and leadership: The Power of Positive Thought and Action in Organization* (Rev. ed.). (pp. 175–204). Euclid, OH: Lakeshore Communications.

Ashcraft, M. (1998). *Fundamentals of cognition*. Reading, MA: Addison-Wesley-Longman.

Ashford, G., & Parry, J. (2001). *Integrating Aboriginal values into land use and resource management*. Winnipeg, Manitoba, Canada: International Institute for Sustainable Development/Skownan First Nation.

Ashford, G., & Patkar, S. (2001). *The positive path: Using appreciative inquiry in rural Indian communities*. Winnipeg, Manitoba, Canada: Kromar Printing Ltd.

Assistance, V. T. (1996). *Appreciative inquiry: An approach to organizational analysis and learning*. Rosslyn, VA: Volunteers in Technical Assistance.

Babcock, P. (2005, September). A calling for change. *Society for Human Resource Management, 50*.

Balousek, M. (2004, September 29). Downtown summit has ideas on freeing up owners. *Wisconsin State Journal*, Retrieved from http://www.madison.com/wsj.

Banaga, G. (1998). A spiritual path to organizational renewal. In S. Hammond & C. Royal (Eds.), *Lessons from the field: Applying appreciative inquiry* (pp. 260–271). Plano, TX: Practical Press, Inc.

Barrett, F. (1995). Creating appreciative learning cultures. *Organizational Dynamics, 24*(2), 36–49.

Barrett, F. (1999). Knowledge creating as dialogical accomplishment: A constructionist perspective. In A. Montuori & R. Purser (Eds.), *Social creativity: Volume 1* (pp. 133–151). Cresskill, NJ: Hampton Press.

Barrett, F. (2000). Cultivating an aesthetic of unfolding: Jazz improvisation as a self-organizing system. In S. Linstead & H. Hopfl (Eds.), *The aesthetics of organization* (pp. 228–245). London: Sage Publications.

Barrett, F. (2000). Learning to appreciate the sublime: Don't knock the rock. In R. Pellegrini & T. R. Sarbin (Eds.), *Between fathers and sons: Pivotal narratives in men's lives*. London: Sage Press.

Barrett, F., & Fry, R. (2005). *Appreciative inquiry: A positive approach to building cooperative capacity*. Chagrin Falls, OH: Taos Institute Publications.

Barrett, F., & Peterson, R. (2000). Appreciative learning cultures: Developing competencies for global organizing. *Organization Development Journal, 18*(2), 10–21.

Barrett, F., Thomas, G. F., & Hocevar, S. P. (1995). The central role of discourse in large-scale change: A social construction perspective. *Journal of Applied Behavioral Science, 31*(3), 352–372.

Barrett, F. J. (1998). Creativity and improvisation in jazz and organizations: Implications for organizational learning. *Organization Science, 9*(5), 605–622.

Barrett, F. J., & Cooperrider, D. L. (1990). Generative metaphor intervention: A new approach for working with systems divided by conflict and caught in defensive perception. *Journal of Applied Behavioral Science, 26*(2), 219–239.

Barrett, F. J., & Cooperrider, D. L. (2001). Generative metaphor intervention: A new approach for working with systems divided by conflict and caught in defensive perception. *Appreciative Inquiry: An Emerging Direction for Organization Development.*

Barros, I., & Cooperrider, D. L. (2000). A story of Nutrimental in Brazil: How wholeness, appreciation, and inquiry bring out the best in human organization. *Organization Development Journal, 18,* 22–28.

Barros, I., & Cooperrider, D. L. (2001, August 14). Appreciative inquiry fostering wholeness in organizations: A story of Nutrimental in Brazil. *Nutrimental Industria e Comercio de Alimentos S.A.*

Bergquist, W. H., Bergquist, W., Merritt, K., & Phillips, S. (1999). *Executive coaching: An appreciative approach.* Sacramento, CA: Pacific Soundings Press.

Bilimoria, D. et al. (1995). A call to organizational scholarship: The organization dimensions of global change: No limits to cooperation. *Journal of Management Inquiry, 4*(1), 71–90.

Bilimoria, D., Wilmot, T. B., et al. (1996). Multi-organizational collaboration for global change: New opportunities for organizational change and development. In R. W. Woodman & W. A. Pasmore (Eds.), *Research in organizational change and development, vol. 9* (pp. 201–236). Greenwich, CT: JAI Press.

Blair, M. (1998). Lessons from using appreciative inquiry in a planning exercise. In S. Hammond & C. Royal (Eds.), *Lessons from the field: Applying appreciative inquiry* (pp. 186–214). Plano, TX: Practical Press, Inc.

Bloom, J. L., & Martin, N. A. (2002, August 29). Incorporating appreciative inquiry into academic advising. *The Mentor.*

Booy, D., & Sena, S. (2000). Capacity building using the appreciative inquiry approach: The experience of world vision Tanzania. *Global Social Innovations, 3*(1), 4–11.

Bosch, L. (1998). Exit interviews with an "appreciative eye." In S. Hammond & C. Royal (Eds.), *Lessons from the field: Applying appreciative inquiry* (pp. 230–243). Plano, TX: Practical Press, Inc.

Bosch, L. (2005). Good leadership: An appreciative discovery of expectations. *OD Practitioner, 37,* 25–30.

Bowling, C., Ludema, J., & Wyss, E. (1997). *Vision twin cities appreciative inquiry report.* Cleveland, OH: Case Western Reserve University.

Branson, M. (2004). *Memories, hopes, and conversations: Appreciative inquiry and congregational change.* Herndon, VA: Alban Institute.

Brittain, J. (1998). Do we really mean it? How we change behavior after the provocative propositions are written. In S. Hammond & C. Royal (Eds.), *Lessons from the field: Applying appreciative inquiry* (pp. 216–229). Plano, TX: Practical Press, Inc.

Browne, B. (1998). Imagine Chicago: A study in intergenerational appreciative inquiry. In S. Hammond & C. Royal (Eds.), *Lessons from the field: Applying appreciative inquiry* (pp. 76–89). Plano, TX: Practical Press, Inc.

Buckingham, S. T. (1999). *Leadership skills in public health nursing: An appreciative inquiry.* Victoria, British Columbia: Royal Roads University.

Bukenya, G. et al. (1997). *Manual of district health management for Uganda.* McKinleyville, CA: Fithian Press.

Bunker, B. B. (1990). Appreciating diversity and modifying organizational cultures: Men and women at work. In S. Srivastva & D. L. Cooperrider (Eds.), *Appreciative management and leadership: The power of positive thought and action in organizations* (Rev. ed.). (pp. 126–149). Euclid, OH: Lakeshore Communications.

Bunker, B. B., & Alban, B. T. (1997). Large group interventions: Engaging the whole system for rapid change. San Francisco: Jossey-Bass.

Bushe, G. R. (1995). Advances in appreciative inquiry as an organization development intervention. *Organization Development Journal, 13*(3), 14–22.

Bushe, G. R. (1997). *Attending to others: Interviewing appreciatively.* Vancouver, BC: Discovery and Design Inc.

Bushe, G. R. (1998). Appreciative inquiry with teams. *Organization Development Journal, 16*(3), 41–50.

Bushe, G. R. (2000). Clear leadership: How outstanding leaders make themselves understood, cut through the mush, and help everyone get real at work, Mountain View, CA: Davies-Black.

Bushe, G. R. (2001). Meaning making in teams: Appreciative inquiry with pre-identity and post-identity groups. In F. Barrett, R. Fry, & D. Whitney (Eds.), *Appreciative inquiry: Applications in the field.*

Bushe, G. R., & Coetzer, G. (1995). Appreciative inquiry as a team-development intervention: A controlled experiment. *Journal of Applied Behavioral Science, 31*(1), 13–30.

Bushe, G. R., & Pitman, T. (1991). Appreciative process: A method for transformational change. *OD Practitioner, 23*(3), 1–4.

Carter, L., Mische, A., & Schwarz, D. R. (1993). *Aspects of hope: The proceedings of a seminar on hope.* New York: ICIS Center for a Science of Hope.

Chaffee, P. (1997). Ring of breath around the world: A report of the United Religions Initiative global conference. *Journal of the United Religions Initiative, 4.*

Chaffee, P. (1997). *Unafraid of the light: Appreciative inquiry and faith communities* (unpublished paper). San Francisco: Interfaith Center at the Presidio.

Chaffee, P. (2005). Claiming the light: Appreciative inquiry and congregational transformation. Herndon, VA: Alban Institute.

Chapagain, C. P. (2005). Appreciative inquiry for building human capacities: An innovative approach for the new millennium. Katmandu, Nepal: Plan-International.

Cobb, N. B. (2002). *Project management workbook.* New York: McGraw-Hill.

Coffey, A., & Atkinson, P. (1996). *Making sense of qualitative data.* Newbury Park, CA: Sage Publications.

Cojocaru, S. (2005). The appreciative perspective in multicultural relations. *Journal for the study of religions and ideologies, 10,* 36–48.

Collins, J., & Porras, J. (1994). *Built to last: Successful habits of visionary companies.* New York: Harper Business.

Cooperrider, D. (2000). An appreciative inquiry conversation guide: Creating a small forum in which leaders of the world religions can gather in mutual respect and dialogue. *Global Social Innovations, 1*(3), 23–26.

Cooperrider, D. (2002). Here's a way to negotiate the Mideast Crisis. *MWorld* (Summer edition).

Cooperrider, D., & Avital, M. (2004). *Advances in appreciative inquiry: Constructive discourse and human organization.* Oxford, UK: Elsevier Publishing.

Cooperrider, D. et al. (2003). *The appreciative inquiry trilogy.* Chagrin Falls, OH: Taos Institute Publications.

Cooperrider, D., & Srivastva, S. (1999). Appreciative inquiry in organizational life. In S. Srivastva & D. L. Cooperrider, *Appreciative management and leadership* (Rev. ed.). (pp. 401–442). Euclid, OH: Lakeshore Communications.

Cooperrider, D., & Srivastva, S. (1999). The emergence of the egalitarian organization. In S. Srivastva & D. L. Cooperrider. *Appreciative management and leadership: The Power of Positive Thought and Action in Organization* (Rev. ed.). (pp. 443–484). Euclid, OH: Lakeshore Communications.

Cooperrider, D. L. (1995). Introduction to appreciative inquiry. In W. French & C. Bell (Eds.), *Organization development.* Englewood Cliffs, NJ: Prentice Hall.

Cooperrider, D. L. (1996). Resources for getting appreciative inquiry started: An example OD proposal. *OD Practitioner, 28*(1 & 2), 23–33.

Cooperrider, D. L. (1996). Special issue: OD and the global agenda. *Organization development journal, 14*(4).

Cooperrider, D. L. (1996). The "child" as agent of inquiry. *OD Practitioner, 28*(1 & 2), 5–11.

Cooperrider, D. L., Barrett, F., & Srivastva, S. (1995). Social construction and appreciative inquiry: A journey in organizational theory. In D. Hosking, P. Dachler, & K. Gergen (Eds.), Management and organization: Relational alternatives to Individualism (pp. 157–200). Aldershot, England: Avebury Press.

Cooperrider, D. L., & Bilimoria, D. (1993). The challenge of global change for strategic management: Opportunities for charting a new course. *Advances in strategic management, 9,* 99–141.

Cooperrider, D. L., & Dutton, J. (1999). *The organizational dimensions of global change: No limits to cooperation.* Thousand Oaks, CA: Sage Publications.

Cooperrider, D. L., & Khalsa, G. S. (1997). The organization dimensions of global environmental change. *Organization and Environment, 10*(4), 331–341.

Cooperrider, D. L., & Pasmore, W. A. (1991). Global social change: A new agenda for social science? *Human Relations, 44*(10), 1037–1055.

Cooperrider, D. L., & Srivastva, S. (1987). *Appreciative inquiry in organizational life.* In W. Pasmore & R. Woodman (Eds.), *Research in organization change and development* (pp. 129–169). Greenwich, CT: JAI Press.

Cooperrider, D. L., & Srivastva, S. (1998). An invitation to organizational wisdom and executive courage. In S. Srivastva & D. L. Cooperrider (Eds.), *Organizational wisdom and executive courage* (pp. 1–24). San Francisco: New Lexington Press.

Cooperrider, D. L., & Whitney, D. (1999). *Collaborating for change: Appreciative inquiry.* San Francisco: Berrett-Koehler.

Cooperrider, D. L., & Whitney, D. (1999). When stories have wings: How "relational responsibility" opens new options for action. In S. McNamee & K. Gergen (Eds.), *Relational responsibility: Resources for sustainable dialogue* (pp. 57–64). Thousand Oaks, CA: Sage Publications.

Cooperrider, D. L., & Whitney, D. (2005). *Appreciative inquiry: A positive revolution in change.* San Francisco: Berrett-Koehler.

Cottor, R., Asher, A., Levin, J., & Weiser, C. (2004). *Experiential learning exercises in social construction: A field book for creating change.* Chagrin Falls, OH: Taos Institute Publications.

Covey, S. (1990). *The 7 Habits of Highly Effective People.* New York: Simon & Schuster.

Cowling, W. R. (2004, Jul/Aug/Sept). Pattern, participation, praxis, and power in unitary appreciative inquiry. *Advances in Nursing Science, 27*(3), 202–214.

Cummings, T. G. (1990). The role of executive appreciation in creating transorganizational alliances. In S. Srivastva & D. L. Cooperrider (Eds.), *Appreciative management and leadership: The power of positive thought and action in organizations* (Rev. ed.). (pp. 205–227). Euclid, OH: Lakeshore Communications.

Cummings, L. L., & Anton, R. J. (1990). The logical and appreciative dimensions of accountability. In S. Srivastva & D. L. Cooperrider (Eds.), *Appreciative management and leadership: The power of positive thought and action in organizations* (Rev. ed.). (pp. 257–286). Euclid, OH: Lakeshore Communications.

Curran, M. (1991, December). Appreciative inquiry: A third wave approach to OD. *Vision/Action,* 12–14.

DeKluyver, C. (2000). *Strategic thinking: An executive perspective.* New York: Prentice Hall.

Easley, C., Yaeger, T., & Sorensen, P. (2002, July 24). Appreciative inquiry: Evoking new ways of understanding, valuing and loving and changing the youth we have lost to gangs. *Proceedings of the Organization Discourse: From Micro-Utterances to Macro-Inferences Conference.* The Management Centre, Kings College, University of London, England.

Elkington, J. (1998). *Cannibals with forks.* Gabriola Island, BC: New Society Publishing.

Elliott, C. (1999). *Locating the energy for change: An introduction to appreciative inquiry.* Winnipeg, Manitoba, Canada: International Institute for Sustainable Development.

Finegold, M. A., Holland, B. M., & Lingham, T. (2002). Appreciative inquiry and public dialogue: An approach to community change. *Public Organization Review, 2,* 235–252.

Fitzgerald, S., Murrell, K., & Miller, M. (Spring 2003). Appreciative inquiry: Accentuating the positive. *Business Strategy Review, 14*(1), 5–7.

Fredrickson, B. L. (2001). The role of positive emotions in positive psychology: The broaden-and-build theory of positive emotions. *American Psychologist, 56.*

Fredrickson, B. L. (2003, July). The value of positive emotions. *American Scientist, 91.*

Frost, P. J., & Egri, C. P. (1990). Appreciating executive action. In S. Srivastva & D. L. Cooperrider (Eds.), *Appreciative management and leadership: The power of positive thought and action in organizations* (Rev. ed.). (pp. 289–322). Euclid, OH: Lakeshore Communications.

Fry, R., Whitney D., Seiling, J., & Barrett, F. (2001). *Appreciative inquiry and organizational transformation: Reports from the field.* Westport, CT: Quorum Books.

Fuller, C., Griffin, T., & Ludema, J. (2000). Appreciative future search: Involving the whole system in positive organization change. *Organization Development Journal, 18*(2), 29–41.

Gergen, K. J. (1990). Affect and organization in postmodern society. In S. Srivastva and D. L. Cooperrider (Eds.), *Appreciative management and leadership: The power of positive thought and action in organizations* (Rev. ed.). (pp. 153–174). Euclid, OH: Lakeshore Communications.

Gergen, K. J. (1991). *The saturated self.* New York: Basic Books Publishing.

Gergen, K. J. (1994). *Realities and relationships: Soundings in social construction.* Cambridge, MA: Harvard University Press.

Gergen, K. J. (1999). *An invitation to social construction.* Thousand Oaks, CA: Sage Publishing.

Gergen, K. J., & Gergen, M. (2004). *Social construction: Entering the dialogue.* Chagrin Falls, OH: Taos Institute Publications.

Gergen, K. J., McNamee, S., & Barrett, F. J. (2001). Toward transformative dialogue. *International Journal of Public Administration, 24*(7), 679–709.

Gibbs, C. (2002). The United Religions Initiative at work: Interfaith dialogue through appreciative inquiry, sowing seeds of transformation, interfaith dialogue and peace-building. Washington, DC: United States Institute of Peace.

Gibbs, C., & Ackerly, S. (1997). United Religions Initiative global summit summary report. Paper presented at the United Religions Initiative Global Summit, San Francisco.

Goldberg, R. A. (2001, March 21). Implementing a professional development system through appreciative inquiry. *Leadership and Organization Development Journal, 22,* 56–61.

Golembiewski, B. (2000). Three perspectives on appreciative inquiry. *OD Practitioner, 32*(1), 54–58.

Golembiewski, R. T. (1998). Appreciating appreciative inquiry: Diagnosis and perspectives on how to do better. In R. W. Woodman and W. A. Pasmore (Eds.), *Research in organizational change and development* (pp. 1–45). Greenwich, CT: JAI Press.

Golembiewski, R. T. (1999). Fine-tuning appreciative inquiry: Two ways of circumscribing the concept's value-added. *Organization Development Journal, 17*(3), 21–28.

Gordon, J. (2003, January 20). Meet the freight fairy. *Forbes, 171.*

Gotches, G., & Ludema, J. (1995). Appreciative inquiry and the future of OD. *Organization Development Journal, 13*(3), 5–13.

GTE. (1997). GTE asks employees to start a grassroots movement to make GTE unbeatable in the marketplace. *GTE Together.*

Hagevik, S. (2000). Appreciative inquiry and your career. *Journal of Environmental Health, 63*(1), 39, 44.

Hammonds, K. (2001, July). Leaders for the long haul, *Fast* Company, 56–58.

Hammond, S. (1996). *The thin book of appreciative inquiry*. Plano, TX: Thin Book Publishing.

Hammond, S. (1998). What is appreciative inquiry? *The Inner Edge, 1*(2), 36–27.

Hammond, S. (2006). *Chinese translation of the thin book of appreciative inquiry*. Plano, TX: Thin Book Publishing.

Harman, W. W. (1990). Shifting context for executive behavior: Signs of change and revaluation. In S. Srivastva and D. L. Cooperrider (Eds.), *Appreciative management and leadership: The power of positive thought and action in organizations* (Rev. ed.). San Francisco: Jossey-Bass.

Hart, S. (2005). *Capitalism at the crossroads*. Upper Saddle River, NJ: Pearson Education.

Head, R. (1999). *School of management*. Cleveland, OH: Case Western Reserve University.

Head, R. L. (1999). Appreciative inquiry as a team-development intervention for newly formed heterogeneous groups. *OD Practitioner, 32*(1), 59–66.

Head, R. L., & Young, M. M. (1998). Initiating culture change in higher education through appreciative inquiry. *Organization Development Journal, 16*(2), 65–72.

Head, T. (2006, Summer). Appreciative inquiry in the graduate classroom: Making group dynamics a practical topic to address. *Organization Development Journal, 24*(2), 83–88.

Head, T. C. (2000). Appreciative inquiry: Debunking the mythology behind resistance to change. *OD Practitioner, 32*(1), 27–32.

Head, T. C., Sorensen, P. F., Jr., Preston, J. C., & Yaeger, T. (2000). Is appreciative inquiry OD's philosopher's stone? In D. L. Cooperrider, P. F. Sorensen, Jr., D. Whitney, & T. F. Yaeger (Eds.), *Appreciative inquiry: An emerging direction for organizational development* (pp. 363–378). Champaign, IL: Stipes Publishing.

Henry, R. (2004). Leadership at every level: Appreciative inquiry in education. *New Horizons for Learning*, Retrieved from http://www.newhorizons.org.

Henry, R. (2005, February). Discovering and growing what gives life: Appreciative inquiry in community colleges. *Instructional Leadership Abstracts, 3*.

Herasymowych, M. (1997, May). Tapping into the power of learning part 4A: Appreciating potential and possibilities. *InfoMine, 4*.

Herrick, C., & Stoneham, D. (2005). Unleashing a positive revolution in medicine: The power of appreciative inquiry. *Utah Medical Association Bulletin, 52*.

Hock, D. (1999). *Birth of the chaordic age*. San Francisco: Berrett-Koehler.

Hubbard, B. M. (1998). Conscious evolution: Awakening the power of our social potential. Novato, CA: New World Library.

Isen, A. M., Estrada, C. A., & Young, M. J. (1998). Positive affect facilitates integration of information and decreases anchoring in reasoning among physicians. *Organizational Behavior and Human Decision Processes, 72*, 117–135.

Jacobsgaard, M. (2000). Appreciative inquiry in action. *Global Social Innovations, 1*, 59–60.

Johnson, G., & Leavitt, W. (2001, March 22). Building on success: Transforming organizations through appreciative inquiry. *Public Personnel Management, 30,* 129.

Johnson, G., & Leavitt, W. (2005). Building on success: Transforming organizations through appreciative inquiry. *Public Personal Management, 30.*

Johnson, P. C., & Cooperrider, D. L. (1991). Finding a path with heart: Global social change organizations and their challenge for the field of organizational development. In R. W. Woodman & W. A. Pasmore (Eds.), *Research in organizational change and development* (pp. 223–284). Greenwich, CT: JAI Press.

Johnson, P. C., & Cooperrider, D. L. (1991). Global integrity: Beyond instrumental rationality in transnational organizing. *Journal of Transnational Associations.*

Johnson, S., & Ludema, J. (1997). Partnering to build and measure organizational capacity: Lessons from NGOs around the world. Grand Rapids, MI: CRC Publications.

Johnston, C. (2002, May 1). The best possible world. *CWRU Magazine, 14.*

Jonas, H., Fry, R., & Srivastva, S. (1989). The office of the CEO: Understanding the executive experience, *Academy of Management Executive, 3*(4).

Jones, D. A. (1998). A field experiment in appreciative inquiry. *Organization Development Journal, 16*(4), 69–78.

Kaczmarski, K. M., & Cooperrider, D. L. (1997). Constructionist leadership in the global relational age. *Organization and Environment, 10*(3), 235–258.

Kaczmarski, K. M., & Cooperrider, D. L. (1998). Constructionist leadership in the global relational age: The case of the mountain forum. In D. L. Cooperrider & J. E. Dutton (Eds.), *The organizational dimensions of global change: No limits to cooperation* (pp. 57–87). Thousand Oaks, CA: Sage Publications.

Kamini, R. S., & Soon, S. (2002, August 9). Appreciative inquiry and the media (SWOT ed.). *New Straits Times,* Malaysia.

Kanungo, R. N., & Conger, J. A. (1990). The quest for altruism in organizations. In S. Srivastva & D. L. Cooperrider (Eds.), *Appreciative management and leadership: The power of positive thought and action in organizations* (Rev. ed.). (pp. 228–256). Euclid: OH: Lakeshore Communications.

Kaye, B., & Jacobson, B. (1999). True tales and tall tales: The power of organizational storytelling. *Training & Development, 53*(3), 44–50.

Kelm, J. B. (2005). *Appreciative living.* Wake Forest, NC: Venet Publishers.

Khalsa, G. S. (2000). A case story of the United Religions Initiative first global summit. Paper presented at the Appreciative Summit Conference, Cleveland, OH.

Khalsa, G. S. (2000). The pilgrimage toward global dialogue: A practical visionary approach. *Breakthrough News,* 8–10.

Khalsa, G. S., & Kaczmarski, K. M. (1996). The United Religions Initiative summit conference summary. Paper presented at the United Religions Initiative Summit Conference, San Francisco.

Khalsa, G. S., & Kaczmarski, K. M. (1997). Chartering and appreciative future search. *Global Social Innovations, 1*(2), 45–52.

Khalsa, G. S., & Steingard, D. S. (1999). The relational healing dimension of organizational development: Transformative stories and dialogue in life-cycle transitions. In W. A. Pasmore & R. W. Woodman (Eds.), *Research in organizational change and development* (pp. 269–318). Stamford, CT: JAI Press.

Kind, M. (2004, January 16). Yellow roadway will keep area workers, expand with terminals in other towns. *Kansas City Business Journal.*

Kinni, T. (2003, September 22). The art of appreciative inquiry. Harvard Business School—Working Knowledge for Business Leaders, Retrieved from http://hbswk.hbs.edu/archive/3684.html.

Knight, P. (2002). Small-scale research: Pragmatic inquiry in social science and the caring professional. London: Sage Publications.

Krattenmaker, T. (2001, October). Change through appreciative inquiry. *Harvard Management Communication Newsletter, 4.*

Krouse, P. (2006, October 25). Global compact recruits locally. *The Plain Dealer,* Cleveland, OH.

Krouse, P. (2006, October 23). Using business to make the world better. *The Plain Dealer,* Cleveland, OH.

Lawn, M., & Morris, D. (2005, February). A positive approach to shaping the future. *Perdido: Leadership with a Conscience, 11,* 19–24.

LeJeune, M. (1999, February). Companies turning to appreciative inquiry to ask staff what's right. *Boulder County Business Report.*

Liebler, C. J. (1997). Getting comfortable with appreciative inquiry: Questions and answers. *Global Social Innovations, 1*(2), 30–40.

Liebling, A., Elliott, C., & Arnold, H. (2001, May). Transforming the prison: Romantic optimism or appreciative realism? *Criminal Justice, 1,* 161–180.

Liebling, A., Price, D., & Elliott, C. (1999). Appreciative inquiry and relationships in prison. *Punishment & Society, 1*(1), 71–98.

Liedman, J. (2002, January). HR pros may favor appreciative inquiry. *Human Resource Executive.*

Livingston, J. (1999). The human and organizational dimensions of global change: An appreciative inquiry interview with Robert Golembiewski. *Organization Development Journal, 17*(1), 109–115.

Lord, J. G. (1995). The philanthropic quest: A generative approach for professionals engaged in the development process. Cleveland, Ohio: Philanthropic Quest International.

Lord, J. G. (1998). The practice of the quest: Evolving a new paradigm for philanthropy and social innovation—A casebook for advancement professionals grounded in the quest. Cleveland, OH: Philanthropic Quest International.

Ludema, J., Wilmot, T., & Srivastva, S. (1997). Organizational hope: Reaffirming the constructive task of social and organizational inquiry. *Human Relations, 50*(8), 1015–1052.

Ludema, J. D. (2000). Leadership symposium 2000: Global staffing and retention. Appreciative Inquiry report on global staffing and retention presented at McDonald's Worldwide Convention, Orlando.

Ludema, J. D., Cooperrider, D. L., & Barrett, F. (2001). Appreciative inquiry: The power of the unconditional positive question. In P. Reason & H. Bradbury (Eds.), *Handbook of action research: Participative inquiry and practice* (pp. 189–199). London: Sage Publications.

Ludema, J.D., Whitney, D., Mohr, B., & Griffin, T. (2003). The appreciative inquiry summit: A practitioner's guide for leading positive large-group change. San Francisco: Berrett-Koehler.

Luechauer, D. L. (1999). Applying appreciative inquiry instead of problem-solving techniques to facilitate change. *Management Development Forum, 2*(1).

Mahé, S., & Gibbs, C. (2003). Birth of a global community: Appreciative inquiry as midwife to the United Religions Initiative. Euclid, OH: Lakeshore Communications.

Mann, A. et al. (2006, January). Adapting appreciative inquiry. *Consulting Today*, Retrieved from http://www.consultingtoday.com/topicindex/index.html.

Mann, A. J. (1997). An appreciative inquiry model for building partnerships. *Global Social Innovations, 1*(2), 41–44.

Mann, A. J. (2000). Variations on a theme: The flexibility of the 4-D model. *Global Social Innovations, 1*(3), 12–15.

Mantel, M. J., & Ludema, J. D. (2000). From local conversations to global change: Experiencing the worldwide web effect of appreciative inquiry. *Organization Development Journal, 18*(2), 42–53.

Markova, D., & Holland, B. (2006). Appreciative inquiry: A strategy for change in systemic leadership that builds on organizational strengths, not deficits. *School Administrator, 62.*

Marshak, R. J. (2005, March). Is there a new OD? *Seasonings: A Journal by Senior OD Practitioners.*

Martinetz, C. F. (2002, September). Appreciative inquiry as an organizational development tool. *Performance Improvement.*

McGehee, T. (200a). WHOOSH: Business in the fast lane: Unleashing the power of a creation company. Cambridge, MA: Perseus Publishing.

Mead, Margaret and her work on intergenerational learning, the Mead Centennial 2001, The Institute for Intercultural Studies, http://www.interculturalstudies.org/Mead/2001centennial.html.

Mellish, L. (2001). Appreciative inquiry at work. *AI Newsletter, 12,* 8.

Miller, C. J., Aguilar, C. R., Maslowski, L., & McDaniel, D. (2003). *The nonprofit's guide to the power of appreciative inquiry.* Denver: Community Development Institute.

Miller, M. G., Fitzgerald, S. P., Murrell, K. L., Preston, J., & Ambekar, R. (2005, March). Appreciative inquiry in building a transcultural strategic alliance. *Journal of Applied Behavioral Science, 42*(1), 91–110.

Mirvis, P. H. (1988). Organization development: Part I—An evolutionary perspective. In W. A. Pasmore & R. W. Woodman (Eds.), *Research in organizational change and development* (pp. 1–57). Greenwich, CT: JAI Press.

Mirvis, P. H. (1990). Merging of executive heart and mind in crisis management. In S. Srivastva & D. L. Cooperrider (Eds.), *Appreciative management and leadership: The power of positive thought and action in organizations* (pp. 55–90). San Francisco: Jossey-Bass.

Mirvis, P. H. (1997). "Soul work" in organizations. *Organization Science, 8*(2), 193–206.

Mohr, B. (2001). *A guide to appreciative inquiry.* Waltham, MA: Pegasus Communications.

Mohr, B., & Watkins, J. (2002). *The essentials of appreciative inquiry: A roadmap for creating positive futures.* Waltham, MA: Pegasus Communications.

Mohr, B. J. (2001). Appreciative inquiry: Igniting transformative action. *The Systems Thinker, 12*(1), 1–5.

Mohr, B. J., Smith, E. J, & Watkins, J. M. (2000). Appreciative inquiry and learning assessment. *OD Practitioner, 32*(1), 33–53.

Muscat, M. (1998). Imagine Chicago: Dreams and visions for a 'second city' of the future. *The Inner Edge, 1*(2), 23–24.

Muscat, M. (1998). The federal quality consulting group: Using the vision story process to rebuild an organization. *The Inner Edge, 1*(2), 18–19.

Newman, H. L., & Fitzgerald, S. P. (2001). Appreciative inquiry with an executive team: Moving along the action research continuum. *Organization Development Journal, 19,* 37–44.

Nicholas, S. (2005). Appreciative inquiry in hypnotherapy. *Hypnotherapy News.*

Nordbye, M., & Yaeger, T. (2003, November). Team development, the appreciative inquiry way. *Training Today.*

Odell, M. (2000). From conflict to cooperation: Approaches to building rural partnerships. *Global Social Innovations, 1*(3), 16–22.

Olson, E. E., & Eoyang, G. H. (2001). *Facilitating organization change: Lessons from complexity science.* San Francisco: Jossey-Bass/Pfeiffer.

Orem, S., Binkert, J., & Clancy, A. (2007). *Appreciative coaching: A positive process for change.* San Francisco: Jossey-Bass.

Paddock, S. S. (2003). *Appreciative inquiry in the Catholic Church.* Plano, TX: Thin Book Publishing.

Pages, M. (1990). The illusion and disillusion of appreciative management. In S. Srivastva & D. L. Cooperrider (Eds.), *Appreciative management and leadership: The power of positive thought and action in organizations* (Rev. ed.). (pp. 353–380). Euclid, OH: Lakeshore Communications.

Paine, L. S., & Rogers, G. C. (2001, July 27). Avon products. *Harvard Business Review.*

Pascale, R. T., & Sternin, J. (2005). Your company's secret change agents. *Harvard Business Review.*

Pepitone, J. S. (1995). Future training: A roadmap for restructuring the training Function. Dallas: AddVantage Learning Press.

Peterson, R. (1993). Design aid ™: A multimedia tool for appreciative organization design. *Organizational Development and Transformation.* California Institute of Integral Studies, 87.

Polak, F. (1973). *The image of the future.* San Francisco: Jossey-Bass.

Preskill, H., & Catsambas, T. T. (2006). *Reframing evaluation through appreciative inquiry.* Thousand Oaks, CA: Sage Publications.

Preskill, H., & Coghlan, A. (2004). *Using appreciative inquiry in evaluation: New directions for evaluation: No. 100.* San Francisco: Jossey-Bass.

Pullen, C. (2001, October). Appreciative inquiry in financial planning and life. *Journal of Financial Planning, 14,* 52–54.

Quinn, R. E. (2000). Change the world: How ordinary people can achieve extraordinary results. San Francisco: Jossey-Bass.

Radford, A. (1998–2007). Appreciative Inquiry Newsletter.

Raimy, E. (1998). Precious moments. *Human Resource Executive, 12*(11), 1, 26–29.

Rainey, M. A. (1996). An appreciative inquiry into the factors of culture continuity during leadership transition. *Organization Development Practitioner, 28*(1 & 2), 34–41.

Reed, J. (2006). *Appreciative inquiry: Research for change.* Thousand Oaks, CA: Sage Publications.

Reed, J., Pearson, P., Douglas, B., Swinburne, S., & Wilding, H. (2002, January). Going home from hospital—An appreciative inquiry study. *Health & Social Care in the Community, 10,* 36–45.

Reed, J., & Turner, J. (2005). Appreciating change in cancer services—An evaluation of service development strategies. *Journal of Health Organization Management, 19*(3), 163–176.

Ricketts, M. (2002). The glass is half full—Appreciative inquiry, experiential learning and organizational change. *Association of Experiential Education's AEE Horizon Newsletter* (Summer ed.).

Ricketts, M., & Willis, J. (2001). *Experience AI: A practitioner's guide to integrating appreciative inquiry and experiential learning.* Chagrin Falls, OH: Taos Institute Publications.

Rosenthal, R. (1969). *Pygmalion in the classroom.* New York: Holt, Rinehart and Winston.

Royal, C. (1994). The NTL diversity study: The use of appreciative inquiry to discover best experiences around diversity in a professional OD organization. Alexandra, VA: NTL Institute for Applied Behavioral Science.

Royal, C., & Hammond, S. (Eds.). (2001). *Lessons from the field: Applying appreciative inquiry.* Plano, TX: Thin Book Publishing.

Ryan, F. J., Soven, M., Smither, J., Sullivan, W. M., & VanBuskirk, W. R. (1999). Appreciative inquiry: Using personal narratives for initiating school reform. *The Clearing House, 72*(3), 164–167.

Salter, C. (2000, November). We're trying to change world history. *Fast* Company, 230.

Schiller, M. (1998). A dialogue about leadership & appreciative inquiry. *Organization Development Journal, 16*(4), 79–84.

Schiller, M., Riley, D., & Holland, B. M. (Eds.). (2001). *Appreciative leaders: In the eye of the beholder.* Chagrin Falls, OH: Taos Institute Publications.

Seligman, M. (1992). Helplessness: On development, depression and death. New York: W.H. Freeman.

Snyder, C. R., & McCullough, M. E. (2000). A positive psychology field of dreams: If you build it they will come. *Journal of Social and Clinical Psychology, 19.*

Sorensen, P. F., Gironda, L. A., Head, T. C., & Larsen, H. H. (1996). Global organization development: Lessons from Scandinavia. *Organization Development Journal, 14*(4), 46–52.

Sorensen, P. F., & Yaeger, T. F. (1997). Exploring organizational possibilities: Appreciative inquiry. *Training Today*, 7–8.

Sorensen, P. F., & Yaeger, T. F. (1998). A universal approach to change: Appreciative inquiry. *Training Today*, 7–8.

Sorensen, P. F., Yaeger, T. F., & Nicoll, D. (2000). Appreciative inquiry 2000: Fad or important new focus for OD? *OD Practitioner, 32*(1), 3–5.

Srivastva, S., & Barrett, F. J. (1986). *Executive power.* San Francisco: Jossey-Bass.

Srivastva, S., & Barrett, F. J. (1988). Foundations for executive integrity: Dialogue, diversity, development. In S. Srivastva (Ed.), *Executive integrity: The search for high human values in organizational life* (pp. 290–319). San Francisco: Jossey-Bass.

Srivastva, S., Bilimoria, D., Cooperrider, D. L., & Fry, R. E. (1995). Management and organization learning for positive global change. *Management Learning, 26*(1), 37–54.

Srivastva, S., & Cooperrider, D. L. (1986). The emergence of the egalitarian organization. *Human Relations, 39*(8), 683–724.

Srivastva, S., & Cooperrider, D. L. (Eds.). (1998). *Organizational wisdom and executive courage.* San Francisco: New Lexington Press.

Srivastva, S., & Cooperrider, D. L. (Eds.). (1999). *Appreciative management and leadership: The power of positive thought and action in organization* (Rev. ed.). Euclid, OH: Lakeshore Communications.

Stavros, J. M. (2000, Winter). Northern and southern perspectives of capacity building using an appreciative inquiry approach. *Journal of Global Social Innovations.*

Stavros, J. M., Cooperrider, D., & Kelley, L. (2003). Appreciative intent: Inspiration to SOAR. *AI Practitioner.*

Stavros, J. M., & Meda, A. K. (2003). An assisted living center: Cultivating the positive core through appreciative inquiry. Paper presented at the Southwest Academy of Management Annual Meeting, Houston, TX, and the Organization Development Institute Annual Conference, Williamsburg, VA.

Stavros, J. M., & Torres, C. B. (2005). *Dynamic relationships: Unleashing the power of appreciative inquiry in daily living.* Chagrin Falls, OH: Taos Institute Publications.

Stavros, J. M., Seiling, J., & Castelli, P. (2007). Appreciative form of capacity building for organizational accomplishment: Lessons from a network of nonprofit organizations. *Journal of North American Management Society.*

Stavros, J. M., & Sprangel, J. (in press). Applying appreciative inquiry to deliver strategic change: OTC. In *Creative conversations for organisational change.* United Kingdom: Kogan Page.

Stetson, N., & Miller, C. (2003, April 1). Appreciative inquiry: A new way of leading change without resistance. *Community College Times, 15.*

Stetson, N., & Miller, C. (2003, May). Lead change in educational organizations with appreciative inquiry. *Consulting Today.*

Stetson, N. E., & Miller, C. R. (2004). *Appreciative inquiry in the community college: Early stories of success.* Phoenix: League for Innovation in the Community College.

Strauss, A., & Corbin, J. (1990). *Basics of qualitative research: Grounded theory procedures and techniques.* Newbury Park, CA: Sage Publications.

Sullivan, M. (2004, June). The promise of appreciative inquiry in library organizations. *Library Trends.*

Sutherland, J., & Stavros, J. (2003, November). The heart of appreciative strategy. *AI Practitioner.*

Tang, Y., & Joiner, C. (2006). *Synergic inquiry: A collaboration action methodology.* Thousand Oaks, CA: Sage Publications.

Tenkasi, R. (2000). The dynamics of cultural knowledge and learning in creating viable theories of global change and action. *Organization Development Journal, 18*(2), 74–90.

Thatchenkery, T. J. (1996). Affirmation as facilitation: A postmodernist paradigm in change management. *OD Practitioner, 28*(1), 12–22.

Thatchenkery, T. (2005). *Appreciative sharing of knowledge.* Chagrin Falls, OH: Taos Institute Publications.

Thatchenkery, T. (2007). *Appreciative inquiry and knowledge management: A social constructionist perspective.* Cheltenham, United Kingdom: Edward Elgar Publishing.

Thatchenkery, T., & Metzker, C. (2006). *Appreciative intelligence: Seeing the mighty oak in the acorn.* San Francisco: Berrett-Koehler.

Trosten-Bloom, A., & Whitney, D. (1999). Appreciative inquiry: The path to positive change. In Key, M. K. (Ed.), *Managing change in healthcare: Innovative solutions for people-based organization.* New York: McGraw-Hill Healthcare Financial Management Association.

Trosten-Bloom, A., & Whitney, D. (2001). Creative AI approaches for whole-system culture change: Hunter Douglas Window Fashions Division. Golden, CO: Corporation for Positive Change.

Trosten-Bloom, A., & Whitney, D. (2001). *Positive change @ work: The appreciative inquiry approach to whole system change at Hunter.* [Videotape and accompanying workbook]. (Available from Corporation for Positive Change, PO Box 3257, Taos, NM, 87571)

UC Berkeley Extension guides higher education to positive change. (2002, April 18). Business Wire, Retrieved from http://home.businesswire.com.

Van Marter, J. (2006, September 27). Executives Look for "A New Way." Article archived at http://www.pcusa.org/pcnews/2006/06491.htm.

Van Vuuren, L. J., & Crous, F. (2005, April). Utilizing appreciative inquiry (AI) in creating a shared meaning of ethics in organizations. *Journal of Business Ethics, 57*(4), 399–412.

Watkins, J. M., & Cooperrider, D. L. (1996). Organizational inquiry model for global social change organizations. *Organization Development Journal, 14*(4), 97–112.

Watkins, J. M., & Cooperrider, D. L. (2000). Appreciative inquiry: A transformative paradigm. *OD Practitioner, 32*(1), 6–12.

Watkins, J. M., & Mohr, B. J. (2001). *Appreciative inquiry: Change at the speed of imagination.* San Francisco: Jossey-Bass/Pfeiffer.

Webb, L., & Rockey, S. (2005). Organizational change inside and out. *Journal for Non-profit Management,* 17–27.

Webb, L. D. (1999). Appreciative inquiry as a way to jump start change. *At Work, 8*(2), 16–18.

Weisbord, M. (1994). *Discovering common ground.* San Francisco: Berrett-Koehler.

Weisbord, M., & Janoff, S. (2000). *Future search: An action guide to finding common ground in organizations and communities,* (2nd ed.). San Francisco: Berrett-Koehler.

West, D., & Thomas, L. (2001). *Looking for the 'bigger picture': An application of the appreciative inquiry method in Renfrewshire Council for Voluntary Services.* Weinheim, Germany: Beltz Publishing.

Whalley, C. (1998). Using appreciative inquiry to overcome post-OFSTED syndrome. *Management in Education, 12*(3), 6–7.

White, T. H. (1996). Working in interesting times. *Vital Speeches of the Day, 62*(15), 472–474.

Whitney, D. (1996). Postmodern principles and practices for large scale organization change and global cooperation. *Organization Development Journal, 14*(4), 53–68.

Whitney, D. (1998). Let's change the subject and change our organization: An appreciative inquiry approach to organization change. *Career Development International, 3*(7), 314–319.

Whitney, D. (2001). Postmodern challenges to organization development. *HRD Strategies for 2000 AD.*

Whitney, D. (2004). Appreciative inquiry and the elevation of organizational consciousness. In D.L. Cooperrider & M. Avital (Eds.), *Constructive discourse and human organization: Advances in appreciative inquiry* (Vol. 1). Oxford, UK: Elsevier Science.

Whitney, D. (2007). Designing organizations as if life matters: Principles of appreciative organizing. In M. Avital, R. J. Boland, & D. L. Cooperrider (Eds.), *Designing information and organizations with a positive lens: Advances in appreciative inquiry* (Vol. 2). Oxford, UK: Elsevier Science.

Whitney, D., & Cooperrider, D. L. (1998). The appreciative inquiry summit: Overview and applications. *Employment Relations Today, 25*(2), 17–28.

Whitney, D., & Cooperrider, D. L. (2000). The appreciative inquiry summit: An emerging methodology for whole system positive change. *OD Practitioner, 32*(1), 13–26.

Whitney, D., Cooperrider, D. L., Garrison, M., & Moore, J. (2001). Appreciative inquiry and culture change at GET: Launching a positive revolution. In *Appreciative inquiry and organization transformation.* Westport, CT: Quorum Books.

Whitney, D., Cooperrider, D. L., Kaplin, B., & Trosten-Bloom, A. (2001). *Encyclopedia of positive questions, volume one: Using appreciative inquiry to bring out the best in your organization.* Euclid, OH: Lakeshore Communications.

Whitney, D., & Schau, C. (1998). Appreciative inquiry: An innovative process for organization change. *Employment Relations Today, 25*(1), 11–21.

Whitney D., & Trosten-Bloom, A. (2003). *The power of appreciative inquiry: A practical guide to positive change.* San Francisco: Berrett-Koehler.

Whitney, D., Trosten-Bloom, A., Cherney, J., & Fry, R. (2004). Appreciative team building: Positive questions to bring out the best in your team. *iUniverse.*

Williams, R. F. (1996). Survey guided appreciative inquiry: A case study. *OD Practitioner, 28*(1&2), 43–51.

Wilmot, T. B., & Ludema, J. D. (1995). Odyssey into organizational hope. In D. Marcic (Ed.), *Organizational behavior: Experiences and cases* (3rd ed.). (pp. 109–112). Eagan, MN: West Publishing.

Wilson, T. (1995). Imagine shaping a better Chicago. *Chicago Tribune*, p. 2.

Woodman, R. W., & Pasmore, W. A. (Eds.). (1987). *Research in organizational change and development: An annual series featuring advances in theory, methodology and research.* Greenwich, CT: JAI Press.

Yaeger, T. (1999). Responses from Russia: An appreciative inquiry interview with Konstantin Korotov, RODP. *Organization Development Journal, 17*(3), 85–87.

Yaeger, T. F., & Sorensen, P. F. (2005, July). A seasoned perspective on appreciative inquiry. *Seasonings: A Journal by Senior OD Practitioners.*

Yballe, L., & O'Connor, D. (2000). Appreciative pedagogy: Constructing positive models for learning. *Journal of Management Education, 24*(4), 474–483.

Zakariasen, K. L., Zakariasen, K. A., & Lodding, D. (2002, February). The practice of your future: Creating a vision. *JADA, 133,* 213–218.

Zantua, M. (2005, Oct 17). Appreciative inquiry as a tool for self-sufficiency and peace. Center for Learning Connections, Retrieved from http://learningconnections.org.

Zemke, R. (1999, June 1). Don't fix that company. *Training Magazine, 36,* 26.

Zemke, R. (2000). David Cooperrider: Man on a mission. *Training, 37*(11), 52–53.

Zhexembayeva, N. (2006, August). Becoming sustainable: Tools and resources for successful organizational transformation. GreenBiz.com, Retrieved from http://www.greenbiz.com/news/columns_third.cfm?NewsID=33335.

Zhexembayeva, N. (2006, November). Management knowledge leading positive change: Are we ready to tip? GreenBiz.com, Retrieved from http://www.greenbiz.com/news/columns_third.cfm?NewsID=34204.

Zolno, S. (2002). Appreciative inquiry: New thinking at work. In E. Biech, *The 2002 Annual: Developing human resources.* San Francisco: Jossey-Bass/Pfeiffer.

ZurBonsen, M., & Maleh, C. (2001). *Appreciative inquiry (AI): Der Weg zu Spitzenleistungen.* Weinheim, Basel, Germany: Beltz Publishing.

AI Dissertations and Theses

(Unless noted, dissertations can be found on the AI Commons.)

Aitken, J. (1996). *Growing the empowerment organization.* San Francisco: California Institute of Integral Studies.

Allen, M. D. (in progress). *What makes an effective public service agency?* San Francisco: California Institute of Integral Studies.

Arcoleo, D. P. (2001). *Underneath appreciative inquiry.* Santa Barbara, CA: The Fielding Institute.

Bieschke, J. M. (in progress). *Transgenerational transference of organizational values.* Culver City, CA: Pepperdine University.

Bowling, C. J. (2000). *Human cooperation: Appreciative processes for creating images of governance.* Cleveland, OH: Case Western Reserve University.

Buckingham, S. T. (1998). *Leadership skills in public health nursing: An appreciative inquiry.* Victoria, British Columbia, Canada: Royal Roads University.

Chandler, D. T. (1998). *Appreciative inquiry as a means of engaging commitment, loyalty, and involvement among members of an organization.* Malibu, CA: Pepperdine University.

Chapagain, C. P. (2004). *Human resource capacity building through appreciative inquiry approach in achieving developmental goals.* Gulfport, MS: College of Business and Economics, Human Resource Management, Madison University.

Cockell, J. (2005). *Making magic: Facilitating collaborative processes.* Vancouver, British Columbia, Canada: University of British Columbia.

Cooperrider, D. L. (1986). *Appreciative inquiry: Toward a methodology for understanding and enhancing organizational innovation.* Cleveland, OH: Case Western Reserve University.

Drabczyk, A. L. (2005). *Citizen and emergency responder shared values.* Terre Haute, IN: Indiana State University.

Drogin, S. L. (1997). *An appreciative inquiry into spirituality and work.* Seattle, WA: Seattle University.

Furman, D. (in progress). *The qwest for excellence in formal education in the United States: The Mexican experience.* Rexburg, ID: University of Idaho.

Hargis, L. C. (2006). *Appreciative inquiry in higher education as an effective communication tool: A case study.* ProQuest/UMI.

Head, R. L. (1999). *Appreciative inquiry as a team development intervention for newly formed heterogeneous groups.* Lisle, IL: Benedictine University.

Hlatshwayo, G. (2001). *Innovative strategies for building collaborative capacity in large-scale global organizing: A case narrative of birthing the United Religions Initiative.* Cleveland, OH: Case Western Reserve University.

Hopper, V. L. (1991). *An appreciative study of highest human values in a major healthcare organization.* Cleveland, OH: Case Western Reserve University.

Johnson, P. C. (1998). *Straight to the heart: Cleveland leaders shaping the next millennium.* Cleveland, OH: Case Western Reserve University.

Johnson, P. C. (1992). *Organizing for global social change: Toward a global integrity ethic.* Cleveland, OH: Case Western Reserve University.

Jones, D. A. (1999). *Appreciative inquiry: A field experiment focusing on turnover in the fast food industry*. Lisle, IL: Benedictine University.

Ludema, J. A. (1997). *Narrative inquiry: Collective storytelling as a source of hope, knowledge, and action in organizational life*. Cleveland, OH: Case Western Reserve University.

Maber, T. B. (2006). *Creating a great workplace: Exploring shared values and employee engagement through appreciative inquiry*. Victoria, British Columbia, Canada: Royal Roads University.

Magee, J. A. (2002). *A condition of the heart*. Victoria, British Columbia, Canada: Royal Roads University.

McGough, L. (2006). *A comparison of appreciative inquiry and nominal group techniques in the evaluation of a college counseling center*. Buffalo, NY: University at Buffalo, State University of New York.

Mellish, L. E. (2000). *Appreciative inquiry at work*. Brisbane, Australia: Mellish & Associates.

Moehle, M. R. (in progress). *Student perceptions of band*. Cleveland, OH: Case Western Reserve University.

Ohs, A. (in progress). *Appreciative inquiry supporting literacy coach empowerment*. Prescott, AZ: Prescott College.

Peelle, III, H. E. (2005). *Appreciative inquiry and creative problem solving in cross-functional teams*. Phoenix, AZ: University of Phoenix.

Petersen, B. A. (2001). *Developing effective staff teams*. Vermillion, SD: University of South Dakota.

Peterson, R. A. (1993). *Designaid ™: A multimedia tool for appreciative organization design*. San Francisco, CA: California Institute of Integral Studies.

Portzline, B. J. (2006). *An appreciative inquiry approach to evaluation practice*. Albuquerque, NM: University of New Mexico.

Pratt, C. S. (1996). *Constructing unitary reality: An appreciative inquiry*. Cleveland, OH: Case Western Reserve University.

Pullicino, E. J. (2002). *Information technology as a marketing tool*. Ibragg, Malta: C. Testa & Co.

Quintanilla, G. L. (1999). *An appreciative inquiry evaluation of a science enrichment program for children and youth: Preliminary findings*. San Diego, CA: San Diego State University.

Rabinowitz, S. L. (2005). *Organizational stress management: A case for positive psychology-based psychoeducational interventions*. Silver Spring, MD: Pepperdine University: MSOD Program.

Rafferty, T. M. (1999). *Whose children are these? An appreciative inquiry*. Cincinnati, OH: The Union Institute.

Richer, M. (in progress). *Effect of appreciative inquiry on personnel retention in healthcare*. Montreal, Quebec, Canada: McGill University School of Nursing.

Robinson-Easley, C. A. (1998). *The role of appreciative inquiry in the fight to save our youth*. Lisle, IL: Benedictine University.

Royal, C. A. (1997). *The fractal initiative: Appreciative inquiry and rethinking social identities*. Santa Barbara, CA: Fielding Institute.

Seifert, T. (2001). *Creating exceptional customer service in a register of deeds office*. Vermillion, SD: University of South Dakota.

Smith, S. R. (2003). *Creating a growth oriented environment using appreciate inquiry in a nondenominational church*. Cleveland, OH: Cleveland State University.

Sperry, S. L. (1999). *A descriptive study of the impact of appreciative processes on self and organization-based self-esteem*. Malibu, CA: Pepperdine University.

Stavros, J. M. (1998). *Capacity building: An appreciative approach: A relational process of building your organization's future*. Cleveland, OH: Case Western Reserve University.

Tamang, B. B. (2004). *Appreciative inquiry approach*. Kathmandu, Nepal: Central Department of Sociology/Anthropology, Tribhuvan University.

Thatchenkery, T. J. (1994). *Hermeneutic processes in organizations: A study in relationships between observers and those observed*. Cleveland, OH: Case Western Reserve University.

Tripp, P., & Zipsie, M. (2002). *The introduction of appreciative inquiry to the U.S. Navy using appreciative inquiry interviews and the large group intervention with applications to U.S. Marine Corps logistics strategic management*. Monterey, CA: Naval Postgraduate School.

van der Haar, D. (2002). *A positive change*. Tilburg, Netherlands: University of Tilburg.

Wasserman, I. C. (2004). *Discursive processes that foster dialogic moments*. Santa Barbara, CA: The Fielding Graduate Institute.

Wilmot, T. M. (1995). *The global excellence in management program: A two year evaluation of 25 organizations using appreciative inquiry*. Cleveland, OH: Case Western Reserve University.

Wishart, C. G. (1998). *Toward a language of human abundance: The holistic human logic of sustainable development*. Cleveland, OH: Case Western Reserve University.

Withers, D. A. (2006). *Appreciative inquiry: Designing for engagement in technology-mediated learning*. Vancouver, British Columbia, Canada: Simon Fraser University.

Wood, K. D. (in progress). *Appreciative inquiry participant's understanding and meaning making of transformative experiences and transformative learning*. Santa Barbara, CA: Fielding Graduate University.

Web Sites

Appreciative Inquiry Commons: http://appreciativeinquiry.cwru.edu

AI Practitioner: http://www.aipractitioner.com

Case Western Reserve University Weatherhead School of Management, Center for Business as an Agent of World Benefit: http://worldbenefit.cwru.edu

IISD (International Institute of Sustainable Development) MYRADA Appreciative Inquiry Project: http://iisd.ca/ai/myrada.htm

Images and Voices of Hope: http://www.ivofhope.org

Imagine Chicago: http://www.imaginechicago.org

Nepal Appreciative Inquiry National Network (NAINN): http://nainn.blogspot.com

SIKT, Scandinavian Institute for Creative Thinking: http://www.sikt.se

The Taos Institue: http://www.taosinstitute.net

United Religions Initiative: http://www.uri.org

Glossary

A

Affirmative competence—The organization draws on the human capacity to appreciate positive possibilities by selectively focusing on current and past strengths, successes, and potentials.

Affirmative topic choice—A topic identified in the *Discovery* phase that guides the formation of the interview guide. It is a positive descriptive phase representing the organization's focus for change.

AI Summit—A large-scale meeting process that focuses on discovering and developing an organization's positive change core and designing it into the organization's strategic business processes, systems, and culture.

Anticipatory learning—A type of learning that creates positive images of the future.

Anticipatory Principle—A fundamental principle that says one's positive images of the future lead one's positive actions. This is the increasingly energizing basis and presumption of Appreciative Inquiry.

Appreciate—A verb that means "to value something." It's the act of recognizing the best in the people or the world around us; to affirm the past and present strengths, successes and potentials; to perceive those things that give life (health, vitality, and excellence) to living systems. It also means to increase in value (e.g., the economy has appreciated in value). Synonyms: valuing, prizing, esteeming, and honoring.

Appreciative Inquiry—The cooperative search for the best in people, their organizations, and the world around them. It involves systematic discovery of what gives a system "life" when the system is most effective and capable in economic, ecological, and human terms.

Appreciative Inquiry Summit—A three- to four-day Appreciative Inquiry intervention that seeks to gather the whole system in one room to collectively go through all phases of the 4-D Cycle. This process can include hundreds to thousands of participants.

Appreciative interview—An interview that uncovers what gives life to an organization, a department, or a community when at its best.

Appreciative learning culture—An organizational culture that fosters and develops the following competencies to create an appreciative learning system: affirmative, expansive, generative, and collaborative competencies.

Appreciative paradigm—A unique perspective of the organizational world that views organizations as mysteries to be embraced.

C

Capacity building—A relational process that builds an organization's future to pursue its vision, mission, and goals and sustain its existence. This process pushes boundaries to develop and strengthen an organization and its people.

Change agent—A person adept in the art of reading, understanding, and analyzing organizations as living, human constructions.

Chaordic organization—An organizational structure (such as Appreciative Inquiry Consulting, LLC) that allows its owners to be autonomous while at the same time connecting all of them around a compelling shared identity and meaningful purpose.

Coconstruct (cocreate)—A term used to describe a collaborative construction of an organization's future state. It is developed out of social construction theory, which states that human systems create their social reality by the words they speak.

Cognitivism—In contrast to behaviorism, this school of thought claims that psychology should be concerned with a person's internal representations of the world and with the internal or functional organization of the mind.

Collaborative competence—The organization creates forums in which members engage in ongoing dialogue and exchange unique perspectives.

Constructionist Principle—A fundamental principle and belief in Appreciative Inquiry that says human knowledge and organizational destiny are interwoven. To be effective, organizations must be understood as human constructs.

Continuity—A part of the Appreciative Inquiry process that seeks to maintain the best of an organization's history, image, and culture during the time of the organization's transformation into the future state envisioned by its stakeholders.

Continuity search—A search that seeks out and then preserves what the organization does best.

Core competencies—The value capabilities that assist an organization in creating strength bases relative to key competition.

D

Deficit-based approach to problem solving—An approach that begins with seeking out the problem, the weak link in the system. Then diagnosis and alternative solutions are recommended. Appreciative Inquiry challenges this traditional paradigm with an "affirmative" approach to embrace an organization's challenges in a positive light.

Design—The third phase of the 4-D model in which participants create the provocative proposition by determining the ideal, "how can it be?" The organization's future is coconstructed. This is where the stakeholders work together to transfer the dreams.

Design elements—Those elements that are considered in the social architecture of the organization's future.

Destiny—The fourth phase of the 4-D model in which participants continue to coconstruct their preferred future by defining "what will be?" Stakeholders begin the planning and implementation process to bring to life the dreams that have been designed. Stakeholders create action plans and assign responsibility commitments.

Dialogue—An exchange of ideas or opinions: *achieving constructive dialogue with all elements*. It is about understanding and learning that builds trust and enables people to create new possibilities.

Discover, Dream, Design, Destiny—4-D Cycle—The model that displays the Appreciative Inquiry approach in four phases that is designed to meet the unique challenges of an organization and its industry.

Discovery—The first phase of the 4-D model in which participants inquire into the life-giving forces of the organization to begin to understand and build their positive core. Participants uncover and value the best of "what is?" This information is generated through the engaging appreciative interviews.

Distinctive competencies—Strengths that give an organization a superior advantage in the marketplace.

Dream—The second phase of the 4-D model in which participants dialogue and create a dream for the organization. A collective vision is defined as "What might be?"

E

Expansive competence—The organization challenges habits and conventional practices, provoking stakeholders to experiment in the margins, make expansive promises that challenges them to stretch in new directions, and evoke a set of higher values and ideals that inspire them to passionate engagement.

F

Fateful—The words one chooses and the questions one asks determine the events and answers one finds.

Future Search—A methodology created by Marv Weisbord and Sandra Janoff that allows the whole system (stakeholders) to cocreate the organization's future.

G

Generative competence—The organization constructs integrative systems that allow stakeholders to see the results of their actions, to recognize that they are making a meaningful contribution, and to experience a sense of progress.

Generative learning—The type of organizational learning that emphasizes continuous experimentation, systematic thinking, and a willingness to think outside the limits of an issue.

Generative metaphor intervention—A form of intervention used to help a group build (1) liberated aspirations and the development of hope, (2) interpersonal relationships, (3) strategic consensus around a positive vision for the future, (4) a renewed collective will to act, and (5) egalitarian language to reflect a new sense of unity and mutuality in the joint creation of the group's future. (Definition is from the article "Generative Metaphor Intervention: A New Approach for Working with Systems Divided by Conflict and Caught in Defensive Perception" by Frank J. Barrett.)

H

Habitus mentalis—Habitual styles of thought.

Heliotropic—A term that implies that people have an observable and largely "automatic" tendency to move in the direction of affirming images of the future.

I

Imagination—The phase of the AI approach to strategic planning when time is spent dreaming and coconstructing the preferred future.

Improvisational capacity—The capacity to allow for change to happen with endless variation. Appreciative Inquiry is not just one way of change; there are infinite ways for the *Destiny* phase to occur.

Indra's Net—A web of relationships that sparkle, nourish, and amplify. It is an ancient image of oneness and diversity.

Inner dialogue—A term used to describe the conversation that goes on within the mind of a person and within the collective mind of the organization. An organization's inner dialogue can typically be ascertained by listening to the informal communication channels within the organization.

Innovation—The phase of the AI approach to strategic planning that begins the strategic design of short-term objectives, tactical and functional plans, integrated programs, structures, and systems to best achieve the desired future.

Inquiry—A verb that describes the act of exploration and discovery. It also refers to the act of asking questions and of being open to seeing new potentials and possibilities. Synonyms: discovery, search, study, and systematic exploration.

Interview guide—The primary data collection tool used during the *Discovery* phase of Appreciative Inquiry. Interview questions are determined based on the affirmative topic choice. These questions are open-ended and designed to elicit rich storytelling from the interviewee. Also known as the interview protocol.

L

Learned helpfulness—Learning that understands what went well and applies what might be done to strengthen the next time.

Life-giving forces—Those elements or experiences within an organization's past and/or present that represent the organization's strengths when it is operating at its very best. A life-giving force can be a single moment in time, such as a particular customer transaction; or it can be large in scope. It can be any aspect that contributes to the organization's highest points and most valued experiences or characteristics.

Logical empiricism—Logical positivism (later referred to as logical empiricism) holds that philosophy should aspire to the same sort of rigor as science. Philosophy should provide strict criteria for judging sentences true, false, and meaningless.

M

Metacognitive—The awareness of one's own cognitive systems and knowledge and insight into its workings. It is the awareness that prompts a person to write reminders to himself or herself to avoid forgetting something.

Metaphor—An element or a figure of speech in which an expression is used to refer to something that denotes a suggested similarity. In Appreciative Inquiry, metaphors are used because they have the power to facilitate "meaning making" and to generate a better understanding within the minds of the receiver and listener.

N

Novelty—Taking the new parts of the positive core identified in the Discovery and Dream phases and integrating them with the past strengths of the system to design what it takes to move the system forward.

O

Open space technology—A process created by Harrison Owen that allows the stakeholder to discuss what he or she can and will do to contribute to the realization of the organizational dream as articulated in the provocative propositions. This technique can be used during the *Design* phase and Appreciative Inquiry Summit.

Organization architecture—The model for designing an organization's future. This is where the design elements are selected to create the ideal organization.

P

Paradigm—The generally accepted perspective of a particular discipline, theory, or mind-set at a given time.

Placebo effect—A process created in the twentieth century in which projected images, as reflected in positive belief, ignite a healing process that can be as powerful as conventional therapy.

Poetic Principle—A fundamental principle and belief in the Appreciative Inquiry approach that says human organizations are like open books. The story of the system is constantly being coauthored, and it is open to infinite presentations.

Positive core—That which makes up the best of an organization and its people.

Positive image—positive action—An Appreciative Inquiry theory that posits the more positive and hopeful the image of the future, the more positive the present day action.

Positive Principle—A fundamental principle and belief in the Appreciative Inquiry approach that says that momentum for change requires large amounts of positive affect and social bonding, attitudes such as hope, inspiration, and the sheer joy of creating with one another.

Pragmatic—A school of philosophy that is characterized by consequences, utility, and practicality as vital components of truth.

Principle of Simultaneity—A fundamental principle and belief within Appreciative Inquiry thought that recognizes that inquiry and change are not separate moments, but are simultaneous.

Problem-solving paradigm—A fundamental perspective that views organizations as problems to be solved.

Provocative propositions—Statements that bridge the best of "what is" with an organization's vision of "what might be." It becomes a written articulation of the organization's desired future state that is written in the present tense to guide the planning and operations in the future. Also known as possibility proposition and possibility statements.

Pygmalion effect—An area of research that provides empirical understanding of the relational pathways of the positive image-positive action dynamic.

S

Sense-making—A term from action research that represents the analytical process within Appreciative Inquiry where the organization defines and learns about the change.

Social architecture—It addresses the design elements critical to an organization to support the positive core. The first step in the *Design* phase is to identify this architecture.

Social constructionism—The idea that a social system creates or determines its own reality.

Strategic inquiry—Part of the SOAR approach to strategy in which an organization's greatest Strengths and Opportunities are discovered and explored among the participants. The participants are invited to share their Aspirations and coconstruct their most preferred future. Then recognition and reward programs are designed to inspire employees to achieve measurable Results.

Sustainable development—Forms of progress that meet the needs of the present without compromising the ability of future generations to meet their needs.

Sustainable enterprise—A firm or an organization that maintains and re-creates itself over time while simultaneously attending to the triple bottom line of social, environmental, and economic benefits being distributed to the entire world..

Systematic management—A style of management that uses a fixed and organized plan.

T

Theme identification—Part of the *Dream* phase of the Appreciative Inquiry process where participants identify important threads from the interview data and summary sheets that pinpoint life-giving forces within the organization.

Transformative—Having the power or tendency to transform. To change a system in nature, disposition, heart, character, or the like; to convert. Appreciative Inquiry is a transformative process for any organization.

Triple bottom line—Focuses on economic prosperity, environmental quality, and (the element business has tended to overlook) social justice and people. Also, financial well-being is one of three important criteria for success; the other two are environmental sustainability and social well-being.

U

Utopian—Utopia, in its most common and general meaning, refers to a hypothetical perfect society. The word has also been used to describe actual communities founded in attempts to create such a society. The adjective *utopian* is often used to refer to good (physically, socially, economically, or politically) but impossible proposals.

W

Whole system—In an AI organizational summit, a cross section of as many interested parties as is practical.

Whole System Change—A term used to refer to the ultimate goal of Appreciative Inquiry to transform an entire organization at one time. Methodologies used include AI Summits, Future Search, and Open Space Technologies.

Whole systems process—A framework for integrating multiple organizational change initiatives into a well-designed, highly effective coherent whole.

Wonder—Rapt attention or astonishment at something awesomely mysterious or new to one's experience.

Index

The Taos Institute is a community of scholars and practitioners concerned with the social processes essential for the construction of reason, knowledge, and human value. We are committed to exploring, developing, and disseminating ideas and practices that promote creative, appreciative, and collaborative processes in families, communities, and organizations around the world. We achieve our educational ends through conferences, workshops, publications, a PhD program, a distance learning program, newsletters, and web-based offerings. We work at the interface between the scholarly community and societal practitioners from communities of mental health, social work, counseling, organizational change, education, community building, gerontology, and medicine. We develop and explore the ways in which scholarly research can enrich professional practices and practices can stimulate scholarly inquiry.

Social constructionist dialogues—of cutting-edge significance within the social sciences and humanities—concern the processes by which humans generate meaning together.
Our focus is on how social groups create and sustain beliefs in the real, the rational, and the good.
We recognize that as people create meaning together, so do they sow the seeds of action.
Meaning and action are entwined.
As we generate meaning together we create the future.

To learn more about social construction and Appreciative Inquiry, visit the Taos Institute web site (http://www.taosinstitute.net) for resources, articles, and learning opportunities or send an e-mail to info@taosinstitute.net.

Taos Institute Board of Directors

Harlene Anderson	Sally St. George
David Cooperrider	Jane Watkins
Robert Cottor	Dan Wulff
Kenneth J. Gergen	Diana Whitney, Emerita
Mary Gergen	Suresh Srivastva, Emeritus
Sheila McNamee	

Phone and Fax: 1-440-338-6733
Toll-free: 1-888-999-TAOS

THE

TA☉S

INSTITUTE PUBLICATIONS
▲▲▲▲▲▲▲▲▲▲▲▲▲▲▲▲▲▲▲▲▲▲

The Taos Institute is a nonprofit organization dedicated to the development of social constructionist theory and practices for purposes of world benefit. Constructionist theory and practice locates the source of meaning, value, and action in communicative relations among people. Chief importance is placed on relational process and its outcomes for the welfare of all. Taos Institute Publications (TIP) offers contributions to cutting-edge theory and practice in social construction. These books are designed for scholars, practitioners, students, and the openly curious. The **Focus Book Series** provides brief introductions and overviews that illuminate theories, concepts, and useful practices. The **Books for Professionals Series** provides in-depth works focusing on recent developments in theory and practice. Books in both series are particularly relevant to social scientists and to practitioners concerned with individual, family, organizational, community, and societal change. Some of the earliest and leading books on Appreciative Inquiry and one of the core principles of AI— social construction—are found within the series of TIP books. We invite you to join in the conversation through these books.

Kenneth J. Gergen
President, Board of Directors
The Taos Institute

For information about the Taos Institute, visit http://www.taosinstitute.net.

Taos Institute Publications

Focus Book Series

Appreciative Inquiry: A Positive Approach to Building Cooperative Capacity (2005), by Frank Barrett and Ronald Fry

Dynamic Relationships: Unleashing the Power of Appreciative Inquiry in Daily Living (2005), by Jacqueline Stavros and Cheri B. Torres

Appreciative Sharing of Knowledge: Leveraging Knowledge Management for Strategic Change (2004), by Tojo Thatchekery

Social Construction: Entering the Dialogue (2004), by Kenneth J. Gergen and Mary Gergen

The Appreciative Organization (2001), by Harlene Anderson, David Cooperrider, Ken Gergen, Mary Gergen, Sheila McNamee, and Diana Whitney

Appreciative Leaders: In the Eye of the Beholder (2001), edited by Marge Schiller, Bea Mah Holland, and Deanna Riley

Experience AI: A Practitioner's Guide to Integrating Appreciative Inquiry and Experiential Learning (2001) by Miriam Ricketts and Jim Willis

Books for Professionals Series

Horizons in Buddhist Psychology: Practice, Research & Theory (2006), edited by Maurits Kwee, Kenneth J. Gergen, and Fusako Koshikawa

Therapeutic Realities: Collaboration, Oppression and Relational Flow (2006), by Kenneth J. Gergen

SocioDynamic Counselling: A Practical Guide to Meaning Making (2004), by R. Vance Peavy

Experiential Exercises in Social Construction: A Fieldbook for Creating Change (2004), by Robert Cottor, Alan Asher, Judith Levin, and Cindy Weiser

Dialogues About a New Psychology (2004), by Jan Smedslund

For online ordering of books from Taos Institute Publications, visit

http://www.taospub.net or http://www.taosinstitutepublications.net.

For further information, call 1-888-999-TAOS or 1-440-338-6733 or write books@taosinstitute.net or taosinstitutepublishing@alltel.net.

Mission

The Center for Positive Organizational Scholarship is a community of scholars devoted to energizing and transforming organizations through research on the theory and practice of positive organizing and leadership.

Key Activities

- Create and test new theories of positive organizational behavior and research instruments to measure positive organizational phenomena
- Develop and market POS educational cases and tools
- Disseminate POS ideas and intellectual products to scholars, students, corporations, nonprofits, and communities.
- Develop co-learning partnerships with select companies and nonprofit organizations.

Domains of Excellence

- Compassion
- Organizational Virtuousness
- Positive Emotions
- Positive Identity
  - Reflected Best Self
- Positive Leadership
  - Empowerment
  - Fundamental State of Leadership

- Positive Social Capital
  - Energy Networks
  - Generalized Reciprocity
  - High-Quality Connections
- Resilience
- Thriving
- Values

Faculty

The Core Faculty of the Center are Wayne Baker (director), Kim Cameron, Jane Dutton, Bob Quinn, Gretchen Spreitzer, and Lynn Wooten, who are joined by Faculty Associates (POS scholars at the University of Michigan) and Faculty Affiliates (POS scholars at institutions and organizations around the world). The faculty of the Center are members of a large, global network of scholars working to push the frontiers of POS.

Positive Organizational Scholarship

Positive Organizational Scholarship (POS) is an exciting new movement in organizational studies that draws on path-breaking work in the organizational and social sciences. "Positive" indicates the discipline's affirmative bias; "organizational" focuses on processes and conditions in organizational contexts; and "scholarship" reflects the rigor, theory, and scientific procedures that ground the POS approach.

The premise of POS research is that by understanding the drivers of positive behavior in the workplace, organizations and individuals can flourish. POS does not adopt one particular theory or research method but draws from the full spectrum of theories and methods to understand, explain, predict, and create high performance.

Center for Positive Organizational Scholarship • 701 Tappan Avenue • Stephen M. Ross School of Business

• University of Michigan • Ann Arbor, MI 48109

(734) 647-8154 • positiveorg@umich.edu • http://www.bus.umich.edu/Positive/ • Projects Coordinator: Janet Max

STEPHEN M. ROSS SCHOOL OF BUSINESS
AT THE UNIVERSITY OF MICHIGAN

Statement of Appreciative Inquiry Consulting

Appreciative Inquiry Consulting, LLC (AIC) is a global network of consultants, academic researchers, business leaders, and individuals committed to creating a positive revolution in change by using Appreciative Inquiry (AI) to engage the "positive core" of all people and all living systems and to expand that rich potential, creating organizations that are themselves agents of world benefit.

AIC is committed to the conceptual and practical advancement of Appreciative Inquiry, including its constructionist, scientific, and spiritual foundations. As a community, we realize that AI is in a state of evolution; and as long as the inquiry part of AI is alive, it will continue to contribute to break new ground. We as a community are constantly seeking creative links and synergies with related and diverse approaches that share in the search for new frontiers of positive change. At the heart of AIC is the sharing of knowledge and practices, the collaboration on projects and research of mutual interest, and peer-to-peer sharing and conferences. The AIC community benefits from a common identity in creating marketing materials, products, and services.

The AIC web site showcases our members' work and provides an evolving resource pool of designs, templates, working papers, protocols, and other artifacts of members' collective work and learning in AIC. Our office and web site can assist those looking for AI practitioners and coordinate a referral system to link practitioners throughout the network for global consulting and collaboration.

Membership in AIC is open to all who share its purpose and principles. The web site (www.aiconsulting.org) lists the purpose and principles and includes a description of the process for joining the positive revolution in change for which AIC stands.

Appreciative Inquiry Consulting, LLC
ManagingPartner@aiconsulting.org
www.aiconsulting.org

About the Authors

Dr. David L. Cooperrider is professor and chair of the SIGMA Program for Human Cooperation and Global Action at the Weatherhead School of Management at Case Western Reserve University. He has served as researcher and consultant to a wide variety of organizations, including Allstate, Capgemini, Ernst & Young, GTE-Verizon, Roadway Express, Nutrimental, World Vision, Cleveland Clinic, Imagine Chicago, American Red Cross, and United Religions Initiative. These projects are inspired by the Appreciative Inquiry (AI) methodology, of which he is co-originator. He has been recipient of Best Paper of the Year Awards at the Academy of Management. GTE was awarded the 1998 Best Organization Change Program by ASTD.

David has designed a series of dialogues using AI with 25 of the world's top religious leaders, started in 1998 by His Holiness the Dalai Lama, who said, "If only the world's religious leaders could just know each other . . . the world will be a better place." Using AI, the group has held meetings in Jerusalem and at the Carter Center in Atlanta. David was recognized in 2000 as among "the top ten visionaries" in the field by Training magazine and has been named in *Five Hundred People of Influence*. He is past president of the National Academy of Management's Division of Organization Development and a cofounder of the Taos Institute. He has lectured and taught at Stanford University, MIT, the University of Chicago, Katholieke University in Belgium, Pepperdine University, and others. David has published 7 books and authored more than 40 articles and book chapters.

His wife Nancy is an artist, and his daughter and two sons are in college. The AI Commons web site he helped create is http://appreciativeinquiry.case.edu. David's e-mail address is david.cooperrider@case.edu.

Dr. Diana Whitney, president of Corporation for Positive Change is cofounder and director emeritus of the Taos Institute. She is an internationally recognized consultant and keynote speaker and a pioneering thought leader on the subjects of Appreciative Inquiry, positive change, and spirituality at work. She is a fellow of the World Business Academy.

She is an award-winning writer and author of six books and dozens of articles and chapters, including *Appreciative Inquiry* with David Cooperrider and *The Power of Appreciative Inquiry* with Amanda Trosten-Bloom. In addition, Diana has edited five collections on Appreciative Inquiry, including *Appreciative Inquiry and Organizational Transformation* and *Positive Approaches to Peace Building*.

Diana teaches and consults in the Americas, Europe, and Asia. She has lectured and taught at Antioch University, Case Western Reserve University, Ashridge Management Institute in London, and Eisher Institute in India and for Human Value in Japan. She is a Distinguished Consulting Faculty at Saybrook Graduate School and Research Center.

The focus of Diana's consulting is the application of Appreciative Inquiry to strategic planning, mergers, large-scale transformation, service excellence and leadership, and management development. With 30 years of consulting, her clients include business, government, and social profit organizations: Merck, British Airways, Hunter Douglas, GTE-Verizon, GE Capital, Johnson & Johnson, and Sandia National Labs.

Diana serves as adviser to the United Religions Initiative, a global interfaith organization dedicated to peace and cooperation among people of different religions, faiths, and spiritual traditions.

Diana lives in Chapel Hill, North Carolina, and can be reached at diana@positivechange.org.

Dr. Jacqueline (Jackie) M. Stavros possesses 20 years of strategic planning, international, and organizational development and change experience. Jackie is an associate professor for the College of Management, Lawrence Technological University, where she teaches and integrates Appreciative Inquiry and other approaches to strength-based change in her MBA and DBA course work.

She uses Appreciative Inquiry (AI) to work with clients to build dynamic relationships and to facilitate strategic planning and leadership development sessions. Clients have included ACCI Business System; BAE Systems; Fasteners, Inc.; General Motors of Mexico; Jefferson Wells; NASA; Tendercare; United Way; Girl Scouts USA; Orbseal Technologies; and several Tier 1 and Tier 2 automotive suppliers and organizations in education.

Jackie has worked and traveled to more than a dozen countries in Asia, Europe, and North America. She has presented on AI and SOAR framework at Hewlett-Packard, the American Dietetic Association, PricewaterhouseCoopers, National City Bank, and the Detroit Chamber of Commerce. She has coauthored another book in AI, *Dynamic Relationships: Unleashing the Power of Appreciative Inquiry in Daily Living,* and dozens of book chapters and articles. She recently coauthored a book chapter for Berrett-Koehler's new *Change Handbook* titled "SOAR™: A New Approach to Strategic Planning" and coedited a series of articles for the international journal The Ai Practitioner on "SOARing to High and Engaging Performance: An Appreciative Approach to Strategy (http://www.aipractitioner.com).

She earned a doctorate in Management at Case Western Reserve University on *Capacity Building Using an Appreciative Approach: A Relational Process of Building Your Organization's Future.* Her MBA is from Michigan State University, and she has a BA from Wayne State University. Jackie is an associate for the Taos Institute and an editor for Taos Institute Publishing. She is a board member of the Positive Change Corps, a virtual global organization that focuses on strength-based approaches to teaching and learning in primary education (Pk–12th grade). She is a member of the Academy of Management, the Organization Development Network, and the Organization Development Institute.

Jackie lives with her family in Brighton, Michigan, and can be reached at jstavros@comcast.net.

Encyclopedia of Positive Questions, Vol. 1

Using AI to Bring Out the Best in Your Organization

Diana Whitney, David L. Cooperrider,
Amanda Trosten-Bloom, and Brian S. Kaplan

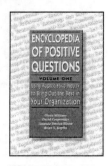

This timely book is composed of generic interview questions central to the "Discovery" phase of the Appreciative Inquiry process. This workbook on the power of positive questions has implications for every aspect of business—measurement systems, custom focus groups, quality management, team building, performance appraisal, surveys—indeed everywhere we ask questions or gather data related to positive change efforts.

ISBN: 1933403-055
212 pp
$18.95

Birth of a Global Community: Appreciative Inquiry in Action

The Story of the United Religions Initiative
Charles Gibbs and Sally Mahé

The birth of the United Religions Initiative (URI) is the story of how hundreds, then thousands of people across cultures, oceans, and faith traditions began to share a common call to make the world they live in more like the world they yearned for in their dreams. The book also tells the story of how an emergent processs of organizational change—the Appreciative Inquiry (AI) process—came along at just the right time to provide the engine for the new organization and its development.

ISBN: 1893435-423
384 pp
$24.95

Appreciative Management and Leadership Revised Edition

The Power of Positive Thought and Action in Organizations
Suresh Srivasta and David L. Cooperrider

"Based on the theory and practice of Appreciative Inquiry, Appreciative Management and Leadership offers a revolutionary alternative—a positive approach to organizing intended to unleash the entrepre- neurial spirit of all organizational members and mobilize system-wide action in pursuit of a common purpose. This book is a "must read" for all thought leaders—chief executives, managers, change agents, scholars, and practitioners—who want to create and sustain vital organizations in a world of rapid change."

ISBN: 1893435-059
548 pp
$49.50

James D. Ludema
Professor of Organization Development
Benedictine University, Chicago, IL

Crown Custom Publishing, Inc.
Brunswick, OH

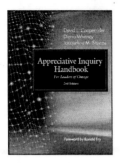